For the Love of God

For the Love of God

Principles and Practice of Compassion in Missions

Edited by
JERRY M. IRELAND

WIPF & STOCK · Eugene, Oregon

FOR THE LOVE OF GOD
Principles and Practice of Compassion in Missions

Wipf & Stock
An Imprint of Wipf and Stock Publishers
199 W. 8th Ave., Suite 3
Eugene, OR 97401

www.wipfandstock.com

PAPERBACK ISBN: 978-1-5326-1638-9
HARDCOVER ISBN: 978-1-4982-4013-0
EBOOK ISBN: 978-1-4982-4012-3

Manufactured in the U.S.A.   MARCH 13, 2017

Dedicated to the poor and needy the world over,
whom Jesus calls by name.

Contents

List of Contributors

JoAnn Butrin, PhD, director of International Ministries for Assemblies of God World Missions and adjunct faculty at Assemblies of God Theological Seminary in Springfield, MO. She served as a missionary to central Africa and is the author of *From the Roots Up*.

Brian Fikkert, PhD, Professor of Economics and Community Development at Covenant College in Lookout Mountain, Georgia. He is also founder and president of the Chalmers Center and co-author of the best-selling book, *When Helping Hurts*.

Jeff Hartensveld, director of mobilization for Assemblies of God World Missions and served many years as a missionary to Indonesia.

Lynda Hausfeld, missionary in Muslim contexts for over twenty-five years, and International Director for Say Hello, a ministry of Global Initiative. She also teaches Spanish at Evangel University in Springfield MO.

Karen Herrera, RN, MSN, missionary with Health Care Ministries and contributing author for the *Hands that Heal Community Curriculum* with the Faith Alliance against Slavery and Trafficking (FAAST).

Suzanne Hurst, BSN, MPH, DrPH (Candidate), missionary to Central Africa where she has served for 25 years working with local churches on community development initiatives.

Jerry M. Ireland, PhD, missionary to sub-Saharan Africa, director of Africa AG Care. His publications include *Evangelism and Social Concern in the Theology of Carl F. H. Henry*.

Paula Ireland, MA, MPH, missionary to sub-Saharan Africa and director of the Cry Africa Network, which helps local churches respond to the HIV/AIDs crisis.

Alan R. Johnson, PhD, missionary to Thailand and author of *Apostolic Function in 21st Century Missiology*. In addition, he has authored numerous scholarly articles on frontier missions.

Jean Johnson, long-time missionary to Cambodia and currently executive director of World Missions Associates (WMA). Her publications include *We Are Not the Hero: A Missionaries Guide to Sharing Christ, Not a Culture of Dependency*.

Jeff Palmer, executive director of Baptist Global Response, a Southern Baptist relief and development agency working closely with the International Mission Board of the Southern Baptist Convention.

Jason Paltzer, PhD, MPH, Global Health Director, Kingdom Workers, assistant professor of public health at Grand Canyon University and has served as a missionary in southern Africa.

A. Chadwick Thornhill, PhD, Chair of Theological Studies at Liberty University School of Divinity. His publications include *The Chosen People: Election, Paul, and Second Temple Judaism* and *Greek for Everyone: Introductory Greek for Bible Study and Application*.

Brandy Tuesday Wilson, MACM, DMin (Participant), Coordinator for Serve4Justice, a team of Nurture Hope, with International Ministries in the Assemblies of God. She served as a missionary in Latin America and Europe before accepting her current assignment.

**Special thanks to Laverne Smith and John Higgins for their editorial work on this project.

PART 1

1

Introduction

JERRY M. IRELAND

PERHAPS MORE THAN EVER before, there exists a profound need to clarify a biblical and responsible approach to the church's compassion mandate in cross-cultural missions. Though Christian missions has a long history of demonstrating compassion, today's missionary faces an ever-growing number of challenges and pitfalls in this area. In recent times, cross-cultural Christian workers[1] have responded to a wide range of issues, including the Ebola epidemic in West Africa, HIV/AIDS in Swaziland, human trafficking in India, a Tsunami in East Asia, and extreme poverty with its many devastating effects in many places around the globe. These tragedies all demonstrate that missionary work frequently intersects with human need and suffering. Sometimes missionary responses to these needs have been well thought out and guided by sound biblical and indigenous principles. Other times, the well-intentioned but ill-conceived efforts of missionaries in response to various compassion-oriented issues have created dependency and exhibited little or no connection to the local community. Such efforts can have a net effect of leaving those we would help worse off than they were before.[2]

---

1. In this volume, "missionary" and "cross-cultural Christian worker" are used synonymously. See also the definitions of "mission" and "missions" in this chapter.

2. Corbett and Fikkert, *When Helping Hurts*; Lupton, *Toxic Charity*.

Some missions agencies have also witnessed an astonishingly sharp increase in new missionary candidates and short-term mission teams interested primarily or solely in "social justice"—which has become something of a catch-all term for all things related to compassion. Others have noticed an increase in giving toward relief and development type ministries, while funds going to evangelism and discipleship have declined.[3] These realities have forced at least one major American denomination to articulate more clearly its approach to compassion ministries when it noticed that many candidates wanting to work in the area of social justice saw no need to connect their work to evangelism or discipleship.[4] Yet, when compassionate missions stand apart from evangelistic efforts and apart from the work of the local church, the uniquely redemptive role of the church is either diminished or lost altogether. Therefore, missionaries must find ways to engage in compassion in ways that are more directly linked to the evangelistic calling of the church. The biblical paradigm is one in which word and deed are not two separate tracks of ministry, but rather are inherently connected and interwoven.

This book is designed to help bridge the gap that sometimes exists between compassion and evangelism. To accomplish this, we not only address the theoretical and biblical principles of compassion in what we hope is a sound and somewhat expansive manner (part one), but also provide some practical guidelines intended to help missionaries navigate the difficult terrain of compassionate missions (part two).

All of the contributors to this volume have at least one advanced degree related to the topic they address. This formal training is buttressed by years of hands-on experience. Together they have well over two hundred years of missions involvement. They have worked in Asia, Africa, Europe, the Middle East, and Latin America. As they have traveled the globe and taught on compassion in missions and worked with local believers to build healthy churches that exhibit a robust understanding of God's own concern for the poor and marginalized, they have found themselves searching in vain for a single volume that addresses both the theoretical and practical side of compassionate missions. This book was born out of that search.

Another reason for this text is that dominant issues in compassionate missions change frequently, and not always for good reasons. Not long ago, HIV/AIDS and orphans were a primary concern. Nearly every evangelical church in the United States had heard of Heidi and Rolland Baker and their

3. On the increase in funds toward relief and development, see Weber, *Missions Handbook*, 52.

4. Author's conversation with members of the Assemblies of God World Missions missiology committee, Springfield, MO, June 16, 2015.

ministry to street children in Mozambique. In early 2015, as this book was being written, the Ebola crisis in West Africa and its once non-stop coverage by Western news outlets had begun to fade. At the same time, human trafficking had been a dominant focus of evangelical compassionate missions for at least a decade. [5] By the time this book goes to press, it seems likely that a new crisis will have captured the attention of evangelicals, and some will demand that we drop everything and turn our attention there. Yet, some of these issues never went away or even subsided to any significant degree on the world stage. Consider, for example, the HIV/AIDS pandemic. Though significant milestones have been reached, this virus continues its devastating spread in countries around the world, and though the emphasis on HIV/AIDS as a major concern in missions has diminished, the need has not.[6] To put it plainly, our tendency to change course in pursuit of what appears to be "the next big thing," even before we have sufficiently addressed the last big thing, merely points to the enduring need to direct emotional and cultural currents with solid biblical foundations and best practices. When this does not happen disaster often ensues. In short, to paraphrase the late Carl F. H. Henry, a reactionary theology will not do.[7] As Scott W. Sunquist puts it, "Christian missionary involvement must not be bound to what is popular, popularly known, or even what seems like 'viable' mission."[8]

Another reality that presses the need for this text centers on the fact that evangelical missionaries have not always done a good job of integrating compassionate work with the national and local churches in the country where they serve.[9] Because of this, we are forced to ask some searching questions. Are our compassionate efforts in missions driven by real needs and by biblical mandates, or by whatever captivates our attention? Do we engage in compassionate ministries out of a need to feel good about ourselves or out of a clear understanding of what the Bible teaches? Does the manner in which we conduct compassionate missions focus on the needs of those we are helping or on their assets? Do we involve those we seek to help in the process, or do we merely presume to know what they need and forge ahead? What is the difference between compassionate work done by missionaries and that done by any number of Non-Governmental Organizations (NGOs)

---

5. See for example, Stafford, "Miracles in Mozambique: How Mama Heidi Reaches the Abandoned."

6. For a helpful discussion on the importance of HIV/AIDS being incorporated into theological education, see Chitando, "HIV and AIDS and Theological Education: Mainstreaming HIV and AIDS in Theological Education," 242–250.

7. Henry, *The Uneasy Conscience of Modern Fundamentalism*, 41–54.

8. Sunquist, *Understanding Christian Mission*, 18.

9. This statement refers to places where the church has been planted.

and parachurch organizations? Should there be a difference? These are questions every missionary working in compassionate ministry should take the time to consider and work through, and this volume has been conceived with these very questions in mind. We have made a conscious attempt to not be driven by the ever-changing and fickle winds of a consumer culture, but by realities that we know, from first-hand experience, directly impact the task of reaching the lost for Christ.

OVERVIEW

Part one of this text focuses on guiding and foundational principles. In chapter 2, Jerry Ireland explores the theological foundations for compassion through a study of the biblical concept of the kingdom of God, wherein compassion constitutes a fundamental aspect of what it means to be the people of God. He then looks at how this biblical understanding should inform the praxis of missionaries and the flourishing of indigenous local churches. Following this, Alan Johnson further develops the idea of how compassion can be done according to indigenous principles. Following Ralph Winter, he distinguishes between the marks of the church and the purpose of the missions band, noting important differences in purpose and function. In chapter 4, JoAnn Butrin and Chad Thornhill articulate social and biblical definitions of poverty. They adopt the widely held view that poverty should be defined by more than economic factors and set the definition within a scriptural framework. Rounding out part one of the text and this section on guiding principles, Suzanne Hurst introduces the essence of a development approach to compassion. Development focuses on the dignity of every person and seeks to avoid the creation of dependency. It also focuses on assets rather than on needs.

In part two, we turn to specific applications of the principles outlined in part one. This section opens with a chapter by Jeff Palmer and Lynda Hausfeld on unreached people groups (UPGs). Included in this chapter is a discussion of how simple acts of compassion can be an effective means of reaching Muslim women. Then, Jean Johnson looks at sustainability in compassionate missions. She proposes ways that missionaries can respond to compassionate needs without depending on outside resources or creating systems that cannot be locally run and locally supported. Following this, several authors propose some specific guidelines that focus on the church's response to dominant issues in contemporary missiology. Brian Fikkert discusses economic development, focusing especially on micro-financing. JoAnn Butrin, Brandy Wilson, Jerry Ireland, and Suzanne Hurst provide guidelines for the churches response to injustice, including issues such as human trafficking, gender inequality, and war and genocide. Jerry Ireland discusses the church's response to the needs of children and considers the value of things such as child sponsorship and orphanages. Karen Herrera and Paula Ireland address the church's response to health issues, looking specifically at some of the most common global challenges, such as malaria, HIV/AIDS, malnutrition, diarrhea and others. Jeffrey Hartensveld writes about church-based responses to natural disasters, based on his experiences in Indonesia during the 2004 tsunami that hit that area. Finally, Jason Paltzer provides some helpful guidelines for how faith-based organizations (FBOs) might more effectively work with local churches.

THE APPROACH OF THIS TEXT

This text addresses compassion in missions from a thoroughly evangelical perspective. As such, this text will center around three themes to which we will often return: *biblical foundations, the local church,* and *development principles.* The central thesis of this text is that these themes must guide evangelical responses to compassion if we are to be faithful to Scripture and to the church's uniquely redemptive purpose. We will argue that Christian compassion is fundamentally a matter of discipleship and that modern Christian missions often tends, contrarily, toward the professionalization of compassionate ministry. Such an approach robs local believers of their God-given mandate to love their neighbors (Matt 22:39).

Defining Mission(s)

What is "missions" and what does it mean to be a "missionary"? As Ott and Strauss have observed, since the 1960s, the singular form "mission" has been increasingly used to mean all of "God's sending activity in the world: God's mission in the world." The plural "missions" generally refers more precisely to cross-cultural efforts to plant the church and thereby take part in the expansion of God's kingdom.[10] This seems like a helpful way to understand these concepts and we will generally follow this pattern. A *missionary* then would be those who engage in *missions* (plural). All believers should participate in mission (singular), as all of God's people are called to involve themselves broadly in God's redemptive plan. Such activities would include near-neighbor evangelism and compassionate acts of service to one's church

10. Ott and Strauss, *Encountering Theology of Missions*, xiv–xv.

and community. In Scripture, though, there are those who are set apart and specifically called to the task of planting and nurturing churches. We see this especially in Acts 11–13, where Paul and Barnabas first go to strengthen the newly planted church at Antioch, and then are later sent by the Antioch church on a church-planting mission among gentiles. "Set apart for me Barnabas and Saul for the work to which I have called them" (Acts 13:2b).

We are primarily concerned with understanding compassion within the context of the cross-cultural movement of God's people to plant the church where it does not exist and to strengthen the church where it does exist. As Christians help plant churches where there are no churches, we inevitably enter into partnerships with local believers, and these partnerships, ideally, become a means for the continued movement of the gospel into new territory.

Biblical Principles

Biblical principles must guide all that we do as the people of God, no less in compassion than in church planting and evangelism. As Evangelicals, we hold that the Bible is the primary source for knowing God and His purposes. Yet when it comes to taking our cue from the Bible in compassionate missions, we must pay attention to both the question of compassion and the question of missions. In other words, we must first ask, "what does the Bible say about compassion?" Then we must follow that by inquiring, "how should we interpret that in the context of missions?" It would be an illegitimate move simply to discern what the Bible says about compassion and then go out and do that in a cross-cultural context. This is because, as we will see in chapters two and three, what is true of the local church and of every disciple is not necessarily true for missionaries. Each operates under a somewhat different biblical mandate.

To be Evangelical means to give primary place to the gospel, the good news about Jesus Christ.[11] This means that concern for the lost always occu-

11. Cf. Bebbington's famous and often cited quadrilateral, which begins with the primary and unequivocal place afforded the Bible; Bebbington, *Evangelicals in Modern Britain*, 2–17. Beyond this though, the key word in the term "evangelical" is the word "evangel", which refers especially to the good news concerning Jesus Christ; see Mark 1:1; 8:35; 10:29; 13:10; et al. Though some would separate Pentecostals and Charismatics from Evangelicals based on epistemological and pneumatological differences, we do not make that distinction for the purpose of this text, and consider an Evangelical to be those who fit within the broader category of theologically conservative Christians who believe in the Trinity, the inspiration of Scripture, virgin birth, the deity of Christ, Jesus' atoning sacrifice upon the cross, and His bodily, historical resurrection from the dead, and immanent return.

pies the central place in the mission of the church. Evangelical compassion must consistently exhibit a robust concern for the lost, with the understanding that only Jesus can redeem sinful humanity from its fallen state. We shall return shortly to the issue of precisely how evangelistic and compassionate missions relate to one another. First, it is important to establish the primacy of the local church in evangelical compassionate missions.

The Local Church

Disciples of Jesus, those who make up the local church, should function as salt and light in their communities (Matt 5:13–16). The church exists to both proclaim and interpret God's revealed Word, and to show forth the moral standards of the Kingdom of God.[12] Missionaries should work to plant and strengthen local churches. Yet sadly, some missionaries have approached compassion as a stand-alone enterprise. For example, one missionary working in a restricted-access country was invited to a meeting in which his colleagues were discussing their team's church planting and evangelism strategies. After sitting silently for an extended period of time during the meeting, this missionary finally spoke up and declared that they were not there to do church planting and evangelism, but only social justice work. When he said this, the other team members sat back in disbelief. Where did this person get the idea that social justice work, important as it is, could legitimately be divorced from the work of establishing churches or making disciples? Do not those being given relief from temporal sufferings also need relief from eternal suffering? How could anyone think that a denominationally-sent missions team, including each member, could neglect its only unique role, that of proclaiming God's gracious offer of salvation to all persons?

In the context of Christian missions, the reality of human suffering cannot be interpreted apart from the larger biblical narrative and its overarching redemptive structure. The need for compassionate responses must be understood within the context of the fall and human rebellion against God (Genesis 3) and God's gracious offer of salvation in and through Christ. Injustice exists because creation is in rebellion against the Creator. Not only this, but the church, defined as the people of God, and it alone, is tasked with the divine purpose of proclaiming that the same God who wills justice will also one day judge all people.[13] Therefore, when Christian missionaries

12. The precise biblical foundations for this will be developed in chapter 2.

13. Cf. Carl Henry's observation that justice and justification must go together in a Biblical faith; Henry, *A Plea for Evangelical Demonstration*, 46.

engage in compassionate outreach, if they are to be true to their calling as part of the church, they must set forth the reality of God's coming judgment and the offer of hope in Christ. Furthermore, this is a function that can *only* be achieved by the church, which is tasked with providing entrance to the Kingdom and standing sentry against the forces of evil (Matt 16:16–20).

The role of missionaries is to equip local believers to be the primary responders. We see this pattern in Acts 11:19–30. Here we are introduced to the church at Antioch, which is the first majority gentile church in the New Testament, and the first place where believers were called Christians. Paul (referred to here as Saul) and Barnabas spent a year teaching and equipping the disciples. When a prophet announces a coming famine, the local church responds of its own initiative and out of its own resources. "The disciples, each according to his ability, decided to provide help for the brothers living in Judea" (Acts 11:29). In other words, the teaching/equipping ministry of the missionaries led directly to the indigenous compassionate response of the local church. The disciples, not the missionaries, decided on an appropriate response and financed that response out of the resources they could muster themselves. This in fact appears to be a New Testament pattern, as we see much the same thing in 2 Corinthians. Paul, speaking this time of the Macedonian believers, says, "For I testify that according to their ability, and beyond their ability, they gave of their own accord" (2 Cor 8:3).

When we focus on empowering and equipping local churches for compassionate outreach, we are helping prepare those churches for cross-cultural missions. By this, we simply mean that people often do not begin to love people across the border until they have started to love people across the street. The global missionary impulse of God's people has always moved from the local to the global, from Israel to the nations, from Jerusalem to the utter most parts, from the community of faith to the broader human family. Consider for example the apostle Paul, who instructs, "while we have opportunity, let us do good to all people, and especially to those who are of the household of the faith" (Gal 6:10; NASB). Though the church has an obligation to the larger community in which it resides, its compassionate mandate must begin at home. From that starting point, the church then discovers the infinite resources bound up in loving God and neighbor.

Development

The term "development" in this text refers to an approach to compassionate missions that starts with people's assets rather than their needs. Furthermore, a development approach to compassion has as its primary objective, do no harm. Compassionate efforts that are most fruitful are those that avoid the creation of dependency, which often robs those we would serve of their God-given dignity as divine image bearers. Development can also be distinguished from short-term relief efforts aimed primarily at alleviating immediate needs arising from disasters or catastrophe. Development requires long-term commitment and emphasizes local ownership and resources. As such, it shuns the quick fix.

A driving idea behind development principles is that of sustainability. This means simply that compassionate efforts should be able not only to persist, but thrive, even without missionary presence and involvement. Such an approach requires tremendous humility and long-term commitment. The missionary who engages in development work cannot be in the spotlight or play the dominant role. Development requires empowering and training local people. This idea finds its ultimate basis in Jesus' own mission, as He came not to be served, but to serve (Matt 20:28).

THE PRIORITISM-HOLISM DEBATE

Evangelicals have, for decades, been locked in a somewhat bitter and often divisive debate over the relationship between compassionate service (deed) and evangelistic efforts (word). How should we understand these issues as they relate to the mission of the church? Is there a priority, and if so what does priority mean? Does prioritizing one thing mean that the other thing is optional, as some have claimed?[14] Or, does priority simply refer to an *ontological priority* that especially defines the nature of the church, but does not necessarily apply to every concrete situation?[15]

To answer these questions a brief survey of some of the historical circumstances that have given rise to this debate will prove helpful. It is widely acknowledged that much of the modern confusion over the relationship between compassion and evangelism can be traced to the fundamentalist-modernist controversy that peaked in the early decades of the twentieth century. Prior to this, as Ed Smither has pointed out regarding the early church, the relationship was somewhat intuitive, as church leaders declared, "of course we preach the gospel; of course we feed the poor."[16]

---

14. Bosch, *Transforming Missions*, 405.

15. Litfin, *Word Vs. Deed*.

16. Smither, "Foreword," ix.

The Enlightenment

To understand modern developments, we must begin with the Enlightenment, which has dramatically shaped modern thinking on numerous fronts,
including the place of moral or compassionate virtue in the Christian life.
The Enlightenment, also called the "Age of Reason," can somewhat sim-
plistically be defined as "an emphasis upon the ability of human reason to
penetrate the mysteries of the world."[17]

The Enlightenment, perhaps more than any other era in human history, has shaped and defined the modern western mind. Specifically, the Enlightenment represented a challenge to or shift in traditional views regarding
several key areas of human thought, especially (1) individual autonomy, (2)
the role and usage of reason, (3) an emphasis on the natural, entailing a
de-emphasis on the supernatural, (4) the power of human progress, and
(5) a tendency toward pluralism and tolerance.[18] These were the primary
themes of the Enlightenment. It was an era that would radically transform
approaches to religion in general and to Christianity in particular.

Liberal Theology

Liberal theology embodied Enlightenment ideology and came to emphasize especially the supposed moral agenda of Jesus, and moved away from
classic orthodox understandings of historical dogma. By emphasizing Jesus'
ethical teachings, liberal theology sought to rescue Christianity from the
devastating effects of the Enlightenment, which in denying the supernatural
left both the nature and content of Scripture, along with many Christian
doctrines, unstable.

Fundamentalism answered with militant opposition to liberalism
coupled with cultural retreat and often overly simplistic defenses of classic
Christian doctrines.[19] Because social concern had become the very center of
liberal theology, fundamentalism tended to reject social justice issues as being too focused on temporal things rather than on the weightier matters of
eternity. In fundamentalism the Kingdom of God came to be understood primarily in futuristic, spiritual terms with little or no practical relevance to the

17. McGrath, "Enlightenment," 151.

18. Livingston, *Modern Christian Thought*, 6–11.

19. For example, see Marsden's comment that William Jennings Bryan's "defense of
Christianity was essentially pragmatic," and that Bryan himself admitted to not having
had much time to study theology; Marsden, *Fundamentalism and American Culture*, 134.

present church age. Yet, this understanding marked a significant departure from orthodox Christianity, which had long embodied a vibrant social ethic.

The Scopes Trial

The clash between fundamentalists and their modernist, liberal counterparts took center stage in the infamous Scopes Trial that took place in Dayton, Tennessee in 1925. That year, twenty-four-year-old teacher John T. Scopes, at the urging of others, taught evolution in his classroom, thereby violating state law. This very deliberate act led to an indictment and trial for Scopes that attracted a flood of media attention, as two of the nation's top lawyers took opposing sides of the case. In many ways, the Scopes trial was a circus. As Kenneth J. Collins observes, "complex intellectual issues emerged cartoonlike in some of the national papers, with the fundamentalists being characterized as buffoons."[20]

Clarence Darrow, an agnostic, led the defense of Scopes, while three-time presidential candidate for the Democratic Party, William Jennings Bryan, a fundamentalist Christian, led the prosecution. Biased press coverage, epitomized by that of H. L. Mencken with *The Baltimore Sun*, frequently misrepresented Bryan to the public, making him appear ignorant and out of touch. Bryan, for his part though, contributed to this through a number of missteps at the trial that resulted in Darrow consistently having the upper hand. In the end, the result was clear. It had not been Scopes who was on trial, but fundamentalism. At least in the public eye, fundamentalism was found guilty of being behind the times and woefully ignorant of developments in science and critical studies of the Bible. Shortly after the trial concluded, Bryan died of a heart attack. And indeed, fundamentalism itself suffered a mortal wound from which it never quite recovered.

About this same time, the Social Gospel of Walter Rauschenbusch and others was gaining momentum. As Collins observes, this movement was characterized by a de-emphasis on personal salvation in favor of a focus on social sins, and by a conscious move away from a belief in instantaneous conversion. Many social gospel advocates preferred to understand salvation in terms of human service toward others and conversion was participation in those types of activities.[21] Fundamentalists reacted strongly to this, decrying "'social service Christianity' that left out the soul."[22]

---

20. Collins, *Power, Politics, and the Fragmentation of Evangelicalism*, 41.

21. Ibid., 50.

22. Ibid., 51.

The Emergence of neo-Evangelicalism

Following these setbacks, fundamentalists began to withdraw from culture altogether and, for the most part, abandoned what had once been a vibrant approach to social needs. World War II (WWII) also marked a serious setback for modernists who had set their hopes on the supposed inevitability of human progress in the social arena. As R. Hilberg says of the Holocaust that lay at the center of WWII: "All our assumptions about the world and its progress prior to the years when this event burst forth have been upset. The certainties of the late nineteenth and twentieth century vanished in its face. What we once understood, we no longer comprehend."[23]

Immediately following WWII, Carl F. H. Henry wrote one of the most important books of the late twentieth century concerning the needed revival of Christian compassion and social concern. In *The Uneasy Conscience of Modern Fundamentalism*, Henry directly challenged the fundamentalist withdrawal from social concern as a knee-jerk reaction to liberal theology that was also un-tethered from the concerns of Scripture. Henry's critique was especially poignant given Henry's own fundamentalist roots and that he was writing as something of an insider. In this text, Henry argued from within a priority framework for the necessity of evangelical social concern.[24]

Not only this text, but much of Henry's career would center on efforts to reclaim the social relevance of biblical Christianity that had evaporated during the fundamentalist-modernist controversy. As a result, Henry, along with Harold Ockenga, can be credited with launching neo-Evangelicalism, which by definition sought to advance a more socially engaged and intellectually rigorous form of conservative Christianity. Included in these efforts were the launching of *Christianity Today* (CT) in 1955, which included in its founding principles the necessity of a socially active faith.[25]

The Lausanne Movement

After the launching of neo-Evangelicalism by Henry and others, Billy Graham, with the help of Carl Henry and CT, founded the Lausanne Movement by holding *The First International Congress on World Evangelization* in

---

23. Hilberg, "Opening Remarks: 'The Discovery of the Holocaust,'" 11; cited in Garrand and Scarre, *Moral Philosophy and the Holocaust*, 75.

24. Henry, *Uneasy Conscience*, 30.

25. Ireland, *Evangelism and Social Concern*, 49. Also, *Christianity Today*, when launched, embodied a more scholarly bent than it does now.

Lausanne, Switzerland in July of 1974. This movement would play a major role in the unfolding prioritism-holism debate.

Billy Graham had specifically asked that the 1974 Congress clarify the relationship between evangelism and social concern. It did so, declaring, "In the church's mission of sacrificial service evangelism is primary."[26] However, as a follow-up to Lausanne, the Consultation on World Evangelization (COWE) convened in Pattaya, Thailand in 1980 and emphasized the necessity of social concern, but reaffirmed the priority of evangelism as stated in the original covenant. However, some thought this resulted from the conference being hijacked by church growth advocates from North America, who were also accused of ignoring voices from the global south and of too narrowly defining the task of evangelism.[27] This led to the 1982 Consultation on the Relationship between Evangelism and Social Responsibility (CRESR). This consultation allowed for three possible approaches to the question of how evangelism and social concern relate to one another. First, social concern can be seen as a consequence of evangelism, since conversion should result in a transformed life directed toward the service of others. Second, it may be viewed as a bridge to evangelism in that it can help overcome hindrances to the reception of the gospel. Finally, social concern functions as a partner of evangelism, given that the two belong together, "like two blades of a pair of scissors or the two wings of a bird."[28] The CRESR also upheld "the primacy" of evangelism on two grounds: first, evangelism relates more directly to people's eternal destiny, and second, in order for there to be Christians involved in social action, there must first have been Christian evangelism. There is, by necessity, a logical order between the two, for Christian social action depends on people having already been converted to Christianity.[29]

Mission as Transformation

In addition to Lausanne, several conferences leading up to it, including the 1966 *Wheaton Declaration* and Ron Sider's 1973 *Chicago Declaration of Evangelical Social Concern,* have contributed to the growth of a new movement within evangelicalism, variously termed *Integral Mission, Holistic Mission,* or *Mission as Transformation.*[30] Leading voices in this movement

26. Stott, *Making Christ Known,* xix; see §6 of the original covenant.

27. Kirk, *Good News of the Coming Kingdom,* 15.

28. Stott, *Making Christ Known,* xx.

29. Ibid.; Sider, *Good News and Good,* 170.

30. Padilla, "Integral Mission and its Historical Development," 42–58.

include Vinay Samuel, Chris Sugden, René Padilla, Orlando Costas, Samuel Escobar, David Bosch, Ronald Sider, David Gitari, and Kwame Bediako, among others.[31]

When Lausanne I affirmed the priority of evangelism, it also, ironically, helped birth the modern holistic movement. As Tizon has shown, Lausanne produced a number of subsequent evangelical conferences, such as Wheaton '83, that first began to develop the theological and practical understanding of holistic missions. In this, the idea of "transformation", defined as "the change from a condition of human existence contrary to God's purpose to one in which people are able to enjoy fullness of life in harmony with God," featured prominently.[32] This framework also not only set forth an integral relationship between evangelism and social concern, but also tended to equate the two as being equally important.[33] Furthermore, there was within this movement a conscious effort to read Scripture through the lens of poverty and concern for the poor. As Sugden has said, "the revelation of God in Christ was given in a particular context, the context of the poor—whether that was the Hebrew slaves escaping Egypt or the people of the land among whom Jesus ministered—so the context of the poor took priority in exegeting the meaning of the Gospel."[34] Thus, the primary starting point within mission as transformation was poverty. From there, advocates also pointed to what they believed to be unbiblical dichotomies between the eternal and the temporal, and between body and soul.[35]

Today missionaries continue to polarize around various ends of the spectrum when it comes to evangelism and compassion. The mission as transformation movement has helped Western missionaries to rediscover what the Bible says about God's own concern for the poor and marginalized. This movement is not without its problems, however; the most significant of which is that it has, as so often happens in the correction of theological error, swung the pendulum too far in the opposite direction. If, for example, we take Sugden's observation above concerning the giving of revelation, it seems far more accurate to say that God's revelation was given in a specific context, and that context was the fundamental need of God's redemption, and not poverty *per se*. In other words, we need not eisegetically place poverty as the central concern of the Bible in order to fully appreciate that God's

31. Tizon, *Transformation After Lausanne*, 5.

32. Lausanne Movement.

33. See comments by the radical discipleship element at Lausanne, in Stott, *Making Christ Known*, 24.

34. Sugden, "Mission as Transformation," 31.

35. Ibid., 32.

Word says a great deal about the poor and the necessary response of God's covenant people.

In addition, the holistic mission movement has tended to set evangelism and compassion on a level plane by locating the theological foundations for both within the biblical concept of the Kingdom of God.[36] Because of this, there has been a tendency within this movement to describe the evangelistic and compassionate mandates of the church in parallel terms, as "two sides of the same coin," or "two wings of the same bird." The genesis of this perspective in fact can especially be traced to the Grand Rapids Consultation, as we have indicated.[37]

A Proposed Way Forward

So where do we go from here? How should evangelicals wanting to be faithful to Scripture engage in compassion, and how should compassion in missions be related to evangelism? The approach of this text is that first, evangelism and compassion should never be equated with one another as being essentially the same thing. Sometimes the language of mission as transformation moves dangerously in this direction. Just because evangelism and compassion both find theological backing in the concept of the Kingdom of God, this actually tells us nothing about how these two mandates relate to one another, because it fails to either ask or answer the question of what other theological weight might be attached to these issues. Second, the question of relationship only solves part of the problem for missionaries. As already noted, we must know both the nature of Christian compassion *and* what that should look like in missions. Too often we have only sought after the nature of Christian compassion, and failed to ask the second, equally important question. As we work through this in chapter two, we will see that compassion rightly understood is necessarily integrated within the Christian life. However, in response to the second question, we discover that there is a strong biblical basis for missionaries to focus more on equipping rather than on doing.

We are indebted to the mission as transformation movement for helping to recover the integrated nature of evangelism and social concern. However, the theological misstep of the mission as transformation movement was that it seemed to presume that some ontological equality (two wings of a bird or two sides of a coin) was necessary to achieve integration. But this is simply not so. Within a biblical worldview, things can be of unequal

36. Cray, "A Theology of the Kingdom," 26.
37. Stott, *Making Christ Known*, 169–173, 182.

status and yet still be integrated. The verbal proclamation of God's revealed word and its unique role in God's redemptive plan defines the church's mission in the world in a way that nothing else quite does. But this need not relegate compassion to optional status. Compassion cannot be thought of, at least biblically, as an add-on to the Christian faith or as optional. How then should we best understand the relationship between evangelism and compassion? In answering this question, Christopher Wright helpfully uses a wheel analogy to describe these two functions of the church in terms of integration and interdependence, even while upholding distinction and difference:

> A wheel is an integrated object that necessarily must have both a hub at the center (connected to the axle and an engine), and a rim (connected to the road). Without a rim, a hub is just a rotating axle end. Without a hub, a rim is just a hoop, spinning anywhere and soon falling over. A hub and a rim are distinct things, but unless they are integrally working together, neither constitutes a wheel. If evangelism is like the hub, connected to the engine of the Gospel of God, then it also takes the living demonstration of the gospel in Christian's engagement with the world to give the hub connection and traction with the context—the road.[38]

By differentiating both evangelism and compassion, and by understanding their unique role in the Christian life, we can keep central to the missionary task the uniquely redemptive role of the church in God's salvific plan. The wheel of missionary endeavor works best when both evangelism and compassion are properly defined and practiced. What follows in this text will therefore be the unfolding of these two things as they relate to the compassionate mandate: proper definitions and best practices.

---

38. Wright, *The Mission of God's People*, 278.

2

A Missionary Theology of Compassion

JERRY M. IRELAND

IN THE BIBLE, COMPASSION consists of a whole system of interrelated
terms and ideas that define human response to God's own compassion
and mercy. These ideas especially include compassion (or mercy), love,
justice and righteousness, and peace. Furthermore, these terms all lay at
the center of what it means to be the people of God. They are inseparable
from a vibrant and God-honoring faith. For missionaries, the challenge is
not only to understand the biblical mandate for God's people as it relates
to compassion, but also to discern the best methods for advancing that
mandate in a cross-cultural context.

This chapter will set forth three key ideas related to a theology of
Christian compassion. First, the kingdom of God is the unifying theme
of Scripture. As such, the kingdom (or reign) of God forms the primary
theological basis for the compassionate response of God's people. Second,
Christian compassion is primarily a matter of discipleship and should be
seen as the proper response to God's own mercy and grace. Third, the local church as a compassionate community exists as the preeminent sign of
God's present and coming kingdom. Because of this, missionaries should
work to strengthen the work of local churches so that they become all God
intends them to be.

BIBLICAL THEOLOGY

A sound theology of compassion requires a canonical reading of Scripture that takes into consideration the various contexts of each passage. These contexts include the natural divisions within each chapter, the entire book in which a passage is found, as well as the overarching context of the entire Bible. This approach is known as *biblical theology*. As Brian Rosner has observed, "Biblical theology is principally concerned with the overall theological message of the whole Bible."[1] It is that overall theological message that will serve as the glue that holds together the varied components of Christian compassion and provides an understanding that stands on solid biblical footing. When carefully followed, this approach will help us overcome many of the common blunders related to proof-texting.

A common case of failing to consider the broader context in establishing the theological basis for compassion involves Matthew 25:31–46. This passage is often cited as the quintessential statement by Jesus calling the church to an active concern for the poor and needy.[2] In fact, Jesus says that when compassion is demonstrated for the hungry, the thirsty, the sick and those in prison, it is as if those things were done to him directly. "The King will answer and say to them, 'Truly I say to you, to the extent that you did it to one of these brothers of mine, even the least of them, you did it to Me'" (Matt 25:40).[3]

But a crucial and often overlooked phrase in this passage is "these brothers of mine." To whom is Jesus referring? It is difficult to answer that question simply by looking at Matthew 25. However, when we look to the entirety of Matthew's Gospel, we discover that "these brothers of mine" always refers to the disciples. So, as one commentator observes, "This passage thus expands on the message of 10:40–42: how people respond to Jesus' *representatives* is both a sign of their attitude to him and the basis for their reward."[4]

That "these brothers of mine" refers to Jesus' disciples ("representatives") and not the poor in general would be difficult if not impossible to know apart from reading the passage in the context of the whole Gospel of Matthew. Furthermore, the proper understanding of this passage in its context does not excuse neglecting the poor in general. As Leon Morris points

1. Rosner, "Biblical Theology," 4–11.

2. Kirk, *The Good News of the Kingdom Coming*, 92; Sider, *Good News and Good Works*, 106.

3. All Bible quotations in this chapter unless otherwise noted are from the Lockman Foundation, *New American Standard Bible*, updated edition, 1995 (NASB95).

4. France, *The Gospel of Matthew*, n.p (emphasis added).

out, "such an attitude is foreign to the teachings of Jesus. Everyone in need is to be the object of Christian benevolence."[5] We just must look elsewhere for the biblical basis. In other words, the wider we expand our interpretive horizon to include more of the biblical text, the more likely we are to arrive at a faithful interpretation of the Bible's teaching on compassion.

Normally a biblical theology progresses book by book through the Bible. Space however does not allow for this. Instead, we must look to the Bible as a whole and ask, what is the dominant theme? Then we can look for the basis for compassion by asking how passages dealing with compassion fit within and relate to that theme.

WHY COMPASSION?

"Compassion" constitutes the primary focus of this book and of this chapter. The reason for this lies in that discussions of the benevolent aspects of missions praxis have often centered around language that either inaccurately or only partially captures the biblical picture. This is evident in the tendency to describe every kind of compassion-type work as "social justice."[6] While justice is an important theme in Scripture (and a topic we deal with in some depth later on), it is not the same thing as mercy or compassion. Compassion constitutes a broader theme encompassing social justice and other important concepts as well, such as love and peacemaking. Also, in common usage, the word compassion often refers to any number of humanitarian-type endeavors done by missionaries. Because of this we will use "compassion" to broadly refer to all that the church does in missions in response to physical human need.

WHAT IS THE CENTRAL THEME OF SCRIPTURE?

If our starting point should be the dominant theme of Scripture, then what is that theme? To answer this, we could start with the Old Testament and look for recurring emphases and then ask how these emphases are carried over into the New Testament. Better still, we could start with the New Testament, and especially with the Gospels and ask, did Jesus ascribe a unifying theme to the Old Testament? Was there a central theme to Jesus' own preaching and teaching? If so, how did that theme inform His own life and ministry?

---

5. Morris, *The Gospel According to Matthew*, 639.

6. McKnight, *Kingdom Conspiracy: Returning to the Radical Mission of the Local Church*, 206.

This approach helpfully rests final authority on Jesus' understanding of the Old Testament and, importantly, emphasizes that a faithful Christian interpretation of the Old Testament depends on reading it in light of the New Testament. In asking these questions, we allow Jesus' own understanding of the Scriptures He inherited (the Old Testament), and the direction He gave to the Scriptures He was commissioning (the New Testament), to act as the foundational hermeneutic for a theology of compassion. Plus, it allows us to overcome ambiguities about how the Old Testament should function for the church. Scripture rarely gives us the specifics of how to demonstrate compassion. Rather, as we shall see, it most often provides guiding principles. Our goal then becomes to show compassion in ways that aim for the Bible's highest ideals.

When we look for the central emphasis in the teaching of Jesus, the biblical concept of the Kingdom of God clearly emerges. There does exist some debate among scholars as to whether or not the Kingdom of God, or reign of God, constitutes *a* central theme or *the* central theme of Scripture.[7] However, scholars agree that the Kingdom of God constituted the center of Jesus' own preaching. For example, George Eldon Ladd observed decades ago that "modern scholarship is quite unanimous in the opinion that the kingdom of God was the central message of Jesus."[8] Gordon Fee agrees, noting that "the universal witness of the synoptic tradition is that the absolutely central theme of Jesus' mission and message was 'the good news of the kingdom of God."[9] In other words, Jesus especially framed his own life and ministry within the concept of the Kingdom of God. As Carl Henry observes, "no subject was more frequently on the lips of Jesus Christ than the kingdom."[10] Furthermore, Jesus drew his understanding of the kingdom from the Old Testament. For Jesus, this was *the* central focus of Scripture.

DEFINING THE KINGDOM OF GOD

The Kingdom of God refers to the rule or reign of God. This is the meaning behind both the Hebrew word *malakh* and the Greek word *basileia*.[11] The exact phrase "Kingdom of God" is not found in the Old Testament, even though the concept of God as King occurs frequently. The Old Testa-

7. Allison, *Sojourners and Strangers*, 89, n.59.

8. Ladd, *Theology of the New Testament*, 57. For an excellent treatment of the emergence of this scholarly consensus see Moore, *The Kingdom of Christ*.

9. Fee, "The Kingdom of God and the Church's Global Mission," 8.

10. Henry, *Uneasy Conscience*, 46.

11. Ladd, *The Gospel of the Kingdom*, 19.

ment portrays God as king over all creation, and declares His reign would be without end. "The LORD (Yahweh) shall reign forever and ever" (Exod 15:18). God established Israel as a theocratic nation, in which human kings served as representatives of God the divine King (Deut 17:14–20; 2 Sam 23:1–7; Ps 61:6–7; Ps 72:1–4). Plus, God's judgment was meted out according to whether or not kings and nations upheld God's righteous standards (Isa 1:23). Thus even though God reigned particularly over Israel as His chosen people, He reigned also over the whole world and all were subject to His judgment.

The Old Testament prophets anticipated the coming of a truly righteous King, a Son of David, who would fully restore God's righteous reign over all of creation. Toward this end, Isaiah prophesied saying, "There will be no end to the increase of His government or of peace, on the throne of David and over his kingdom, to establish it and uphold it with justice and righteousness" (Isa 9:7). Both Matthew and Luke in their Gospels immediately describe Jesus as the fulfillment of this declaration. Luke records the angel saying of Jesus, "He will be great, and will be called the son of the Most High; and the Lord God will give Him the throne of His father David; and He will reign over the house of Jacob; and *His kingdom* will have no end" (Luke 1:32–33; cf. Matt 1:1).

Jesus himself taught that his own ministry was the inauguration of God's promised Kingdom. "Jesus came into Galilee, preaching the gospel of God, and saying, 'The time is fulfilled, and the kingdom of God is at hand; repent and believe the Gospel'" (Mark 1:14). Notice that repentance is the first-order response to the kingdom. But not only does the coming kingdom entail a spiritual deliverance, but physical deliverance as well. When John the Baptist found himself in prison, he wondered if indeed Jesus was the promised Davidic King. Jesus sent a telling response. "Go and report to John what you have seen and heard: the blind receive sight, the lame walk, the lepers are cleansed, the deaf hear, the dead are raised, the poor have the Gospel preached to them" (Luke 7:22). In other words, the appearance of the promised King of Righteousness brings both spiritual and physical deliverance. John questioned whether Jesus was truly the King he expected because his own literal release from captivity had not taken place. John's question highlights the expectation that the promised Son of David would bring about such a deliverance. Jesus' answer indicates that He would indeed do both. The physical and spiritual aspects pick up on Jesus' inaugural sermon of Luke 4:18–19 and underscores the totality of the salvation that Jesus offers. Jesus' life, and especially his resurrection, overturns the effects of the fall and points to the coming consummation when all things will be put right.

Because of this dual emphasis on the "already" aspects of the Kingdom and the "not yet" aspects, scholars now widely agree that the biblical Kingdom of God should be understood as in a sense both present and future, or what theologians call *inaugurated eschatology*. The reign of God exists now and is demonstrated in and through God's covenant people—Israel in the Old Testament and the Church in the New Testament. Jesus declared that the Kingdom had come in His Person (Matt 12:28). That reign, however, is not yet perfectly realized, as John the Baptist had discovered. The world awaits the full appearance of God's reign, when Jesus will return, destroy evil once and for all, and the entirety of creation will again be declared "good," as it was in the beginning (1 Cor 15:24–28).

COMPASSION, COMMUNITY, AND THE KINGDOM OF GOD

Both in the Old Testament anticipation and in the New Testament's partial realization of God's righteous reign, a key concern was the formation of a community of chosen people who reflect the character of God in their daily lives. This compassionate community functioned in two ways according to God's redemptive purposes. First, it functioned redemptively and formatively in that the compassion of the community was intended toward the creation of a people who reflected the mercy and compassion of God. Second, this compassionate community functioned missiologically. The missiological aspect itself functioned in two ways. First, the compassionate character of God's people was meant to attract the attention of outsiders and draw them in. This is evident in Jesus instruction to His disciples, when he said, "let your light shine before men in such a way that they may see your good works, and glorify your father who is in heaven" (Matt 5:16; cf. 1 Pet 2:11–12). It also served in judgment as God's Kingdom people set forth in their behavior the standards by which God will judge the world.[12]

A number of biblical terms inform the compassionate outlook of God's people. These terms, as we have seen, figure prominently in discussions about the kingdom of God. What exactly do they mean? As we unpack these terms, the dual emphasis described above will become clear.

12. Henry, *Christian Countermoves*, 26; Matt 5:16.

Mercy and Compassion

Usually compassion in Scripture refers to the compassion or mercy of God in offering the opportunity for repentance. For example, in Exodus 34:6–7 we read "The LORD, the LORD God, compassionate and gracious, slow to anger, and abounding in lovingkindness and truth; who keeps loving-kindness for thousands, who forgives iniquity, transgression and sin." This redemptive thrust and assurance of God's unfailing compassion toward sinners and a rebellious people is carried throughout the prophetic literature of the Old Testament. A similar emphasis appears in Isaiah 54:8, where compassion and redemption are explicitly tied together: "'In an outburst of anger I hid My face from you for a moment, But with everlasting lovingkindness I will have compassion on you,' Says the Lord your Redeemer" (also Isa 49:13; 55:7).

That said, God's compassion also demanded of this redeemed people a compassionate response to the needs of others, and thereby fashioned the people of God to reflect God's nature. "Be merciful, just as your Father is merciful," said Jesus (Luke 6:36). Consider also the following verses which link compassion for the poor and needy to faithful obedience to God:

- Proverbs 14:31 He who oppresses the poor taunts his Maker, But he who is gracious to the needy honors Him.

- Proverbs 19:17 One who is gracious to a poor man lends to the LORD, And He will repay him for his good deed.

- Micah 6:8 He has told you, O man, what is good; And what does the LORD require of you But to do justice, to love kindness, And to walk humbly with your God?

- Zechariah 7:9–10 Thus has the LORD of hosts said, 'Dispense true justice and practice kindness and compassion each to his brother; and do not oppress the widow or the orphan, the stranger or the poor; and do not devise evil in your hearts against one another.'

- Colossians 3:12 So, as those who have been chosen of God, holy and beloved, put on a heart of compassion, kindness, humility, gentleness and patience.

- Titus 3:14 Our people must also learn to engage in good deeds to meet pressing needs, so that they will not be unfruitful.

Throughout Scripture, the compassionate response of God's people to human need and suffering is declared more important than the exercise of religious duty. This is the point of Isaiah 58, in which God declares that strict religious devotion, in this case fasting, is fruitless if divorced from an active concern for the poor and needy. Furthermore, in this passage God declares that His people can have no expectation of justice and mercy themselves if they do not dispense it to those in need (Isa 58:2, 10–11; cf. Hos 6:6). This idea is reiterated by Jesus who said "blessed are the merciful, for they shall receive mercy" (Matt 5:7).

A prime example of the formative nature of compassion for God's people can be seen in the events of Israel's exodus from Egypt. God, in an act of compassion, redeemed His people from their bondage. God's mighty and historically situated acts pointed to His presence among His people. "And [God] said, "Certainly I will be with you, and this shall be the sign to you that it is I who have sent you: when you have brought the people out of Egypt, you shall worship God at this mountain" (Exod 3:12). And indeed, the exodus of the Hebrew slaves from Egypt is paradigmatic for the greater redemption provided for in the life, death, and resurrection of Christ.[13]

Nehemiah explicitly attributes the deliverance of the Israelites and His provision for them in the wilderness to the compassion of God (see Neh 9:19–28). As we have observed, God's compassion then is oriented toward deliverance from oppression. But that is only one side of the story. The redemption of God results in God setting forth certain ethical and moral standards for His covenant people, not as conditions of their release, but as the proper response to God's grace. This is most evident in the Ten Commandments in the Old Testament and in the Sermon on the Mount in the New Testament. Both of these articulate what it means to love God and neighbor (Exod 20:1–17; Matt 5–7) and relate the faithful response to God in the context of moral and ethical expectations. To be the covenant people of God meant reflecting the character of God in every relationship. To know God was to honor Him through the merciful and compassionate treatment of others.

The compassion of God also functions missiologically. This was explicit in the promise made to Abraham when God said, "through you the nations will be blessed." This missiological aspect found frequent emphases by the prophets throughout Israel's long cycle of rebellion and repentance. Isaiah for example declares of Israel's Babylonian captivity, "When the LORD will have compassion on Jacob and again choose Israel, and settle them in their own land, then *strangers will join them and attach themselves to the*

---

13. For example, Jesus' encounter with Satan in the desert casts Him as a new Moses (Luke 4:1–13).

house of Jacob" (Isa 14.1). Similarly, Hosea declares "I will sow her for My-self in the land. I will also have compassion on her who had not obtained compassion, And I will say to those who were not My people, 'You are My people!' And they will say, 'You are my God!'" (Hos 2:23). What are the prophets saying here? They are saying that just as it was in the Exodus, when God delivers His people from their Babylonian captivity, He will do so be-cause of His compassion for Israel *and* as a demonstration to the nations of the compassion of Yahweh. Simply put, God's love for His people provides merciful relief for those in need, and signals to those outside that the God of Israel is a compassionate God.

Justice and Righteousness

No qualities are more directly linked to the nature of God's rule or reign than that of justice and righteousness. Scripture describes justice and righ-teousness as the primary characteristics of God's reign, as evident in the twice repeated formula that these "are the foundation of His throne" (Ps 97:1–2; 89:14). This can only mean that these two qualities especially define the reign of God in a way that nothing else does.

The terms justice (Heb. *mishpat*) and righteousness (Heb. *tsedeqah*) occur together about forty times in the Old Testament. As with compassion, these also often refer both to God's own character and to what God expects of His covenant people. The Psalmist declares that God "loves righteousness and justice; the earth is full of the lovingkindness of the Lord" (Ps 33:5). These same qualities are to characterize the lives of those who worship YHWY. Of Abram God declares, "I have chosen him, so that he may com-mand his children and his household after him to keep the way of the Lord by doing justice and righteousness" (Gen 18:19). And Job declares "I put on righteousness, and it clothed me; My justice was like a robe and a turban" (Job 29:14).

Frequently God's justice and righteousness find expression in concern for the poor and needy, especially for orphans and widows. Those who are most vulnerable in society are a special concern of God and thereby of God's people. "He executes justice for the orphan and the widow, and shows His love for the alien by giving them food and clothing" (Deut 10:18). Scripture expresses this care for the vulnerable in both a passive and active sense. The people of God are to take care not to oppress the poor, the needy, orphans, widows, and foreigners, but also to come to their defense when others mis-treat them. For example, Jeremiah captures both senses in the exhortation to "Do justice and righteousness, and deliver the one who has been robbed from the power of his oppressor. Also do not mistreat or do violence to the stranger, the orphan, or the widow; and do not shed blood in this place" (Jer 22:3; cf. Isa 1:17). Justice and righteousness thus require of God's people both the avoidance of repressive behavior toward others as well as rescuing the victims of oppression whenever we become aware of their plight.

The common linking of justice with righteousness indicates that they are to be understood together as referring to a single idea. Amos captures this clearly in the form of a Hebrew parallelism, declaring "Let justice roll on like a river, righteousness like a never ending stream" (Amos 5:24). A parallelism is a poetic device used to express a single idea in two different but similar (parallel) ways. As Cray says, "these things form the basic characteristic of God's rule as King. Righteousness and Justice form one quality, not two. The Old Testament knows no distinction between social justice and private morality."[14]

The Bible's call for the people of God to demonstrate justice and righteousness therefore can be understood as emphasizing both the inherent rights of individuals (justice) and human actions that provide for, ensure, and protect those rights (righteousness).[15] The Ten Commandments in fact are inherently "rights" oriented. Murder is forbidden because others have a right to their own life. Stealing is forbidden because they have a right to their own property. These rights find grounding in that all persons have value by virtue of being created in the image of God.[16] In fact, the prophet Jeremiah specifically links oppression of the poor and needy to neglect of their rights (Jer 5:28). Justice and righteousness then are crucial to the formation of a Kingdom people. As Smedes says:

> The prophets of the Old Testament walked the streets of Israel's cities, probed into Judah's courts, poked around in the market places, and were outraged at what they saw. They saw injustice aplenty, and they roared their indignation at those who had money and power for raping the poor and oppressing the weak. They were not detached philosophers spinning out theories of justice; they were angry prophets attacking injustice as they saw it. Yet when the prophets spoke for justice, they must have been moved by some vision of justice, of a people made whole and right in the kingdom of God.[17]

14. Cray, "A Theology of the Kingdom," 34.

15. On the link between justice and rights in the Ten Commandments, see Smedes, *Mere Morality*, 15–16, 23. See also Mott, who defines "rights" as "God's claim on us." He further says "rights . . . are as much a matter of responsibility as they are of freedom. Every right implies a duty," Mott, *Biblical Ethics and Social Change*, 53.

16. Smedes, *Mere Morality*, 15, 23–24.

17. Ibid., 27.

The New Testament uses a single word, *dikaiosunē,* to express both ideas (justice and righteousness). Unfortunately, most of us think of this term in the New Testament solely in terms of justification, of being made right in the eyes of God through faith in Jesus. And in several passages that is indeed the intended sense. But in other passages, righteousness is used in keeping with the Old Testament pattern of ethical obedience characteristic of God's covenant people. This is evident in Rom 6:13–20, in which righteousness is contrasted with living in sinful disregard of God. In Eph 4:24 the righteousness of those who are a new creation in Christ is to result in kindness and forgiveness toward others, based on God's own undeserved kindness and forgiveness. Righteousness also produces generosity (2 Cor 9:10), and believers are to be trained in righteousness (2 Tim 3:16). For Paul, God's righteousness creates a people whose lives testify to the reconciling love of God. We might also recall that Jesus spoke of righteousness not primarily as a state of being but as an action. It was something to be practiced in a way that surpassed that of the Pharisees (Matt 6:1; Matt 5:20). Jesus and Paul also directly associated righteousness with the Kingdom of God (Matt 6:33; Rom 14:7) and as a quality of God to be imitated.

Love

The basis for the people of God defending and providing for the needs of others is not duty, but love.[18] Two Old Testament passages of Scripture especially emphasize the importance of loving both neighbors and strangers. Leviticus 19:18 instructs the Israelites, "Do not seek revenge or bear a grudge against one of your people, but love your neighbor as yourself. I am the LORD." Later in that same chapter we read, "The alien living with you must be treated as one of your native-born. Love him as yourself, for you were aliens in Egypt. I am the LORD your God." Jesus combines Leviticus 19:18 with Deut 6:4 in declaring that the greatest commandment is loving God and the second is loving one's neighbor (Mark 12:29–31). This means that, as Lewis Smedes has said of the Ten Commandments, they not only point to the minimal requirement of justice, but also to the maximal requirement of love.[19]

If loving our neighbor is the second greatest commandment, we may be inclined like the lawyer in the parable of the Good Samaritan to ask "who is my neighbor?" In his response, Jesus combines the definition of neighbor and stranger, making the point that they can be and often are one in the

18. Mott, *Biblical Ethics,* 48.

19. Smedes, 16.

same. A neighbor is anyone in need and cannot be defined according to race or social or economic status (Luke 10:30–37). The kind of love God requires is not just loving one's family and friends but also one's enemies (Matt 5:43–46). Furthermore, the motivation for enemy love is the indiscriminate compassion of God, who causes "the sun to rise on the evil and the good, and sends rain on the righteous and unrighteous" (5:45b). Once again, the compassion of God provides the model for the compassion of God's people.

In Scripture, love is concrete and action oriented. It is not primarily an emotion. A number of passages bear this out, such as 1 John 3:16–18. Here the loving actions of Jesus in laying down His life for others is described as a paradigm for the loving actions of his followers. "This is how we know what love is: Jesus Christ laid down his life for us. And we ought to lay down our lives for our brothers. If anyone has material possessions and sees his brother in need but has no pity on him, how can the love of God be in him? Dear children, let us not love with words or tongue but with actions and in truth." Jesus' love is not only a pattern to be followed, but makes possible the love of His disciples. "Even as I have loved you, love one another" (John 13:34; RSV). As Mott points out, "Jesus' love is both the source and measure of their love."[20]

Hesed

Another important biblical term that informs our understanding of compassion is the Hebrew noun *hesed*, frequently translated as love, loving-kindness, or mercy. *Hesed* constitutes the highest expectation of God for his people. It is the measure *par excellence* of what God desires in our relationship with Him and with one another. In Hosea 6:6 God says, "For I delight in loyalty (*hesed*) rather than sacrifice, and in the knowledge of God rather than burnt offerings." Likewise, Micah declares of God, "He has showed you, O man, what is good. And what does the LORD require of you? To act justly and to love kindness (*hesed*) and to walk humbly with your God." And in Proverbs we read "What is desirable in a man is his kindness (*hesed*)" (Prov 19:22). All three of these passages emphasize that the people of God should be especially characterized by the expression of kindness and love toward others. In all of this, the goal is that the people of God would reflect the qualities of God's own nature. As we have seen again and again in this chapter, faith and compassion go hand in hand.

20. Mott, *Biblical Ethics*, 41.

Peace

In the Bible, peace (*shalom*) represents a state of being, wholeness, where justice, righteousness, and love are present as the realization of God's will (cf. Isa 52:7). The term occurs roughly 250 times in the Old Testament. The New Testament equivalent (eirēne) occurs about 100 times. From these several important aspects of peace can be discerned. Peace represented the blessing of God (Num 6:26). Jesus instructs his disciples to be peacemakers (Matt 5:9), and his conflict with Satan is described as the absence of peace (Matt 10:34). Paul describes peace as an essential quality of God ("God of Peace"; Rom 15:33, et al.). Paul and other New Testament writers also describe peacemaking as something believers are to actively pursue (Rom 14:19; 2 Tim 2:22; He 12:14, 1 Pet 3:11; James 3:18).[21]

THE KINGDOM OF GOD AND DISCIPLESHIP

The real danger in contemporary missiology when it comes to compassion lies in the tendency toward the professionalization of compassion. Many missionaries today conceive of compassionate missions according to an NGO or parachurch structure. These structures often develop independently of local believers and tend to be funded and run by outsiders. As a missionary living in West Africa, I have heard countless tales told by African pastors describing how donor-driven projects connected to NGOs have ruined the image and effectiveness of the local church. These stories are sadly similar. An organization wanting to do good comes in and starts some sort of benevolence program. Often times the organization offers to provide their service through a local church. I even recently heard of one organization that was using a local church to distribute lump sums of cash in the amount of $100. I presume the idea was that folks would use this money to start small business that would eventually help people escape poverty. Yet, almost all of these programs end the same. Eventually resources run out, but only after having created dependency in the community. Those called to be salt and light are no longer preserving and illuminating, but have become dependent and materialistic. Local church members end up losing sight of the joy of giving and think only in terms of what they can get. And when the handouts disappear, so too does most of the congregation.

All of this results from the loss of compassionate virtues and ethics as part of the disciple-making process. The cure for this malady is to understand Christian compassion primarily as a matter of character formation, or

---

21. Swartley, "Peace," *Dictionary of Scripture and Ethics*, 583–86.

discipleship.[22] In fact, looking back at the early church, one discovers that the compassionate lifestyle of potential converts was a chief concern in the disciple-making process. In some cases, individuals were denied baptism who showed no genuine love toward others. Because of this, the process of conversion involved more than simply saying a short prayer. Instead, the process of discipleship could take years because the development of this compassionate orientation was considered indispensable for true conversion. To cite one example among many, in the early Christian text known as *The Apostolic Tradition*, usually reckoned to be a third-century discipleship document, we read that candidates for baptism should be carefully examined in order to establish "whether they lived uprightly as catechumens, whether they honored the widows, whether they visited the sick, whether they were thorough in performing good works."[23] Early Christians placed great value on the ability of the faith community to demonstrate radical forms of love for both one another and for outsiders. This love attracted unbelievers and made them want to be part of this compassionate community.[24]

Somewhere along the way this emphasis has been lost. Perhaps, when it comes to missions, we have lost this emphasis on character formation because it is not something we can put in a shoebox and ship around the world. We cannot pile it into shipping containers or send a six-person team to build it in a week's time span. But when compassion is understood in terms of character formation, then this has radical implications for the way we go about missions. Most importantly, we should never engage in compassionate missions in a way that robs local congregations of this aspect of their essential Christian identity. As we look to what Scripture says about the compassionate orientation of God's people, we will see that the primary focus is on the development of a community that daily lives out this compassionate disposition, as it loves God and neighbor.

WHAT IS CONVERSION?

This approach of the early church relating to compassion and discipleship is strengthened by looking at the meaning of conversion. In Scripture, conversion is a matter of accepting the merciful offer of God's redemption and of

22. Stassen and Gushee, *Kingdom Ethics*, 58–59.

23. Hippolytus, *On the Apostolic Tradition*, 20:1. *The Didache*, usually dated to the late first or early second century, also highlights the necessity of compassion among new believers as a matter of discipleship.

24. See especially Kreider, *The Change of Conversion and the Origin of Christendom*; Green, *Evangelism in the Early Church*, 20.

living under the rule of the King, as we have already seen. This includes becoming compassionate (merciful) towards others in need. Paul describes this using the imagery of light: "For you were once darkness, but now you are light in the Lord. Live as children of light." Those given entrance to the Kingdom are not to just believe the truth, they are to practice it (John 3:21).

Paul K. Moser has described this interdependence of faith and obedient, loving action as *kardiatheology*, from the Greek word *kardia*, meaning "heart." Moser defines theology of the heart as "an entrustment of oneself to God that involves one's motivational heart and is therefore action-oriented."[25] Moser's point is that true biblical faith is not solely internal and spiritual. Rather true faith should result in obedient and loving action modeled on the loving actions of God. In defense of this idea, Moser refers to Paul. "For neither circumcision counts for anything nor uncircumcision, *but keeping the commandments of God*" (1 Cor 7:19, RSV).[26]

So strong was the link in the early church between conversion-discipleship and the necessity of caring for the needy that later commentators were perplexed that "almsgiving seem[ed] to be encouraged more for salvation of the giver than for alleviation of poverty."[27] In other words, sermons in the early church tended to emphasize that if one was not actively concerned for the poor, then one's salvation was in question. This issue was not so much how much was given, but whether the giving was done freely and joyfully. The basis of this was that one's outward life reflected the attitude of the heart. One's action's revealed one's true beliefs and showed whether a person had truly appreciated the mercy God had shown them.

This idea of the interrelationship between faith and compassionate or loving action is born out in the story of the rich man in Luke 18:18–27. It is also noteworthy to observe that the story is framed in the context of the Kingdom of God, and the need to enter the kingdom as a child (Luke 18:17). The questioner, described as "a ruler" is certainly someone of elevated social status. Indeed, by calling Jesus "Good Teacher" the ruler made an effort to force a return compliment regarding his status. Social norms of the day called for nothing less. But Jesus would have no part in this social game. By asking "why do you call me good?" Jesus challenged the widely held idea that goodness and social status went hand in hand.[28] Specifically, he challenged the man's notion of "goodness" by bringing up the Ten Commandments, which as we have mentioned, formed the theological and ethical basis for

25. Moser, "Faith," 20.

26. Ibid., 21 (emphasis in Moser).

27. Rhee, *Loving the Poor, Saving the Rich*, 75.

28. Green, *The Gospel of Luke*, n.p., Accordance electronic ed.

the people of God. The man responds that he has kept all of them since his youth. To which of course, Jesus responds, "One thing you still lack; sell all that you possess and distribute it to the poor and you shall have treasure in heaven; and come follow Me" (Luke 18:22). Luke then records that the ruler went away sad.

The point of this story is very much in concert with what has been said throughout this chapter. The kingdom of God has both spiritual and ethical dimensions. To be a subject of the King is to care about what the King cares about, including the poor (cf. Exod 23:11; Lev 19:9–16; Deut 15:1–18). As with Isaiah 58, religious duty divorced from caring for those in need misses entirely what it means to be the people of God. True obedience to the commandments (conversion) involves both a change in heart and in actions. God has graciously and freely shown compassion, and his people are to do the same. Religious commitment and obedient actions are inseparable. Faith without works is dead.

Luke goes on to present a stark and surprising contrast to the rich ruler. This time the focus is on someone of low social status, namely Zaccheus, a tax collector. In many ways, Zaccheus is the very antithesis of the rich ruler. Though also rich, Zaccheus is socially despised because of his role as chief tax collector. Plus, in the biblical account he had no influence over the crowd that blocked his view. He had wealth but not power, whereas the young ruler had both. Zaccheus though displays an attitude very different than that of the rich ruler. He is clearly not concerned about social appearances, even risking humiliation by publically climbing up a tree to see Jesus. Jesus not only notices, but honors Zaccheus by coming to his home. Deeply touched by the gracious mercy of Jesus, Zaccheus freely gives half of his possessions to the poor (Luke 19:1–10). Everything that the rich ruler should have been, Zaccheus was. He trusted not in his status, but in Jesus. The mercy of Jesus compelled him to likewise be merciful. Salvation was not something to be earned, but to be received. His conversion resulted in a changed heart from which flowed loving deeds.

In many ways, the contrast between the rich ruler and Zaccheus might also serve as a parable of modern missions endeavors and compassionate outreach. The rich ruler, sadly, represents many western approaches to compassionate missions. We often go trusting in our resources and in our status as highly-educated, well-financed, and knowledgeable experts. We not only know the Ten Commandments but have at our disposal half a dozen different versions of Scripture in which to read them, along with countless commentaries and theological dictionaries. Yet, have we truly understood these commandments? Have we seen in them the necessity and importance of a people of God empowered to freely and voluntarily give out of their own resources, like Zaccheus? Are we instead approaching compassionate missions with vain confidence in ourselves, thinking we have all the answers? If the latter, the solution lies in a renewed emphasis on the compassionate character of the Christian community and engaging in compassionate missions in ways that foster and develop that character.

THE CHURCH AS A COMPASSIONATE COMMUNITY

The people of God under the New Covenant were to embody God's own righteousness. As with the Old Covenant this was never to earn God's favor, but as the proper response to God's grace. The disciples' righteousness was to exceed that of the Pharisees (Matt 5:20). Thus Paul describes the church as helpers in the Kingdom (Col 4:11). He also says, "the kingdom of God is not eating and drinking, but righteousness and peace in the Holy Spirit" (Rom 14:17). He therefore instructs Timothy to pursue righteousness (2 Tim 2:22). To repent in response to God's gracious offer of mercy is to in turn become one whose own life reflects that same mercy toward others. "Be merciful just as your heavenly father is merciful" (Luke 6:36). By their preaching and by their living the church is to declare what good things are to come for those who put their trust in Christ.

What Jesus taught in the parable of the Good Samaritan, he also modeled. This is evident in that Jesus' miracles were often driven by his compassion for social outsiders, including the sick (Mark 5:25–34), the poor and needy (Mark 10:46–52), women (Luke 7:11–17), racial and religious outcasts (Luke 17:11–19: Matt 8:5–13), and sinners (John 9).[29] In each case Jesus, moved with compassion, responded to someone in need through loving action. As such, Jesus' miracles served a dual role. They evidenced His status as the promised Son of David, and pointed forward to the final restoration of all things. Therefore, His miracles are both eschatological evidence—the Kingdom has appeared in the person and work of Jesus, and eschatological sign—the Kingdom is still coming, and healing and wholeness are its essence. So, while the church as the charismatic people of God should seek after and pray for miracles with faith and fervency, to stop there is to miss the full importance of miracles in Jesus's ministry.

There is a direct connection between Jesus' miracles and the compassionate expectations of the Kingdom of God. Jesus' significance as the primary locus of the reign of God gave compassionate direction to the church He called into existence. The church cannot therefore simply pray for the poor and needy, and consider that we have done our duty. James warns

---

29. Verhey, *The Great Reversal: Ethics and the New Testament*, 49.

against precisely this, saying "if a brother or sister is without clothing and in need of daily food, and one of you says to them, 'Go in peace, be warmed and filled,' and yet you do not give them what is necessary for their body, what use is that?" (James 2:16; cf. 2 Cor 8:7–9).

The reality is that Jesus' followers cannot always miraculously heal. We can always ask, seek, and knock, but healing is ultimately the prerogative of God. The church can always engage in loving action even when healings do not take place. The compassionate response of the early church to the needs around them emerged precisely on these grounds. As Verhey points out, Jesus' compassion for everyone regardless of social status "shaped the mind of the early church to a similar indiscriminate compassion."[30] In other words, Jesus' miracles not only compelled his disciples to become a charismatic community in which signs and wonders were present, but to become a compassionate community of practical service as well. If we are to be like Jesus, then it is not enough to simply pray for others. We must also be moved by compassion to take action. Thus, what Jesus said to the lawyer who questioned Him in the parable of the Good Samaritan he says to the whole church in regard to compassion (mercy): "go and do likewise."

THE KINGDOM, MISSION, AND THE LOCAL CHURCH

Since our primary concern is to articulate a theology of compassion for cross-cultural missions, it is worth asking at this point precisely how the concept of the Kingdom of God relates to the concept of *missio Dei*, or mission of God, especially since there is a direct theological connection between the Kingdom of God and *missio Dei*.[31] Furthermore, these concepts directly inform the nature of the local church.

The term *missio Dei* relates to the church's participation in the redemptive mission of God to all nations.[32] God's plan for the redemption of fallen humanity calls forth a covenant people tasked with participation in declaring the Good News of what God has done in Jesus Christ. As such, the Kingdom of God and *missio Dei* overlap in that it is God as King who issues forth divine commands through His revealed Word. Thus, Johannes Verkuyl rightly states that the Kingdom of God is the goal of *missio Dei*.[33] God works in the world to accomplish His redemptive purpose to save creation from the fall

30. Ibid. By "early church" Verhey means the apostolic church, as he refers solely to material contained in the Gospels.

31. For *missio Dei* as the grand narrative of Scripture, see Wright, *The Mission of God*.

32. See Tennent, *Invitation to World Missions*, 55–59.

33. Verkuyl, "The Kingdom of God as the Goal of Missio Dei," 168–175.

and all its effects (Rom 8:22). Missionaries are those called to be involved in this work by engaging directly in cross-cultural ministry. Local churches differ in purpose in that their focus lies primarily, though not exclusively, in reaching and discipling believers in their own context. Local churches too have a missions mandate, as is evident throughout Paul's letters. So, while there is certainly overlap between the nature and function of missions and that of the local church, it is vitally important that we do not confuse the two. Alan Johnson will develop this idea in more detail, but for now a few basic ideas need to be established, and to do so we turn to the important work of Charles Van Engen on this topic.

In his book, *God's Missionary People*, Van Engen discusses the dangers of compassionate missions being divorced from the local church. Pointing to the "baby boomer" generation in America in the 1960's in support, Van Engen shows that compassion came to be separated from a direct attachment to local congregations, as that generation became increasingly dissatisfied with the church as an institution. People gave up participation in local congregations, though still considered themselves part of the Church universal. These "free range" Christians, as I call them, then went out and joined the Peace Corps and any number of other programs geared toward the transformation of society.[34]

The social activism in which they engaged, once divorced from the local church, resulted in a deformed understanding of missions. Believers largely lost sight of participation in *missio Dei* as a cross-cultural endeavor. Instead, they tended to see everything the church does as mission. It was in this context that Stephen Neill responded saying, "if everything is mission, nothing is mission."[35] As Van Engen explains, "they wanted mission without the church, and they would only give allegiance to the church insofar as it fulfilled the political and social functions they considered to be mission."[36]

The solution for overcoming this is two-fold. First, we must understand the local church as a compassionate community such as described above. This compassionate community exhibits first of all, care for needy members of the faith community, and secondarily, for their neighbors who are in need. Second, missionaries working in compassion should direct their efforts toward the strengthening of this capacity among local churches and local believers. As Scot McKnight says, "The only place kingdom work

---

34. Van Engen, *God's Missionary People*, chapter 1, n.p.
35. Neill, *Creative Tension*, 81.
36. Van Engen, *God's Missionary People*, chapter 1, n.p.

is and can be done is in and through the local church when disciples (kingdom citizens, church people) are doing kingdom mission."[37]

To better understand the first aspect of this, we again turn to Van Engen, who has borrowed and expanded on Oscar Cullman's understanding of the reign of God in terms of concentric circles. Cullman referred to an inner and outer circle, designating the inner circle R1, and the outer R2. R1 indicates the reign of Christ in the church, the place where Christ reigns most fully in the present. R2 refers to the reign of Christ over all creation (Ephesians 1; Colossians 1). This reign is exercised over the unwilling and unknowing, who have never made a decision to follow Jesus. To this, Van Engen adds R3, designating to the reign of Christ over "principalities and powers." Missionary churches are planted in R2, where the Lord reigns over the lives of the unwilling. Through their evangelizing and living as re-born citizens of the Kingdom of God, local believers constantly press in and expand the territory of R1 by adding to their own numbers. As it does, the gates of hell cannot prevail against it (Matt16:18), which is presumably what Van Engen means by R3. In all of this, the church does not usher in or bring about the Kingdom, but it points to it as a sign.[38]

The goal then of the local church is not to just do good things in the community. Anyone can do that. Rather as subjects of Jesus the King, churches ultimately want to see those living under R2 pack up their things and take up residence within R1. The aim is to invite the lost into the church and for the church to so powerfully evidence the presence of Christ in both word and deed, that joining the community becomes irresistible. This is the first step in conversion.

In some ways, our missionary endeavors in the realm of compassionate ministry run the risk of doing to the local churches we partner with something very similar to what the baby boomers had done. We run the risk of separating the compassionate mandate inherent in the kingdom of God from its primary locus as a matter of discipleship among local believers. This robs local congregations of their missional mandate. We do this by setting up compassionate programs that do not involve the local church or involve it only as a passive partner. The result is that the local church has no reason to look outward because the outward aspect of its mission is being done by others. Local churches then inevitably turn inward, and all of their activities become about their own people and programs.

Van Engen argues that if the local church is to emerge as a truly missional church being effectively used in the expansion of R1 into R2, then

---

37. McKnight, *Kingdom Conspiracy*, 208.

38. Van Engen, under chapter 7, "The Local Church and the Kingdom of God."

it must demonstrate all of the following marks: *koinonia* (community), *kerygma* (proclamation), *diakonia* (service), and *martyria* (witness). Of these, *koinonia* provides the foundation for all the others. When it does not function properly, neither do the others.

If the church turns all its attention inward and fails to engage the needs of the community, then *koinonia* changes into what C. Peter Wagner calls *koinonitis*.[39] The power of community mutates into the plague of self-interest. Then, not only is *koinonia* left unrealized, but all the other distinguishing marks of the church suffer as well. As Van Engen explains, "being for the world, identification with the oppressed, mission, proclamation witness, and yearning for numerical growth are meaningless outside the light of this supreme mark of the Church."[40] What Paul says in 1 Corinthians 13 holds true. Without love it is all for nothing.[41]

Charity Begins at Home

The importance of *koinonia* means that the church's compassionate activity must begin with those in need within the faith community. A number of passages of Scripture bear this out. Jesus said, "By this all men will know that you are My disciples, if you have love for one another" (John 13:35). Acts emphasizes this communal aspect of caring for one another as well (Acts 2:45). And indeed, the primary meaning of *koinonia* relates to sharing life together, including one's possessions.[42] Paul also argues for prioritizing the needy within the church, but also declares that it must not stop there. "So then, while we have opportunity, let us therefore do good to all people, and especially to those who are of the household of faith" (Gal 6:10). But there are important theological reasons for this. The church in mission functions best when its members are healthy and whole, when they experience *shalom*. This requires community because in Christianity, to be saved is to enter a Christ-centered community.

Therefore, it is not surprising that much of the New Testament emphasis in giving and caring for the needy focuses on the faith community. This brings us back to our main point. Whenever missionaries insert themselves as the sole source of compassionate ministry, the result will always be local churches whose spiritual growth is stunted. When compassion becomes

---

39. Van Engen, under chapter 6, "Kononia: Love One Another."
40. Ibid.
41. Ibid.
42. Gonzalez, *Faith and Wealth*, 85.

professionalized by outsiders, the motivation for intercommunity compassion is lost, and so too is the power for effective outreach.

Howard Synder has argued similarly from Ephesians 2:8–10. This passage says, "For by grace you have been saved through faith; and that not of yourselves, *it is* the gift of God; not as a result of works, so that no one may boast. For we are His workmanship, created in Christ Jesus for good works, which God prepared beforehand so that we would walk in them." From this passage, Snyder draws two conclusions. First, the church accomplishes God's purposes "by what it is (a redeemed community) and by what it does (good works)." Therefore, "the Church's first task is to be the redeemed community."[43] It is to be the people of God being increasingly made whole through their common life together in worship of Christ and service to one another. "The Church is before it does."[44] Missions efforts then that short-circuit the power of "being" do damage also to a local congregation's motivation and impulse to "do." By recasting missionary compassion in terms of building the capacity of local churches, which as we have argued is the biblical paradigm, we avoid overestimating the role of the church in community transformation.[45]

CONCLUSION

This chapter has shown that to be the covenant people of Christ the King means not only believing the right things, but also doing the right things. In Christianity faith and action go together as God's covenant people live in such a way as to reflect the mercy and compassion of God who is Himself merciful and compassionate. Compassion is a vital part of Christian discipleship, and where compassion is absent it is appropriate to question the genuineness of one's commitment. This seems to have been a pattern present in the early church at least up through the third century.

This has profound implications for missions. Missionaries going to majority world nations often find themselves gripped by the vast human suffering they encounter. They find themselves face to face with young children (who perhaps remind them of their own children) standing on street corners dressed in rags and begging for food, or families living in shanty compounds with little or no access to running water or basic necessities. We see these things and we want to help. Where we often go wrong, however, is in forgetting that the role of missionaries differs fundamentally from that

43. Synder, *The Community of the King*, n.p.

44. Snyder, chapter 4.

45. Snyder, chapter 4.

of the local church. It is the local church that is called to push back the darkness inherent in the world (R2) and work for the expansion of God's reign through the church (R1). The local church does this first by caring for its own members, through shared life, through *koinonia*. Church members then experience a degree of shalom, which propels them out into the world as salt and light. Their goal is not the transformation of society, but to see God expand His Kingdom. They serve this goal by living as children of the King and by lavishing mercy and compassion on all those in need, and especially on those who can never repay them. As McKnight points out, "Christian public actions are, then, the 'spillover' of the church's inner workings. A Christian not engaged in the world in 'good works' has failed to live according to the kingdom vision."[46] Christian compassionate missions therefore must work not only to foster this notion of "spillover," but also work in ways which do not hinder it.

46. McKnight, *Kingdom Conspiracy*, 207.

3

Missions and Compassion

The Indigenous Principles

ALAN R. JOHNSON

ON THE SURFACE IT would seem that the practice of cross-cultural mission and the practice of acts of compassion in Jesus' name would go hand in hand. In the history of the Christian faith there has always been what Paul Johnson calls the matrices of proclamation and compassion.[1] Yet in the world of cross-cultural missions people equally committed theologically to the proclamation of the Good News of Jesus and to caring for people in Jesus' name often part company radically in the way these two elements are practiced on the ground.

In this chapter the focus is on how "indigenous church principles" as conceived of in global missions relate to the practice of compassion ministry, specifically in the context of cross-cultural missionary labor. The notion of indigeneity can help to resolve tensions that arise in the practice of compassion in missions and provide the conceptual material to develop integrated practice. This begins with a brief overview of how the split between proclamation and compassion occurred in the modern missionary movement and calls for their reintegration. The second section introduces the notion of indigenous church and discusses its implications in missionary practice. The conclusion examines compassion through the grid of indigenous principles

---

1. Johnson, *A History of Christianity*, 234, 252.

and illustrates how integrated ministry can look at the level of the individual and ministry team.

MISSION, COMPASSION AND THE NEED FOR INTEGRATED PRACTICE

The practical issues that necessitate such a discussion grow out of the legacy of the fundamentalist-liberal divide of the late 19th and early 20th centuries. With the rise of theological liberalism that challenged the authority of the Bible, all that was left was the Fatherhood of God and the brotherhood of man. In cross-cultural missions this meant no need for conversionary evangelism, rather social action and bringing civilization was required. Evangelicals who held to the authority of the Bible rejected this view and reacted against it. Mission came to be seen as only evangelism and the planting of the church. This was a shift from the situation of the late 18th and early 19th centuries when evangelicals of the first and second great awakening periods were very active socially.

In the mid-20th century Carl Henry began to rework through the relationships between Christian social concern and the ministry of compassion and evangelism and church planting.[2] Today in the world of cross-cultural mission there remains a lack of consensus on how the relationship between compassion and mission plays out on the ground. Theologically there is agreement that both are critical but it is the practical questions that remain complex.[3]

This issue of compassion ministry in mission is taking on increasing importance for mission agencies that have traditionally been involved in church planting because an increasing number of those applying are interested in ministry oriented towards Christian social action rather than proclamation of the gospel. This is part of what is known as the "social turn" in American evangelicalism and it creates challenges for agencies and field teams that see church planting as a high priority.

Two kinds of problems emerge in this climate. The first is that there can be situations where people take polar positions. On one side are those

2. Henry, *The Uneasy Conscience of Modern Fundamentalism*. For an in-depth discussion of Henry's theology of evangelism and social concern see Ireland, *Evangelism and Social Concern in the Theology of Carl F. H. Henry*.

3. See Lausanne Covenant, Article 5, "Christian Social Responsibility." This illustrates well the recognition that declaring the good news and social involvement are "part of our Christian duty" and that salvation should be transforming in both the personal and social realms. How this is worked out in local church ministry and cross-cultural mission is where there is ongoing debate.

who see cross-cultural mission as only properly involving proclamation of the gospel and planting the church, while on the other people can only conceive of mission in compassion and humanitarian terms. A second scenario is where a missionary will acknowledge the importance of both dimensions but take a compartmentalized view and see their ministry as only working on one dimension, either proclamation or compassion.

Missionary ministry that seeks full integration in practice along both dimensions best aligns with the biblical data and the current mission realities. Central to the conception of cross-cultural mission as a holistic enterprise are the indigenous mission principles. Traditionally, the indigenous principle of self-support is invoked to argue that compassion ministries need to become self-sustaining. There is now a great deal of literature that provides practical guidelines for avoiding dependency on outside funding.[4] Further, the whole idea of indigeneity points to a holistic conception of cross-cultural mission and provides the guiding parameters for best practices.

INDIGENOUS PRINCIPLES AND THE WORK OF CROSS-CULTURAL MISSION

Wilbert Shenk sees the idea of the indigenous church as the most universally recognized concept to emerge out of the modern missionary movement.[5] He notes that while many associate the idea with the British Anglican Henry Venn (1796–1873) of the Church Mission Society, and Rufus Anderson (1796–1880) who served as the senior secretary of the American Board of Commissioners for Foreign Missions, it has not been possible to trace the actual origins.[6]

In the early phases of the modern missionary movement Shenk notes that among the first generation of workers some began to explicate the goal of mission in terms of the development of churches run by local Christians rather than the missionary.[7] He observes that:

> By 1840 something of a conventional wisdom concerning missionary methods and principles was beginning to take shape. Some missions had by now been established thirty or forty

4. Corbett, and Fikkert, *When Helping Hurts*; Schwartz, *When Charity Destroys Dignity*. For a list of resources on dependency issues see the World Missions Associates website at http://wmausa.org/resources/article/.

5. Shenk, "The Origins and Evolution of the Three-Selfs in Relation to China," 28.

6. Ibid.

7. Ibid.

years, and there was greater realism about the nature of the task. Rufus Anderson and Henry Venn came into leadership as a part of the second generation of the modern missionary movement. Both men saw the need to clarify the aim of missionary work and the means by which the aim might be achieved.[8]

Venn and Anderson emphasized different aspects in their thinking on the indigenous church. For Venn it was the issue of self-support, and for Anderson it was native leadership. Shenk says that by the 1850s both of them were talking about the "Three Selfs" of self-support, governance, and propagation.[9]

Over the years, various criticisms have been leveled against indigenous principles. Experience showed that it was possible to have formal indigeneity with the three-selfs while being completely foreign in its forms. This has led to the suggestion that there are additional selfs that should be considered to help address this issue. These include the areas of theologizing, missionizing, in terms of sending their own cross-cultural workers, and self-caring to express Christian social concern.[10]

What is important to keep in mind here is the kind of logic that is in operation when thinking about Christian world missions. The call to take the gospel to the world originates in Scripture. As the modern missionary movement matured, however, both observation and reflection on Scripture led to the understanding that it was not enough to simply seek conversions. The task of world evangelization required local faith communities, not just missionaries. Mission leaders like Venn and Anderson and practitioners like John Nevius and Roland Allen also observed that churches run by the mission were foreign transplants, dependent on outsider workers and funds, and unable to truly flourish in the local soil of their societies. The realization came that it is the planting of local churches indigenous to their setting that allows them to become the vehicle of world evangelization.[11]

8. Ibid.

9. Ibid., 29. See also Shenk, 1990, 30–31and Newberry, "Contextualizing Indigenous Church Principles: An African Model," 99–102, on the role of John Nevius and Roland Allen in the development of three-self thinking.

10. Newberry, 2005, 110–114. Those who find it more helpful to use only three "selfs" would include these additional dimensions as elements of the primary three.

11. Shenk, "Rufus Anderson and Henry Venn: A Special Relationship?" 171. See Allen, *The Spontaneous Expansion of the Church-and the Causes Which Hinder It*, 111. He argues that the organizations set up in his day by missions could not be used by local Christians without foreign assistance, thus the need for churches that are able to expand spontaneously on their own.

The basis for thinking about indigenous local churches comes from the book of Acts and particularly the ministry of the Apostle Paul that Luke traces there, as well as Paul's letters to the churches. Paul's understanding of his mission was to plant communities of faith, and they were to be responsible for themselves in all dimensions. Local congregations were to participate in God's mission and take the Gospel to their social worlds and beyond. Paul did not stay on with the new churches in order to provide governance, finance, or do the work of evangelism. His own personal call was to go where Christ was not known or named (Romans 15:20) and he expected the local churches to continue the work of proclamation as he moved on.

IMPLICATIONS OF INDIGENOUS PRINCIPLES

Four major implications grow out of the notion of indigeneity as it relates to cross-cultural mission. First, if the indigeneity of a local church or church movement is accepted as a goal, it introduces a very specific conception of the missionary task. It means there is a trajectory to mission in its broadest sense. Participation in God's global redemptive purpose is not about personal fulfillment, or doing things deemed momentarily important. It is about taking the good news to the nations and making disciples and leading them to the obedience that comes from faith. The missionary role as conceived by Paul was always to seek to plant the church where Christ was not known and to develop responsible local expressions of the body of Christ that are able to participate in God's mission as well. Thus the cross-cultural missionary role is to plant the church and set the biblical DNA and then let that church body express Christ to its world.

Second, the goal of indigeneity means the work of the cross-cultural missionary is of necessity going to be of a different character than that of Christians in a local church. This distinction between missionary work, with the goal of indigeneity, and that of a local church is rooted in two key companion ideas: a broad and narrow sense of mission which is based in the idea of the difference between the work of the apostolic mission band and local churches. The broad sense of mission concerns the whole people of God. Andrew Walls and Cathy Ross suggest five marks of mission:[12]

1. Proclaim good news

2. Teach, baptize and nurture

12. Ross, "Introduction: Taonga," xiv. Ross observes that this is not a complete or perfect definition of mission but does provide a good working basis for holistic mission today.

3. Respond to human need with loving service

4. Seek to transform unjust structures

5. Safeguard the integrity of creation and sustain and renew life on the earth

Although they do not make this distinction, these are the marks that should characterize God's people in their local expressions everywhere. The basis for this assertion comes from the way that Chris Wright explicates the covenant with Abraham and his exegesis of Genesis 18. Wright says that "the Abrahamic covenant is a moral agenda for God's people as well as a mission statement by God.[13] Wright understands Genesis 18:16–21 as weaving together election, ethics and mission into a single theological sequence in 18:19 where:

> Ethics stands as the mid-term between election and mission, as the purpose of the former and the basis for the latter. That is, God's election of Abraham is intended to produce a community committed to ethical reflection of God's character. And God's mission of blessing the nations is predicated on such a community actually existing.[14]

In addition to this, Sodom becomes paradigmatic of the fallen world and the interchange in this passage of Yahweh with Abraham shows that the people of God are to engage broken human society in righteousness and justice.[15] What it means to be the people of God in any particular spot at a given time in history is personal participation in God's redemptive mission, one understanding of which is exemplified in these five marks of mission.

For the narrow sense of missions, Ralph Winter on mission structures and Robert Banks on the Pauline house churches offer helpful guidance. Winter argues that the local church and the apostolic missionary band represent two different redemptive structures in the New Testament, each with its own kind of work.[16] Robert Banks, in his work on Paul's house churches, similarly argues that there are clear distinctions between the churches that Paul planted and what Banks calls "the mission," by which he means the apostolic band. While Paul's mission band and the churches share the similarities of family terminology, gifts and ministries and the equality of

---

13. Wright, *The Mission of God's People*, 221.

14. Ibid., 368.

15. Ibid., 359–360. Wright summarizes his work on the Genesis 18 passage in this way: "The community God seeks for the sake of his mission is to be a community shaped by his own ethical character, with specific attention to righteousness and justice in a world filled with oppression and injustice," 369.

16. Winter, "The Two Structures of God's Redemptive Mission," 220–230.

members, there are key differences.[17] The mission band was a task group
of specialized purpose and not marked by the gathering of its members,
and there is no hint of the body metaphor used of the church. They were
involved in a common task, gifts were aimed at outsiders and it is evangelism rather than edification that is the primary task. While the churches all
had multiple authority figures, in the mission band it was Paul who was in
charge.[18] Banks summarizes the relationship between the mission and the
churches in this way:

> Not only is Paul's conception of the *ekklesia* distinctive, but his
> conception of the *ergon* as well. These two, the church and the
> work, should never be confused, as they generally have been
> in subsequent Christian thinking. Paul views his missionary
> operation not as an *ekklesia* but rather as something existing
> independently alongside the scattered Christian communities
> . . . Paul's mission is a grouping of specialists identified by their
> gifts, backed up by a set of sponsoring families and communi-
> ties, with a specific function and structure. Its purpose is first the
> preaching of the gospel and the founding of churches, and then
> the provision of assistance so that they may reach maturity[19].

If the mission band is not the same as the local church, it means that it
is not bound by the same sensibilities as local churches. It is crucial to note
that each of these structures does different things well in God's redemptive mission. The narrow work of the Pauline apostolic band was to plant
churches with the ability to participate in the mission of God in its broader
sense. The Church, the people of God, lives out their lives as salt and light
in the world. Local churches rooted in their communities and ethnic groups
are much better suited to tackle the kinds of broader issues that are im-
plicated in the five marks of mission. However, the more complex task of
planting the church outside of one's culture requires different skills, commitment and mobility that are appropriate for the mission band. To insist

17. Banks, *Paul's Idea of Community: The Early House Churches in Their Cultural
Setting*, 159–160. Note that Moreau, et al., in *Introducing World Missions*, 72–73, propose some definitions of God's mission, the Church's mission, and missions that are
consonant with the distinction between the local church and the mission band. The
mission of God is everything that God is doing to bring about his kingdom rule in the
world. The mission of God's people, the church, then becomes participating with the
triune God in anything that works towards his kingdom rule. Missions plural becomes
the various activities of the church to proclaim the good news of the Kingdom among
the nations. In this framework the mission of the church then fits well the five broad
marks of missions suggested by Walls and Ross.

18. Banks, 160–162.

19. Ibid., 169.

that mission bands exhibit the five marks of mission in the same way as local churches derails them for their narrower purpose of planting local churches that embrace the vision of the marks of mission.

Some will take issue with the narrow view of the role of the apostolic band and argue that cross-cultural mission efforts have in fact resulted in major social changes. They would rightly point out that there is an impressive and growing base of scholarly research that challenges the claims of some secularists and intellectuals that the Western missionary enterprise has been harmful to non-Western societies.[20] Winter argued that today's evangelical missionary movement needs to recover the broad social vision of what he calls First Inheritance Evangelicals in the late 18th and early 19th centuries.[21]

The primary issue here is about ultimate purpose and trajectory. To argue for a distinction in the work of local churches and mission bands is not to say that there is no overlap or that the individuals involved in the mission band do not respond to their social environment with the compassion of Jesus. Where missionary efforts have brought about positive social change in the modern missionary era it was not because they aimed at social change, but they aimed at conversion. Winter calls it "the informal theological intuition" of missionaries whose primary purpose was to preach the Gospel and plant the church who did massive numbers of good works that brought about temporal change.[22] Woodberry's work on the impact of colonial mission also illustrates how missionaries working towards the goal of bringing people to Christ and planting the church were catalysts of social change.[23] In some cases it was through missionaries as transformed individuals who tackled social issues such as racial attitudes or challenged the colonial policies of their own governments. In other instances, social change was a byproduct of their conversionary labors such as the promoting of literacy so that people could read Scripture.

There are organizations that are called by God to work cross-culturally solely in the arena of Christian social action. Christian organizations like this work *with* and *through* local Christians to affect social change, while classic mission bands *produce* local Christians who become transformed individuals "so very essential to any significant social transformation."[24]

20. As examples see Schmidt, *How Christianity Changed the World*; Stark, *For the glory of God*; and Woodberry, "The Missionary Roots of Liberal Democracy," 244–274.

21. Winter, "The Future of Evangelicals in Mission," 15.

22. Ibid., 12.

23. Woodberry, "Reclaiming the M-Word: The Legacy of Missions in Non-Western Society," 17–23.

24. Winter, "The Future of Evangelicals in Mission," 8.

The distinction between the local church and mission band means that *how* the cross-cultural missionary team works will look different from people doing ministry in their own cultural setting. Local churches and church movements who take seriously the five marks of mission are going to harness people and resources to address these various dimensions. However, a cross-cultural missionary has the goal of planting and developing local churches that can do precisely those kinds of things. That requires a completely different approach than a direct address of a particular dimension of ministry on the part of the missionary. To think in terms of a fully indigenous church movement as the result means that from the beginning all activity is done by the expatriate worker with a view towards local people taking ownership and responsibility.

For example, situations exist where the church does not exist or is very small, and where the church is more robust and larger in size. The local church/mission band distinction, and the goal of indigeneity means that in a place where there are few Christians, evangelism and planting of the church is central, based on the Pauline conception of mission as the controlling paradigm. Then, from the very beginning, as people respond to follow Christ, it is the role of the missionary to help that church embrace God's mission and find ways of expressing themselves along the five dimensions. In situations where the church exists, indigeneity as a goal means that the cross-cultural team works to enable the church to express compassion in their society. This requires skill sets that go beyond direct ministry by the missionary to work together with local Christians, help raise vision from Scripture, model the values, and help work out expressions that can be locally owned and maintained.

Indigenous principles also imply a full integration of practice where evangelism, church planting, training and compassion are brought together. At first glance it would seem that individual missionaries and mission teams could work along single dimensions in terms of developing indigenous churches and movements. Thus the classic clusters of evangelism-discipleship-church planting, leadership training, and compassion ministry could be seen as the primary work of a person or team. The problem with this, as Wright points out, is that new Christians will imitate what they see as priorities and values in those who have brought them to faith.[25] If a fully indigenous church on six dimensions is the goal, cross-cultural workers need to advocate through teaching and modeling in behavior across these dimensions. The nature of the task demands a holistic approach, not one that is compartmentalized.

25. Wright, *The Mission of God*, 319–320.

PRACTICING INTEGRATED
CROSS-CULTURAL MISSION

This section turns specifically to what the practice of compassion ministry looks like when informed by indigenous principles. The goal of a truly indigenous church that lives out the five marks of mission in its context requires an integrated approach on the part of the missionary. What might compassion ministry look like in practice when done with a fully integrated approach? The following section examines some of the problems that accrue when compassion in mission is not done in an integrated fashion and concludes with suggestions for integration based on the Gospels from Wilbur Shenk, and discusses strategy development, concluding by illustrating compassionate ministry in three different ministry settings.

PROBLEMS WITH COMPARTMENTALIZED
COMPASSION APPROACHES

The relationship between evangelism and Christian social concern is not problematic at the theological level as much as it is at the practical implementation on the ground. Missionaries agree that the good news must be proclaimed and that the poor and marginalized need to be helped. In real life, however, that often means picking one of those dimensions as primary and seeing those who choose the other side as having a truncated view of mission. This section will briefly look at some of the problems that arise from ministries of compassion in cross-cultural mission settings that are not integrated into a larger biblical framework.

While there are a number of matters that require attention when considering compassion ministry in cross-cultural mission settings, two particular issues are at the root of some of the common problem sets experienced by mission teams, individuals and ministries. The social turn among evangelical Christianity in the United States of America means that more people are now conceiving of their cross-cultural ministry as issue based. Working on problems such as clean water, adequate housing, human trafficking, and AIDS are seen by some as ends in themselves without reference to the Gospel and planting of the church. This represents a change from theological views of mission as the term was traditionally used; i.e. the propagation of the faith, expansion of the reign of God, conversion of non-Christians and founding new churches.[26] This popular conception of mission is characterized by crossing a geographic and/or cultural bound-

26. Bosch, *Transforming Mission*, 1.

ary in order to address a particular social issue. There are varying degrees of connection in this to local Christians and churches. In some cases, the intervention is completely driven from a concern that starts outside of the social setting and local Christians are hired to manage and provide the delivery system, while in others there is an attempt to meet a felt need of local Christians and involve them in the process. Issue-based ministry, as defined here, is not an entry strategy to a place but a stand-alone work that does not operate with the goal of connecting to classic concerns of mission for planting and strengthening the church.

The local church/mission band distinction helps to highlight the problems and pitfall of an issue-based approach. Social issues are on the radar of local churches that embrace God's mission in their society, but when Christians from one social setting take issues from their setting and address it in a new setting, it is likely not to be a successful intervention from an indigenous church perspective. It may be satisfying to the individuals who do the intervention but not effective on the ground.

An indigenous-principles approach to issues seeks to develop a response on the part of local Christians. This changes the direction of how interventions are developed with local vision, initiative, and ownership being key goals. Issue-based ministry also tends to be driven from the outside, both in terms of the proposed intervention and funding. The problems that entail from this are well documented[27] and there is a growing body of literature to help cross-cultural workers develop sustainable ministries that avoid dependency and that have local ownership and initiative.

WHAT INTEGRATION LOOKS LIKE

The answer to the problems of issue-based compassion ministry in cross-cultural mission is a fully-integrated approach that is undergirded by the notion of an indigenous local church movement as the goal. This section will show how an integrated approach is developed and conducted by starting with a model for personal and corporate ministry based on Jesus and then illustrating an integrated approach in three common mission scenarios. The focus here is on mission agencies that are called "standard missions agencies"[28] that have a broad biblical agenda that includes the planting of the church as well as showing compassion.

---

27. See especially Corbett and Fikkert, *When Helping Hurts*; Lupton, *Toxic Charity*.
28. Winter, "Six Spheres of Mission Overseas," 16–45.

Jesus as Our Model for Integration

Wilbur Shenk argues that word and deed language still does not get to the crux of the matter. He feels that we focus too much on the component parts of word and deed and not enough with God's new order that is announced and embodied in Jesus.[29] Instead, he proposes that Jesus himself models a way of approaching people that does not put things into priorities. Jesus responds to people and, so in that sense, it is the person that sets the agenda. He also responded out of who he was and what he represented. The new reality that Jesus calls people to has personal/social and proximate/ultimate dimensions. Shenk says that in Jesus' ministry:

> Each part is consistently informed by what is central to his very being; and that dynamic center is the way to salvation. Our 'word and deed' perspective continues to fail because it causes us to miss the sense of wholeness which for Jesus was foundational to all else. That wholeness was God's shalom. Our witness to the gospel ought always to have the effect of pointing to the kingdom of God rather than focusing on the particular expression of ministry in which we are engaged.[30]

This is a powerful word that embeds compassion in a larger frame of God's rule in the world. It matches well with the practice of indigenous principles as well because it puts the onus on God's work and not on the interests of the cross-cultural worker. It is too easy for ministries of compassion to be driven by outsider sensibilities and values. While well intentioned, without the larger framework they can perpetuate the word/deed split. Jesus calls people to a new reality and in mission we follow him in calling people to him and teaching them to live out this relationship in their personal and social relations. Responding to people and their need and also who we are in Jesus and as his representatives in the world is something that can be worked out at the personal and ministry team level. To follow Jesus in this way means that we cannot silo off responses into "physical" and "spiritual" dimensions and pick one and think we are doing his mission.

Illustrating Integration in Three Common Missions Scenarios

This section moves from Shenk's proposal that we emulate Jesus in the wholeness he demonstrated to sketching how that can be played out in three

---

29. Shenk, "The Whole Is Greater Than the Sum of the Parts," 73–74.

30. Ibid., 74.

very common missions settings. Compassion ministry is present in each of these scenarios but is shaped by a commitment to developing and nurturing an indigenous church movement. Before looking at specific ministry configurations, it is helpful to reflect on thinking strategically about compassion ministry that is applicable to any kind of ministry situation. Then follows a sketch of compassion ministry in the scenarios of (1) working among an existing church movement, (2) working as a church planting team among an unreached people group, and finally (3) where a compassion ministry serves as the platform for obtaining a visa in order to enter a country for ministry.

How do we make strategic decisions about compassion ministry in a given ministry setting? Compassion ministry that is rooted in indigenous principles has a very different starting point than ministry that simply wants to express compassion and help with social problems. The reason for this is that indigenous church principles are based on the idea that the best way to fulfill the Great Commission is to plant the church of Jesus Christ among the *ethne*. Many times compassion ministry is the starting point and primary template for some people. Thus, in any ministry setting, they are going to look for opportunities to express compassion ministry. However, when the goal is a fully indigenous local church movement rather than ministry based on the pre-formed ministry template, ministry strategy starts from the presence or absence of an existing church movement and makes determinations based on broader scriptural mandates than just compassion. In the current world of missions there are three kinds of focus that have become paradigms. They are church planting and church growth, church planting among unreached peoples, and Christian social action. Each of these areas has strong support in the Bible, but often they become the only framework in which people can conceive of mission. In determining missionary strategy, we should look at a ministry context through all three of the lenses in order to decide which strategy should take the lead. Each of the paradigms produces questions that can be asked of the local situation and after we work through questions posed by each of these frameworks, we are in a better position to see what is most critical in that setting.

This kind of preparatory work means that all approaches are on the table and strategy and practice is based on needs of the local situation. This means that there are no pre-set, templated ministry approaches or interventions. It also means that ministry strategy will be hammered out in a collaborative environment that includes both the missionary team and national church input.

Another scenario that arises is an existing compassion ministry that is not indigenous. Here local Christians had no say in its founding; it is something initiated and funded from the outside. There is abundant literature here on best practices and ways to avoid and reduce dependency. A process over time needs to be engaged that moves towards local resources and ownership.

Scenario #1: What does compassion ministry done in line with indigenous principles look like where the church exists?

The goal of indigenous church planting is local churches and a church movement that is fully responsible along all the critical dimensions, and that embraces its role in God's mission. If the social setting needs ministries of compassion, and the church movement is not yet addressing the situation, following indigenous principles means that ministry development happens along several fronts in conjunction with the local churches and Christians.

In the first step above, the decision to follow indigenous principles at the strategy development level has already steered away from pre-formed responses that are based on expatriate interpretations of the needs on the ground. The work of the cross-cultural team will take place on several levels. The first is a theological level, where local Christians begin to find legitimation for their exercise of compassion and social concern from the Bible itself. In many situations local Christians feel that to become engaged in need is not within the scope of their responsibility. They have a spiritual/secular or church /government kind of split where their role as the church is to evangelize and make Christians and the government or state is to handle social problems.

This kind of theological work takes place on both informal levels in conversations with local and national church leadership and also in formal instructional settings such as Bible school training. When social action happens that is driven by expatriate cross-cultural workers and is based in interventions that are contrived and funded from the outside and proof-texted from the Bible, local Christians and churches will find no reason to own such action.

Another level is to begin to work with the local churches to identify things that they can do on a sustainable basis that serve the needs of the local community. Rather than pulling local Christians in to participate in ministry driven by expatriates, the cross-cultural workers brainstorm and pray with local churches to find creative avenues for ministry. Where local Christians have been exposed to outsider-driven and financed social concern, they often feel that it is impossible for them to do anything on their own without the budget and staffing from cross-cultural workers. Following indigenous principles here means taking more time to work through the issues and let solutions emerge locally. If this happens there will be long term engagement and results because of local ownership.

The cross-cultural worker plays a key role in connecting the theological and action sides because they need to model what it is they are advocating. There are two key mistakes that need to be avoided. One is to tell people what the Bible says they need to do while not doing it themselves. The second is to take action independently of local Christians and model ways that they cannot emulate.

Modeling can be effective when teams and individual members assess needs in cooperation with local believers and propose solutions that are reproducible by local churches. Modeling in this fashion helps to "interpret" what we are teaching from Scripture as people see it fleshed out.

Scenario #2: What does compassion ministry look like in the context of a church planting team working where existing church movements do not exist or are very small?

The scenario here is a church planting team in a place with few or no local Christians and churches where social needs are present. Fully integrated ministry means that the team and its individual members evangelize, disciple, gather believers, train leaders and show God's compassion for hurting people through all of their interactions. The key here is that these functions are not done serially as in some kind of order, nor are they compartmentalized and separated from one another. Following indigenous principles here again means that the expressions of compassion and concern will intentionally be developed so that local people who come to believe will be able to participate in and continue them.

If the church planting team is naturally involved in people's lives the Good News will be shared verbally and modeled in their lives as the community of God's people. Thus when local people believe, they will understand how to engage their non-Christian neighbors in an integrated fashion. As the local churches grow, they will have an understanding of the Bible that encourages them to show God's compassion and will have seen it modeled in ways that they are able to replicate and take ownership.

Scenario #3: How is compassion ministry conducted when it is the entry platform for ministry?

In the previous scenario, the church planting team was on the ground as a church planting team. Their ability to enter and stay in the country was not based on their doing some kind of humanitarian ministry. This meant that they were able to pursue compassion expressions that grew naturally out of the relationships they formed.

There are many places in the world today where the only way to get on the ground and remain is through some kind of humanitarian or social service that is understood by the local authorities as being on par with non-governmental organizations, even when they are known to be Christians. The concern of those working in ministries of compassion is that there are times when it is possible for this entry platform to be pursued as a means of entry and the ministry of compassion itself to be either poorly run or neglected so that evangelism can be done.

This is problematic on a number of levels and can result in impeding the spread of the Gospel rather than facilitating it. Normally an indigenous-principles focus means that the cross-cultural worker starts with local Christians and, working together, ministry is developed that local churches can take ownership for and sustain. If an institutional response is chosen it is because the local churches have chosen this path and can support it. But compassion ministry that is tied to permission for visas and entry is generally an intervention that is conceived and funded from the outside. An integrated approach, in a situation like this, works along several lines. One key area is that the compassion ministry itself be done with excellence and without strings attached. People among the Muslim, Hindu, and Buddhist worlds are very sensitive to issues of manipulation both real and perceived. As Christians, whether we are in a business, educational, or government role, we need to share our story and worldview in every situation where possible. The key is having natural interfaces with people, so that what we are doing makes sense and legitimates our presence. There will usually be opportunities not only for the organizational response of compassion regarding the entity that provides the missionary access, but also as individuals we can demonstrate our values through caring for people outside of our assigned tasks. When people do respond to become Christ followers our teaching of Scripture about local initiative and responsibility for caring will resonate as they will have observed it in our lives.

CONCLUSION

It is a mission reality that the nations and peoples with the least Christians, churches and access to the Gospel are also among the poorest places on earth. For those striving to emulate the wholeness of Jesus in his ministry, compassion for the hurting, broken, harassed and helpless is not an option. The critical question is not whether we should show compassion, but rather how we will proceed in showing compassion in Jesus' name? Will our efforts help people become stronger, freer and more autonomous people? Will the results outlast our own time horizon in ministry? Practicing compassion with a deep commitment to the founding and maturing of an indigenous church movement carries with it the hope of lasting fruit and people with increased capacity to care for their own needs and that of their community and who see God providing for them.

4

Defining Poverty and Need

JoAnn Butrin and A. Chadwick Thornhill

In order to understand clearly what God expects regarding the poor, we first need to establish a definition of poverty. Though this might seem like a simple task, the manner in which poverty is viewed is often defined by worldview, culture, and one's own economic status. Because of this we need to articulate definitions capable of overcoming some of our cultural blinders. Bryant L. Myers' offers a helpful understanding of poverty as fundamentally a matter of broken relationships. This definition, as Myers observes, finds agreement with both Scripture and with several critical studies on the causes of poverty.[1] We will also though move beyond Myers' definition and present a fuller picture of poverty as defined in the Bible. This will help answer the question of how God views poverty and the poor, and give insight into the necessary responses of God's people.

DEFINING POVERTY

Poverty is a fact of life for many people of our world. When viewing poverty from an economic standpoint, statistics say that there is a decrease in the numbers of people living in acute poverty. In 1990, the World Bank, together with other globally interested organizations put forth a set of Millennium Development Goals (MDGs) which included reducing the worldwide

1. Myers, *Walking With the Poor*, 66–81.

poverty rate in half by 2015. According to the World Bank, that goal was achieved by 2010.[2] Their definition of poverty is those persons living on or around $1.25 or less per day. Though each nation has its own metrics of what constitutes poverty for their population, most in the majority world fall on or near the $1.25 figure and persons living on or near that daily earning fall into the category of "extreme poverty."

Despite progress, the number of people living in extreme poverty globally remains unacceptably high. According to the most recent estimates, seventeen percent of people in the majority world live at or below $1.25 a day. That is down from 43 percent in 1990 and 52 percent in 1981.[3] Over two billion people live on less than two dollars a day, which is still considered a metric of deep deprivation.[4]

Economic poverty results in devastation at many levels. It is often associated with inadequate housing and sanitation, lack of food security, malnutrition, lack of education, poor health, and often deplorable exploitation, marginalization, and abuse. Realizing that about one quarter of the world's population is living in poverty should be hard to bear. It should concern us deeply. It is no wonder that God's concern for the poor is portrayed over and over in Scripture and His instructions clearly call upon His covenant people to reach out to those in need.[5]

From an economic and material standpoint, we define poverty as lacking adequate resources to acquire those things necessary to not only survive but to thrive. Thriving would be defined differently by various cultures but would be based on what normal, everyday life looks like for a particular location. The challenge comes when daily survival takes all the resources and energy of an individual or family. When this is the case, thriving is simply not within reach.

Is poverty only about lacking "things," or should it be defined more broadly? When reflecting on poverty, one's thoughts often go to the things that are "lacking" as described above—material and economic resources. If one were to write a list of the characteristics of poverty most certainly the list would include the lack of materials and finances. Truly, many who are poor are lacking, often on many different levels.

In his book, *Walking with the Poor*, Bryant Myers talks about the poor in a relational sense rather than from a material point of view.[6] Accord-

2. "WB-IMF Report Gauges Progress on Development Goals."
3. "World Bank Group: Poverty Overview."
4. Ibid.
5. Cf. Ps 73:13; Prov 19:17; 21:13; 22:19; 28:27; Ezek 16:49, Matt 19:21; et al.
6. Myers, *Walking with the Poor*, 87.

ing to Myers, if one sees poverty only in terms of deficit, then responses are usually developed that seek to replace or fill in what is lacking. So for example, if someone is lacking water, there is a need to give water. If the lack is food, then food needs to be provided. If it is material goods, they are donated and on and on. He warns that because those who "have" can try to "fill in the deficit" for the "have nots", the "haves" can develop a God-complex or a Santa Claus approach to poverty alleviation.[7] Though we may have good intentions in trying to provide for the lacks, we may create an unhealthy dependence. We, without meaning to, place those receiving aid in a recipient rather than participant role, often taking away their dignity and not recognizing either their capacity to help themselves or the various gifts and talents that have enabled them to make it thus far in their life jour- neys. Therefore, Myers suggests "poverty is a result of relationships that do not work, that are not just, that are not for life, that are not harmonious or enjoyable. Poverty is an absence of shalom in all of its meanings."[8] He goes on to suggest that the relationships that result in poverty are fragmented, dysfunctional or oppressive. Myers identifies four main relationships that, when not functioning properly, can produce poverty: one's relationship to God, to self, to others, and to one's environment.

Poverty, when seen through the lens of relationships that do not work, can result in material poverty or in a lack of the foundational elements needed to succeed. However, people can possess wealth, but without Christ as the center of their lives they remain spiritually poor. There may be those who are wealthy and feel that they have power over others and who use that power negatively. They could be said to be suffering from a poverty of being. If poverty then is viewed in terms of relationships that do not work, then instead of trying to "fill in the gaps" one works rather to assist in righting relationships. This way of viewing poverty will profoundly affect the way poverty "alleviation" is undertaken.

WHO ARE THE POOR?

They live in a mud house with a thatch roof, with one room and an outdoor latrine. Behind them is a garden which provides their food. Flowers line the walkway to the house. There are shade trees with a hammock swinging in the breeze and children are laughing and playing with a homemade toy in the dirt lawn. Dad takes the local tuktuk (mini-van) into the small town each day where he works for minimum pay, thankful to have a job. Mom

7. Ibid., 82.
8. Ibid., 86.

tends the garden and sells some of the produce along the road. In total they make about $32.00 per month.

If this family were asked to describe their lives they would likely use terms such as happy, satisfied, enough to eat, serving the Lord, blessed. Yet, if a person from an affluent Western society were to come upon this villager's home in rural Africa, the Westerner would likely describe this family as "poor."

Identifying the poor is done through the lens of one's own status in life, one's worldview, beliefs, values and culture. Each community, in fact, sets the metrics for its own view of "who is poor." For persons outside a particular culture, it is difficult to determine who the poor are, simply because the lens by which it is measured is not always clear. The example we just gave shows that clearly. In this particular community, because dad has a job, the garden is producing and the house is intact and providing good shelter, that family would probably not be considered poor in that location. Some would even say they are thriving.

There are many studies which have interviewed those that would be considered economically poor in various cultures. In one of those studies, many of the respondents, rather than describing what they lack, talk about the psychological trauma that they experience––isolation, humiliation, lacking voice, being treated rudely and their inability to participate fully in community life because of their status. The poor in this study focus on assets rather than income and link their lack of physical, human, social, and environmental assets to their vulnerability and exposure to risk. The particular groups interviewed were populations in Eastern Europe and Central Asia.[9]

This further underscores Myer's definition of poverty as consisting of broken relationships.[10] Looking at the self-descriptors in the study above, it becomes clear that relationships with others (community, governments, local leaders, etc.) are not working and are causing emotional distress. People experience humiliation and feel that others perceive them as "less."

So who are the poor? Every human being is suffering from a poverty of spiritual intimacy, a poverty of being, a poverty of community, and a poverty of stewardship. We are all incapable of being what God created us to be and are unable to experience the fullness of joy that God designed for these relationships.

Therefore, it is imperative that as a necessary first step in working with the poor, Christian workers need to acknowledge their own brokenness and need of redemption and restoration. By doing so, we discover humility

9. "World Development Report, chapter 2."

10. Myers, *Walking with the Poor*, 86.

and we come to view others in love. Acknowledging our own broken relationships keeps us from adopting an over-under approach to compassion
in which we see ourselves as the provider and the poor merely as a part
of a problem to be solved. Paul instructs us to "do nothing from selfishness or empty conceit, but with humility of mind regard one another as
more important than [ourselves]" (Phil 2:3). This perspective opens the
door for understanding our journeys as shared and for recognizing that we
have something in common, namely our own frailty and common needs.
Paul follows this with the instruction, "do not *merely* look out for your own
personal interests, but also for the interests of others" (2:4). Such a sober
assessment helps foster a compassionate view of others. Viewing others and
ourselves as suffering from broken relationships will also keep us constantly
aware of the spiritual side of poverty. This will propel us to share the Good
News, knowing that when our relationship with God is set right, all others
will be positively affected.

THE BIBLICAL VIEW OF POVERTY

The Bible addresses poverty often. In fact, the words "poor" or "poverty"
appear over 150 times in Scripture.[11] According to the *Poverty and Justice
Bible*, produced jointly by World Vision and The American Bible Society,
there are over two thousand passages that in some way address issues of
poverty or injustice. It is important to remember that the Bible speaks of
poverty in two distinct senses. It speaks of both a spiritual poverty and material poverty, and both are important for those engaging in compassionate
missions. Also, there often exists some connection between spiritual poverty and material poverty in Scripture, as it is often the materially poor who
most recognize their need of God and turn to Him.

Poverty in the Old Testament

The Old Testament presents a complex, yet also compelling, portrayal of
poverty and how the people of God should address it. Poverty is certainly
not the divine ideal. Beginning in Genesis, the good creation of God provided more than enough to sustain human life. After the Fall, however, the
misuse of material goods, as seen perhaps most strikingly in the plight of
the people of Israel in Egypt prior to the exodus, becomes a significant part

11. Refers to occurrences in the New American Standard Bible, 1995 edition
(NASB95).

of the biblical script. As the paradigmatic act of salvation in the Old Testament, the exodus represented not just a spiritual freedom, but a freedom from physical and emotional turmoil as well. Blomberg writes, "Exodus [the book] is clear that this liberation is holistic. Physically oppressed people are being physically liberated, but with an unambiguous spiritual objective—to let everyone know that Yahweh alone is God (Exod 6:7; 9:16) and to create a covenant community of followers who will serve him by obeying his laws (Exod 20–40)."[12] A holistic view of salvation permeates both Old and New Testaments. God does not just provide spiritual deliverance, but also brings physical deliverance, and promises an ultimate deliverance from all forms of suffering as well as from death itself.

The oppression experienced by Israel is sometimes cited in her Laws as grounding for the proper treatment of others (Deut 15:15; 24:18, 22).[13] The Law of Moses contained numerous and specific provisions to prevent the growth of poverty and the oppression and exploitation of the poor. For example, when a person became so poor that they were forced to sell their land, a relative could purchase it or they could purchase it back themselves if able. In the year of jubilee, the land reverted back to the original ownership (Lev 25:25–28). When a fellow Israelite became poor, it was also required that they be given temporary residence and not charged interest (Lev 25:35–38). These and other provisions were designed to protect those who fell on hard times. Thus Wright comments, "Indeed, some of the economic regulations of Israel called for the sacrifice of self-interest in favor of the needs of a fellow Israelite."[14] When possible, the immediate or extended family was to bear this burden.[15]

The divine ideal was that God's provisions for Israel in the land and the regulation of fair economic practices would ensure that poverty would not be an issue (Deut 15:4).[16] If, however, there were poor Israelites, their fellow Israelites were to provide willingly for their needs, even if this meant personal loss to the lender (Deut 15:7–11). In the year of jubilee, the Israelite fields and vineyards were to remain uncultivated and the poor allowed

---

12. Blomberg, *Neither Poverty nor Riches*, 37–38.

13. See Kaiser, "Poverty and the Poor in the Old Testament," 40.

14. Wright, *Old Testament Ethics*, 157.

15. So Wright again notes, "The law emphasizes *the kinship/family structure of society* as the key factor in preventing poverty and restoring people from it;" Wright, *Old Testament Ethics*, 173.

16. Burnside comments that the text invokes sympathy for the poor "brother" rather than the poor "other," creating an emotional connection in which the affections have a role to play in moral action; Burnside, *God, Justice, and Society*, 225.

to eat from what remained (Exod 23:10–11; Deut 24:18–22).[17] Likewise, the edges of the fields and any fallen crops were to be left for the needy and the foreigner (Lev 19:9–10; Deut 24:19–21). Further still, a tithe from the harvest was periodically collected and stored in order to provide for foreigners and the needy (Deut 14:28–29).

Beyond these practices of generosity, the commerce of the Israelites was regulated to ensure fair practices were followed. Exploitation for financial gain and delayed wages were strictly forbidden (Lev 19:13). Honest weights and measurements were commanded so that no one was cheated in an economic exchange (Lev 19:35–36). Judicial matters also required fairness, and showing partiality to the rich or powerful was forbidden (Lev 19:15).

In the Psalms,[18] Yahweh hears the cries of the poor and makes provision for them because of His loving-kindness (Ps 12:5; 34:6; 35:10; 68:10; 69:33; 72:2–15; 82:3–4; 102:17; 107:9, 33–43; 109:31; 132:15; 140:12). The Psalms, like the Pentateuch, condemn the oppression of the poor and the afflicted (Ps 10:2, 8–10, 14; 109:14–20; 113:7–8). The wicked are at times equated with the rich who oppress the poor (Ps 37:14–21). In contrast, those who help the poor will be blessed by Yahweh with health and prosperity (Ps 41:1–3). The ultimate hope in the Psalms is that the poor will break free from oppression and no longer experience poverty (Ps 9:18).

Alternatively, in Wisdom Literature, poverty is frequently depicted as the result of either laziness (Prov 6:10–11; 10:4; 13:18; 19:15; 24:30–34) or wickedness (Prov 21:13, 17; 23:21). Ecclesiastes observes that the poor are ignored and afflicted while the rich are remembered (Eccl 5:8; 6:8; 9:15–16). The poor are despised by their neighbors (Prov 14:20) and shunned by their friends (Prov 19:4). Yet, Proverbs also says that it is better to be a poor man with integrity than to be a rich fool (Prov 19:1), a crook (Prov 28:6), or a liar (Prov 19:22). Like the Pentateuch and the Psalms, Proverbs also condemns the mistreatment of the poor (Prov 22:16, 22–23). Those who help the poor are happy and blessed (Prov 14:21, 31; 28:27; 29:7).

The Old Testament's poetic literature also frequently recognizes the poor come to their plight often because of oppression and exploitation (e.g., Eccl 5:8–17).[19] Proverbs 13:23 remarks, "There is much food in the field of

17. Ibid., 221. Burnside notes that the Sabbath itself protected the vulnerable from being overworked or taken advantage of.

18. The following section is largely taken from Thornhill, *The Lexham Bible Dictionary*, "Poverty." Used with permission.

19. Blomberg, *Neither Poverty nor Riches*, 54. Blomberg notes that the monarchy became a source of oppression for the poor in Israel, certainly against the divine intention. He states, "The monarchy would also co-opt the best of the fields, vineyards and roves of the land and demand a tenth of the produce and flocks, so that in essence God's

the poor, but it is swept away by injustice" (LEB). As Wright summarizes, "oppression is by far the major recognized cause of poverty . . . Mostly, people are made poor by the actions of others—directly or indirectly."[20] Wright also notes that the Mosaic regulations are typically directed at regulating those in positions of power rather than the poor (e.g., creditors, employers, slave-owners).[21] In other words, the poor are not always if not even usually to be viewed as the problem; those who fail to care for them or who take advantage of them are.

Throughout the works of the prophets, exploitation of the poor is condemned. Isaiah and Jeremiah commanded the defense of the orphan and widow (Isa 1:17) and condemned the affliction and exploitation of the poor (Isa 3:14–15; 5:8; 10:1–2; 32:6–7; Jer 22:13–17; 34:13–17). In response to oppression, Yahweh Himself defends and cares for the needy and the afflicted (Isa 11:4; 14:30–32; 25:4; 29:19; 19:25; Jer 20:13), though this should have been performed by Israel (Isa 58:7–12). Ezekiel identified the righteous as those who help the needy and condemned those who oppressed the poor (Ezek 16:49; 18:7–32; 22:29–31). Daniel exhorted Nebuchadnezzar to stop sinning against Yahweh and to show mercy to the poor (Dan 4:27). Amos too condemned the abuse of the poor and threatened judgment for those who ignored his warnings (Amos 2:6; 4:1–3; 5:10–13; 8:4–6), as did Micah (Mic 2:1–5), and Zechariah (Zech 7:8–14).

The danger in the portrayal of poverty and wealth in the Old Testament, and in the Bible in general, is that its multi-faceted depiction can be neglected. The Deuteronomic portrayal of cause and effect relationships between obedience/blessing and disobedience/cursing could lead to the conclusion that poverty is a result of disobedience if not counter-balanced with the perspective of the book of Job. The critique of wealth as oppressive could lead to advocacy of ascetic lifestyles or class struggle if not balanced with the example of the patriarchs and others. The picture in Proverbs in which poverty results from laziness could be totalized if not balanced with the prophetic picture of poverty as a result of oppression. Thus a careful approach to the topic will reveal that in the Old Testament, poverty was a complex issue which resulted from a multitude of factors. The major chord which plays throughout, however, is that God and the people of God must show great care and concern for the oppressed and poor.

people would become slaves of the king."
20. Wright, *Old Testament Ethics*, 170.
21. Ibid., 174.

Poverty in the New Testament

In the first century, there was largely not a substantial "middle class." By and large people were either poor or rich, with most being poor.[22] The rich minority tended to be either landowners or public or religious officials of some sort while the poor were laborers.[23] The rich were thus also the powerful, and often this meant they abused their power.[24] Though wealth did not necessarily indicate corruption, the general belief seemed to be that wealth resulted in greed, and thus in oppressive practices to obtain more.[25]

In the New Testament, although Luke places the greatest emphasis upon Jesus' care for and ministry to the poor, all four Gospels evidence this as a central part of Jesus' mission. In Matthew 11 and Luke 4, Jesus summarizes the evidence for his bringing of the kingdom of God by quoting from Isaiah 61, which, in part, affirms he has come to proclaim good news to the poor. This good news undoubtedly included the hope for their deliverance from their impoverished state, if not in the immediate future, certainly in the *eschaton*.[26] In its Old Testament context, Isaiah 61 connects with the year of jubilee, so Jesus' quotation is not simply assurance of spiritual salvation, but a promise that the arrival of the fullness of the kingdom will mean the release from debt and destituteness for all of the people of God.[27]

In the Sermon on the Plain in Luke (6:17–31) and the Beatitudes of the Sermon on the Mount in Matthew (5:1–12), Jesus proclaims blessing upon the poor. Scholars debate the significance of Matthew's modification of the poor as poor "in spirit," but it is clear here that material poverty is at least partly, if not primarily in view.[28] This need not mean that all poor persons were automatically granted kingdom membership, but it does speak to the reality that poverty often developed reliance upon God and riches reliance upon self.

The parable of the rich man in Luke 12:16–21 illustrates the danger of self-reliance. Likewise, the parable of the stewards in Luke 16:1–18 and the

22. Blomberg estimates around 20 percent of the society might be considered to be living above the "poverty line" in the ancient Greco-Roman world; Blomberg, *Neither Poverty nor Riches*, 88.

23. P. H. Davids, "Rich and Poor," 701.

24. Ibid., 702.

25. Ibid., 703.

26. See Marshall, *The Gospel of Luke*, 250.

27. See J Middleton, *A New Heaven and a New Earth*, 254–262.

28. Davids notes, "the so-called metaphorical use of 'poor' is not entirely metaphorical; it always contains an element of real suffering and insecurity, even if the suffering is not necessarily economic"; Davids, "Rich and Poor," 706.

rich man and Lazarus in Luke 16:19–31 warn the wealthy against reliance on wealth and neglect of spiritual matters. Davids notes that while there are wealthy people in the Gospels who receive the kingdom, it is only those engaged in acts of generosity (e.g., Zaccheus in Luke 19:1–10).[29] Witherington summarizes:

> Luke is not satisfied with showing that universalization of the gospel liberates the oppressed (Luke 4:18c). He especially wants to show how it liberates the oppressor as well, whether it is a Zacchaeus or Levi the tax collector (Luke 5:27–29; 19:1–10), or a Simon the Pharisee (Luke 7:36), or a representative of Rome, a centurion (Luke 7:1–10; cf. Acts 10). Salvation is viewed as something that transforms every aspect of the lives of any and all persons.[30]

The earliest church maintained Jesus' concerning for the poor. Acts 4:32–36 famously notes that the community of believers held all things in common "for there was not a needy person among them, for all who were owners of land or houses would sell them and bring the proceeds of the sales and lay them at the apostles' feet, and they would be distributed to each as any had need" (NASB).

Likewise, Paul's ministry evidenced special concern for the poor. In Romans 15:25–29, Paul mentions the collection he was gathering for the poor Jewish believers in Jerusalem (see also 2 Cor 8 and Gal 2). Though Paul encouraged contribution, he emphasized the gift was given voluntarily (2 Cor 8:3) and the Macedonians contributed joyfully in spite of their own deep poverty (8:2).

The epistle of James also has a great deal to say about the poor. In James 2, the author condemns preferential treatment of the rich.[31] James repeats here the widespread opinion that the wealthy often oppressed the poor (2:6). To show preference to the rich was to violate the command to love one's neighbor. It is in this context that James brings up his famous faith/works discussion in 2:14–16. Interestingly, his two examples of those who are vindicated/righteous are Abraham, a wealthy man, and Rahab, a poor female prostitute. Just as rich Abraham and poor Rahab acted obediently and found favor with God, so too the Jewish Christians in James' audience must act faithfully and hospitably to all, regardless of their economic status.[32]

---

29. Davids, "Rich and Poor," 707.

30. Witherington, *The Indelible Image*, 671–672.

31. See Witherington, *The Indelible Image*, 302.

32. See Blomberg and Kamell, *James*, 140.

THE CHURCH'S RESPONSE TO POVERTY

One of the challenges of applying the biblical teachings today is that we often lack exact cultural parallels to what was going on in the first century. A careful hermeneutic must take into consideration the historical and cultural distance between ourselves and the original recipients of the New Testament's instruction. Davids suggests applying Jesus' teachings must involve three steps: 1) examining Jesus' message to his contemporaries in its context; 2) examine how these teachings were enacted in the early Church as evidenced in the Gospels and Acts; and 3) looking at the earliest interpretations and applications of Jesus' teachings within the rest of the New Testament to see how the Church responded to wealth and poverty.[33] But beyond even a careful examination of the trajectory of the New Testament, we must also examine our own cultural situations to determine the most appropriate manner in which to live out these teachings.

In fact, the trajectory of the entire Bible points us toward a generous, voluntary, cruciform, and missional engagement with the poor among us. As Wright comments, "The law makes care for the poor *the litmus test of covenant obedience to the whole of the rest of the law*."[34] Given this injunction, and the biblical trajectory, there should be no doubt that caring for the poor is a duty of the Church. This duty, as Davids notes, is both an individual and communal one.[35] In a Western context, it is most often the communal imperative which we fail to fulfill, as individual Christians may give generously, but most churches lack a strategic means by which they meet the needs of the vulnerable in their community of faith and their community at large. A biblical theology of possessions teaches us that ultimately God owns all things, and thus should free us to give of what we have to meet the needs of others.[36]

We must also recognize, however, that sin, both individual and systemically, often creates poverty. Just as in the biblical world(s), so today often corrupt practices by the wealthy, whether individual or corporate, create or further the reality of poverty. So Wright argues, "It is indeed what poverty implies for human relationships (their abuse, distortion, exploitation, etc.) that constitutes the ethical problem. Poverty cannot therefore be addressed

---

33. Davids, "Rich and Poor," 709.

34. Wright, *Old Testament Ethics for the People of God*, 174.

35. Davids, "Rich and Poor," 708.

36. Wright, *Old Testament Ethics for the People of God*, 147–148.

merely as an economic or material issue without at the same time address-ing the relational issues of social injustice and exploitation."[37]

This means that the struggle against poverty ultimately cannot be one in "this age."[38] Until those forces which create disruption and turmoil in the world are ultimately removed from it in the *eschaton*, human individuals and institutions will continue to have oppressive tendencies. This does not mean, however, that the struggle against poverty should be given up. The Christian life is lived in the tension between the "now" and the "not yet." The kingdom is here, but not yet fully. We have been raised to life, but not yet transformed. The new age has dawned but has not yet been realized. Living in this tension means we struggle now, as Paul remarked, against powers and principalities and spiritual forces of darkness (cf. Eph 6:12). But struggle we must. In Western evangelicalism, this means we struggle often against allowing wealth to distract us from service to God and others. Kai-ser states, "The temptation is ever present to make these goods, instead of God, our lasting companions."[39] As individuals, we must battle against the temptation to accumulate for ourselves (a value deeply permeating Western culture) rather than release to others. And likewise our churches must be committed not to turning inward, but to renewing inwardly in order to turn outward. As Blomberg commends, "The key to evaluating any individual church or nation in terms of its use of material possessions (personally, col-lectively or institutionally) is how well it takes care of the poor and power-less in its midst, that is, its cultural equivalents to the fatherless, widow and alien."[40]

A beautiful example of a Christian response to human need is portrayed by Jesus in the parable of the Good Samaritan found in Luke 10:18–22. It demonstrates the importance of a true commitment and willingness to be interrupted and inconvenienced, to cross cultural barriers, and to provide immediate relief as well as a longer-term responses to need. It is an excellent model for an individual's response when confronted with a need.[41]

But, what if, instead of one wounded person lying in the road, there were one hundred, or a thousand? One person could not begin to meet the overwhelming needs. However, churches filled with the love and compas-sion of Jesus and mandated to love the world around them (I John 3:17) has

37. Wright, *Old Testament Ethics*, 168.

38. So Kotter remarks, "The problem of hungry people can be addressed now with food; but the ultimate solution to poverty is the full realization of the kingdom of God, where hunger will be no more;" Kotter, "Remember the Poor," 64.

39. Kaiser, *Toward Old Testament*, 211.

40. Blomberg, *Neither Poverty nor Riches*, 84.

41. Cf. Butrin, *From the Roots Up*, 48.

the opportunity to respond in the non-discriminatory love and concern that gives glory to God and testifies of His greatness to those who receive care.

Compassion for those in need isn't an add-on task for followers of Jesus. It is the essence of the Church of Jesus Christ. To be incarnational is to be truly compassionate about the needs of others. If one is giving glory to the Father; i.e. in vertical relationship to God, then the horizontal or outward extension of that relationship is service to others, and that service is based in love and motivated by compassion (1 John 3:17, James 2:14–17).

The Church, therefore, as it carries out God's purposes becomes intimately involved with the spiritual, physical, and emotional needs of people. It does this in a uniquely redemptive fashion, in the name of Jesus and by the power of the Holy Spirit as the people of God join in *Missio Dei* , the mission of God. The local church as a gifted body of believers, filled with the love and compassion of Jesus and released together to touch the world, can bring healing and wholeness to multitudes. This is what the church was intended to be, a dynamic community of worship, salvation, reconciliation, and restoration.

When the Holy Spirit comes to a group of believers, a sense of *koinonia*, which embodies unity and fellowship, reigns, and with that unity of purpose and power and anointing, the body becomes able to sustain the reconciling message of Jesus' love to the sinner and hope to the downcast. It is that same power that gives wisdom in righting injustice, and power to come against principalities and powers that are not of the flesh and not always seen or understood by human comprehension" (Ephesians 6).[42]

HUMAN DIGNITY AND THE POOR

A friend and long-time educator with the Assemblies of God, Billie Davis, was the daughter of migrant workers. Growing up, she and her family traveled throughout the Western United States picking fruit and cotton, and selling hand-made baskets and furniture. They lived mostly in their model "A" Ford or in tents.[43]

I recall Dr. Davis speaking in a Sunday School class about the times when a bread truck would roll through the migrant camp. She was sent out by her father to run behind the truck and catch loaves of bread that were tossed out. She said, "I was grateful for the bread, dry and stale though it was, because I was constantly hungry. But I hated that truck and the owners

---

42. Ibid., 50.

43. Davis, "I was a Hobo Kid," 25.

of the farm for taking away my dignity and making me feel like I was a beg-
gar running after their almighty bread!"[44]

As missionaries, we must be careful to not rob the poor of their dignity
by making them chase our handouts, no matter how well intentioned we
might be. Dignity is defined as a sense of worth. From a Christian perspective it can be closely related to identity. Identity, according to Chris Sugden,
answers the question, "who am I?", while dignity asks, "what am I worth?"[45]
Vinay Samuel portrays dignity by the following characteristics:

- When people are affirmed and are discovering a sense of self-worth,
  self-acceptance and a sense of having something to contribute to the
  world and to other

- When people are free to act according to their conscience without a
  threat from others who may control them

- When people begin to make their own contributions to the life of the
  community, especially in decisions which affect them as a family, a
  community, a religious and political entity

- When people begin to share with others in such a way that humanity
  is enhanced rather than reduced, and together there is a fight against
  evil and injustice

- When women, the weak, and the disabled have a role which affords
  them equality and inclusion[46]

All of the above, according to Sudgen and Samuel, are possible only
when people find their identity in Christ and their identity as a "child of
the King" begins to deeply inculcate into who they are. Dignity and worth
are articulated by Scripture as God calls His people to allegiance to Himself
(Deut 7:7–8; Hos 2:2–3; I. Cor. 1:26; Eph 2:12–19; I Pet 2:10). Jesus affirmed
the dignity of those around Him by eating with "sinners," mixing in public
with women, and teaching that entering the kingdom of God requires becoming like children and servants.[47]

The poor through marginalization, inequality of voice, isolation and
oppression often feel like worthless failures. Society can further enforce
that belief by its values, such as materialism, success, and so forth. Sadly,
the church's compassionate responses can affirm a person's feelings of

44. Davis, "I was a Hobo Kid," Lecture, Central Assembly of God, Sunday School,
May 2003, author's notes.

45. Sugden, "What is Good About Good News to the Poor?" 238.

46. Samuel, "God's Intention for the World," 149.

47. Sugden, "What is Good about Good News to the Poor?" 240.

worthlessness by taking approaches that are poorly thought out. Persons who wish to give to the poor often do so from a position of power, simply because they are not "as poor" materially. Rather than involving the poor in working toward their own solutions, they render the poor as recipients of their gifts and handouts, making the poor at some level grateful, yet still afflicted with feelings of inadequacy. Persons who witness to the poor can also unintentionally make the poor feel devalued by initially focusing on their sin and unworthiness rather than presenting a loving, gracious God who cares about them.

Lupton states it well when he says, "Doing for others what they can do for themselves is charity at its worst." Lupton has worked for years in the inner city of Atlanta, Georgia, and has found that, unless the people themselves are a part of coming up with solutions for their own problems and then becoming actively involved in solving them, the community may be "bettered" but the people aren't changed. This is because real transformation at both the personal and community level has not happened. There is something, Lupton says, in one-way giving that erodes human dignity. This kind of compassion subtly communicates to the recipient, "You have nothing of value that I desire in return." [48] One-way mercy ministry , as kindhearted as the giver may be and as well intentioned, is an unmistakable form of put-down.

However, when Christ is introduced to the poor as a loving, gracious Savior and He is received, the transformation begins in a way that can only happen in the realm of the supernatural. The Gospel begins to reconcile the poor to their true selves as God intends them to be and begins to reconcile them to others as they become the "family of God." Barriers of race, of cultural status, of economic difference begin to break down as Christ becomes the center of the person in their community.[49] Families and communities experience renewal as social evils, such as alcoholism, sexual exploitation and abuse, and crime and fighting reduce.

Imagine a man who has spent his life in poverty, feeling like a failure and isolated and without voice or authority, finds Jesus. Imagine him as he understands that he is a child of the King, a part of the Royal Priesthood and this man, who had such a negative identity now has a new identity in Christ. He walks with His head a little higher and his view of himself is gradually transformed. Imagine when he receives spiritual gifts or begins speaking in a heavenly language with a voice he has never known. Imagine the dignity of this man as Christ remakes his identity. Imagine even more when he is

48. Lupton, *Compassion , Justice and the Christian Life*, 26.
49. Samuel, "God's Intention," 251.

treated with respect, and encouraged to participate in his own betterment. Imagine that those who come to help, come as friends, with the agenda of encouraging his walk with the Father, and participating together in solutions that make sense for his life, that of his family and the community of which he is part. Imagine a time when this man is in right relationship with God, himself, others and the environment around him.

5

Best Practices in Compassionate Missions

Suzanne Hurst

THE WORLD IS FULL of suffering and it is easy to be overwhelmed by the plethora of needs facing the world. Many people see these needs and want to help or to problem-solve so that the need goes away. For example, Americans as a whole tend to be generous. In 2014 Americans were tied for the number one spot in the world for charitable giving.[1] A Gallup poll states that in 2013, 65 percent of Americans volunteered for a religious organization while 83 percent gave from their personal finances.[2]

For Christians, helping those who are in need is an integral part of our faith. With an abundance of travel options and a desire to reach beyond our own boundaries, it is no surprise that there has also been a significant increase in the numbers of evangelical Christians who travel overseas for a short-term missions experience.[3] These trips often have a small goal that aims to address a tangible need such as working with orphans, painting a school, holding a soccer camp and so on. These altruistic trips have become so popular that a 2005 study done by Princeton University found that 1.6 million American church members participated in church-sponsored missions trips that were on average eight days long. Approximately $2.4 billion

1. Charities Aid Foundation, "World Giving Index 2014 Report."
2. Gallup, "Most Americans Practice Charitable Giving, Volunteerism."
3. Fanning, "Short Term Missions: A Trend That Is Growing Exponentially," 1.

was spent that year alone on these trips. And this amount continues to grow every year.[4]

While motives may be pure, an abundance of activity and money spent do not necessarily mean an effective response. Good intentions do not guarantee good results. As Christians we not only want to minister in Christ's name, but we want to *do good, well.* Everything we do for the glory of God should be done with excellence. We do not want to do things in the name of Jesus that are haphazard and poorly executed, yielding minimal or even disastrous results. We want our giving, our going, our volunteering and our work to lead to life-giving transformation in communities, and we should settle for nothing less. As Christians our goal should be to minister in a way that brings about total transformation: physically, emotionally, relationally and spiritually. Whether it is a two-week trip or a lifetime commitment, our work for Jesus should be done in the best manner possible with the goal of seeing lives transformed.

As Christians we are commanded to show compassion. Throughout the Bible we see God showing His love for mankind and being concerned with suffering. Passages such as that of the Good Samaritan (Luke 10:25–37) make it clear that we are to reach out and offer help to those who are suffering and in need.

Broadly speaking there are two streams of response to human need and suffering: relief and development. Before discussing what components lead to excellence in compassion ministries, it is important to define what exactly our activities are, as relief and development have vastly different goals and strategies.

RELIEF

One definition of relief as described by Merriam-Webster, is "things (such as food, money, or medicine) that are given to help people who are victims of a war, earthquake, flood, etc."[5] Relief is providing what is needed when some sort of crisis, natural or manmade, brings harm to a community, creating a situation where individuals cannot have the basics for life as they did before the crisis. An example of this type of crisis is the 2010 earthquake in Haiti.

Before the earthquake a large majority of Haitians were very poor[6] and one could easily say that Haiti was in need of development. While it

4. Lupton, *Toxic Charity,* chapter 2.

5. *Merriam Webster Online,* s.v. "Relief."

6. Disasters Emergency Committee, "Haiti Earthquake Facts and Figures: Haiti Before the Earthquake."

could be said that life for most Haitians was very difficult and in need of improvement, the mere fact that a very populated Haiti existed demonstrates that they had figured out a way to survive. They had developed survival strategies.[7] It was not always pretty and it certainly was not ideal, but as a whole, Haitians had strategies that helped them live despite their impoverished circumstances. However, within minutes, all that changed when the earthquake occurred. Haitians who had the skills to survive in the Haiti that they previously knew were now destitute and in eminent danger of injury and death. This is a situation that calls for relief. Relief is given when people are suddenly unable to survive and carry on with life as they did before the crisis event. Relief aims to rescue individuals from eminent danger and is often given free of charge. Healthcare, meals and rescue operations, all provided by others who are often outsiders in an effort to help a population during a time of crisis, is relief. In theory, relief is always short-term and should have a plan to segue into rehabilitation and development, with an emphasis on promoting independence. It is appropriate only during those initial days, or possibly weeks, where people's lives are eminently threatened. As soon as the immediacy of possible injury or death has been dealt with, efforts should be made to change strategies from relief to rehabilitation and development.[8] Jeff Hartensveld deals with this in some detail in chapter twelve. The purpose of the present chapter, however, is to focus on compassion ministry efforts that are more developmental in nature.

DEVELOPMENT

What is "development?" There are many ways to define development. The Center for Global Development talks about development being something that is not confined to simply a change in economic status but as something that has a long-lasting, multi-faceted impact on communities.[9]

Whether we are career missionaries working full-time in Africa or youth pastors taking short-term teams to Mexico, we need to make sure that, like the Hippocratic oath states, we "do no harm." This might seem like an unnecessary statement, and we are inclined to think, "of course a missionary or missions team would not do harm." However, sometimes there are unintended or unforeseen consequences to our actions and harm *is* done. When working in a culture that is not fully understood, it is easy to

7. Myers, *Walking with the* Poor, 141.

8. Corbett and Fikkert, *When Helping Hurts*, under chapter 2 "Not All Poverty Is Created Equal," Kindle.

9. Barber, "What Is Development?"

do something and be unaware of the cascading unintended consequences of that action. A West African proverb says that "the eyes of a stranger are wide open, but he sees nothing." This refers to an individual who visits a place or situation that lies outside their normal context. This person sees new sights and hears new things and quickly comes to conclusions about needs, causes and effects, but does not adequately understand the root context of beliefs, what is really happening, or the possible implications of certain actions when viewed through the eyes of the local culture. As Christians we usually come with good intentions and kind hearts. While our motives need to be pure, good motives and kind hearts do not necessarily guarantee that we understand the context where we are working or that we are cognizant of possible unintended consequences. We need to take the time to understand and to make sure that all we are doing is empowering, encouraging and giving life to the community.

Consider the following story as told by Heather Ruiz who was a journalist for the Seventh-Day Adventist Church Development Agency (ADRA). In 2013 Ruiz traveled in West Africa as a journalist and development worker for ADRA:

> It took me a while to find it. The taxi driver and I were shouting over each other in French about whether the orphanage was another street down or already behind us, but finally the crooked sign "Grace House" appeared in dripping, painted words. The driver lost no time in depositing me on the lonely street, and I felt more orphaned than ever before marching through the creaking gate.
>
> Dirty floors and dim lights welcomed me inside. I did my best to prepare myself for what might come next--coughing invalids or stray chickens or skeleton babies--and I nearly stepped on top of bright red Sanuks.
>
> "Who are you?" The voice caught me first, unmistakable in her accent.
>
> "The journalist from ADRA. I called earlier about stopping by?" I found myself looking at . . . well, a stereotypical American College Student in all her glory: pink tank top shouting Abercrombie like a tag line to her expressionless face; Ray-Bans slipped into a highlight-streaked ponytail; I almost expected an iced Starbucks to appear in her hand.
>
> "Oh, I'm just here for a week before we go on the safari." She shrugged. "I came to volunteer with a group from my university."
>
> I followed her through the halls and corridors to her squad in the main room, and there I found the chaos.

Some children were dancing, others scaling volunteers' laps and arms, still more were jumping in place as the uncontrollable excitement pummeled through their slender bodies.

"Green dress?" A volunteer was pulling clothing out of a cardboard box.

"Miiiiiiine!" screeched every girl voice and, honestly, a few boy voices. They tore and clawed through the crowd, arms flailing out.

"Blue t-shirt? Yellow socks?" The voice continued.

"Hey, I have candy over here!" Another volunteer contributed. Even the walls seemed to be quivering with pleasure.

I discovered the director in the back of the room, smiling wide. "How many volunteer groups do you get here?" I shouted over the din.

"Sometimes two a month," he beamed proudly. "The volunteers cover almost all our staff."

"You aren't providing jobs for any local workers?" I repeated.

"Well, no." He paused a moment, sensing the need to make it sound better. "We have so very many children here at Grace House. They need food and a home. They need help. Here, they get help."

"Where do they come from before here?" I encouraged, reaching for my notepad.

"Terrible families. No food. So poor, you know."

"Wait, they have families?"

"Half of them have families." I was frozen for a moment, but the sad truth is such numbers are typical in African countries. After the wave of volunteers to orphanages in Ghana began to show signs of an abusive business enterprise, the Social Welfare Department organized a survey revealing that 90 percent of Ghanaian orphans have one or more living parent. The presence of volunteers visiting so many orphanages created "jobs" for children from families that could benefit from a few less mouths to feed.

"Some of these children have lost their parents and are emotionally susceptible at this stage," I gently said. "Isn't it damaging to further their never-ending cycle of abandonment from a revolving door of volunteers?"

"This is just the way it is." The director crossed his arms. "We do this to make a difference the best we can, and you need to remember, this is for the volunteer, too. This experience is life-changing."

I glanced at the group of college students, taking selfies with the animated children. No doubt this will be a series of profile pictures. For a moment, I wondered if the unidentified, romping, homeless children seemed reduced to the same status of elephants and zebras on the veld.[10]

Before embarking on any compassion ministry related endeavor we need to make sure that what we are doing is important to the community, that it will empower the local community, will create independence instead of dependence and that when we leave positive effects remain and continue, supported by and carried out by the community. How do we do this? We follow best practice recommendations.

BEST PRACTICE

The Cambridge Dictionary broadly defines best practice as "a working method or set of working methods that is officially accepted as being the best to use in a particular business or industry."[11] Whether we realize it or not, we are daily affected by best practice. Best practice is why we brush our teeth every day. Research has shown that bacteria cause tooth decay and that brushing our teeth can greatly reduce the amount of bacteria in our mouths.[12] Best practice is what, ideally, most Bible schools use to put together a solid curriculum, to use the best teaching methods and to choose quality textbooks. Best practice is what helps missionary aviation ministries to provide safe transportation. Best practice is what we, as cross-cultural Jesus followers, should be referencing when planning compassion ministry outreaches. Why, as Christians, is best practice so important?

- Everything that we do in the name of Jesus should be done in the best way possible.

- Best practice helps us to be good stewards of the resources that God has given us.

- Best practice helps to ensure that we show respect and dignity towards those who we serve or work alongside.

- As people created in God's image everyone deserves the best strategies and methods available. They also deserve methods that aim to build up their capacity and increase their abilities, instead of creating dependence on outside resources.

10. Ruiz, "Voluntourism."
11. Cambridge Dictionaries Online, s.v. "Best Practice."
12. Carr, "When and How Often Should You Brush Your Teeth."

Researchers continuously examine development initiatives around the world in an effort to understand why one method works with great success and another is an abysmal failure. This research has found that there are certain components that tend to lead a project more towards empowering the local community while having a positive, sustained impact. These principles, or competencies, have been determined to have a significant impact on how the project unfolds and ultimately whether or not positive, long-lasting results are produced.[13] This list of competencies can vary, depending on the resource. However basic competencies that are usually present in successful development projects are:

- Community-based
- People-centered
- People-owned
- Participative
- Focuses on targeting the root cause of the problem
- Measurable
- Sustainable

Community-based

While it is certainly possible to improve the life of an individual or one family, true development is about transforming communities. Although everyone is responsible for making their own healthy choices and for their own behavior, the reality is that in many ways the health of a person's neighbors can have an impact on their own health. In Kinshasa, Democratic Republic of Congo the number one cause of death in children under the age of 5 is malaria.[14] There are many things that individual families can do to decrease their exposure to the mosquitos that carry malaria. They can keep their yard tidy and free from standing water and tall grasses that attract mosquitos or they can sleep under a net at night. However, if the community all around them is not cutting the grass and has old tires and other reservoirs for standing water, which attracts mosquitos, they will still have a large mosquito population and will still be at risk of malaria. True development should address communities. Christ calls us to live in community and He calls us to

---

13. Meyers, *Walking with the Poor*, 68.

14. World Health Organization, "Democratic Republic of Congo."

show His love through our community of believers. Communities touching communities are what bring about widespread transformation.[15]

People-centered

Development or compassion ministry projects need to be focused on people. While a structure might be built or painted, the end goal is that people's lives would be touched and changed. Painting a school is not necessarily "development." If once a short-term team leaves, students are abused in the school and parents are forced to pay bribes in order to receive their children's grades, then having a freshly painted school is not having a true impact on the community. This is not to say that painting a school is wrong. It is to say that we are kidding ourselves if we think that because we gave of our time and painted a building that the community is automatically better off.[16]

People-owned

Anything that we do needs to be done in a way that creates a sense of ownership for the local population. When a community feels ownership over a project, they are more likely to be involved, more likely to make sure it continues and more likely to problem solve and work on fixing things when they break.[17]

Participative

This goes hand in hand with the competency of people-owned. For true development to take place, the receiving community needs to participate in the work. This is how people develop a sense of ownership in a project. They should be active participants from the beginning, rather than passive recipients. When we participate in our own growth and development, we celebrate our successes and we feel our failures. We learn during the process and through this learning we are personally empowered and encouraged.[18]

---

15. Narayan, "Designing Community-Based Development."

16. Brown, "People-Centered Development and Participatory Research," 69.

17. Smithers, "The Importance of Stakeholder Ownership for Capacity Development Results."

18. World Health Organization, *Health Promotion and Community Participation*, 202.

Focuses on the Core Issues

True development does not attempt to put a bandage on a gaping chest wound. It takes time to determine the core reasons of why things are the way they are. Consider the following story. On a visit to a Latin American country a team realized that the school children in the village where they were ministering were not academically at the appropriate level. Caught up in the tangible, run-down state of the school they quickly arranged for a second missions trip during which they painted the school, bought desks and benches for every student and put in a brand new blackboard for the teacher. They even brought notebooks and pencils from the U.S. for each student. However, a year later, school performance had not improved. After a further, more in depth examination, it was discovered that over one-half of the students were anemic and most did not eat breakfast before going to school. The teachers were poorly qualified and had not had any value-additive teacher training to improve their methods in over ten years. While having a nice facility can certainly enhance the learning environment, even more important is the nutritional state of the students and the training of the teachers. Therefore, while making capital improvements to the building was a nice gesture, it did not touch the root of the issue and therefore did not bring about lasting change.[19]

Sustainable

The Oxford Dictionary defines sustainable as "able to be maintained at a certain rate or level."[20] A definition cited by Shediac-Rizkallah and Bone is "A development program is sustainable when it is able to deliver an appropriate level of benefits for an extended period of time after major financial, managerial and technical assistance from an external donor is terminated."[21] Sustainability is extremely important and should be kept in mind throughout the entire project. The world is littered with development projects that were successful as long as development workers were there to manage it or outside sources were funding it. However as soon as the workers and funding left, these projects died. Effective development is done in a way that is able to be maintained by the local community and is not dependent on continued outside resources. When outside funds or resources are neces-

19. Lopez, "Analyzing Root Causes of Problems," *Community Tool Box*, chapter 17, Section 4.

20. Oxford Dictionary, s.v. "Sustainable."

21. Shediac-Rizkallah, and Bone, "Planning for Sustainability," 91.

sary for project initiation it is important that, from the beginning, there is a plan to phase out the externally provided resources and build the capacity of the community, so that they can manage their own development.[22]

Consider a water project done in a rural village by outside development workers. A well was put in the village and everyone rejoiced when water began to flow. The development workers left feeling very successful as they had helped to improve the lives of the people in that village. One year later the workers returned to the village to evaluate how the presence of the well had impacted the community. To their surprise, the well sat, unused, and the women were once again trekking several kilometers to the water source. The mechanism for pumping the well had broken. No one in the village knew how to repair it so they left it broken and returned to their former ways. The well was not sustainable because no training had been done on well maintenance, how to problem solve breakdowns, and where to purchase the needed pieces to repair the well.

There are many dimensions to sustainability, depending on the dynamics of the community and the project. Physical or environmental sustainability[23] refers to development that respects and encourages proper management of natural resources. God created the world and all that is in it. The first vocation that he gave to man was to steward this creation. Development activities should encourage environmental sustainability so that man can continue to use the natural resources that God gave us. Physical sustainability also means that communities are empowered to care for themselves, without being dependent on outside resources.

Myers talks about mental sustainability,[24] which addresses the mentality of poverty that is often present among the disadvantaged. Mental sustainability is about encouraging people to see who they are in Christ and that they are loved and valued by Him. This encourages people to believe in themselves, to realize that they can, through Christ, make changes in their lives and in their communities. They do not have to be passive recipients but rather an active part of the solution.

Continued community participation refers to sustaining community interest and involvement in the project. Operational or maintenance sustainability involves the ability to manage and maintain the project.

Sustainability needs to be discussed during the initial phases of project development and not viewed as a latent goal to be addressed towards

22. Meyers, *Walking with the Poor*, 128.

23. Ibid., 129.

24. Ibid., 130.

the end of implementation.[25] Program methods should aim for long-term maintenance and effects. At the beginning of the project or activity, when discussing sustainability and how to promote this concept, the development team needs to ask, "What is it that we want to sustain? What do we want to see continuing into the future when we are gone?" Specifying what you want to continue will help the team during the project design phase to ensure that strategies and resources used are locally accepted and locally available. It is also important to use appropriate technology that can be locally understood and maintained. For example, setting up an internet connection for a rural school could open up doors for increased learning. However, if the connection cannot be maintained or problems cannot be solved locally, it is not appropriate technology. Therefore, it is not locally sustainable.

Measurable

Every project should have a degree of measurability so that at the end of the project, during the evaluation phase, the impact can be determined. The process of evaluation can measure the project outputs and outcomes. Outputs are the results of the actions taken. Outcomes can take longer to manifest and therefore measure. An outcome is related to the initial goal of the project.[26]

For example, a church in an area of high HIV prevalence decides to start an HIV/AIDS awareness and prevention campaign. Their ultimate goal is to see a decrease in the incidence of HIV transmission in their community. An output of their program would be that there is increased knowledge in the church and community on the transmission and prevention of HIV. This would be fairly easy to measure. Before starting the awareness campaigns a simple baseline assessment of HIV knowledge could be performed. At the end of the campaign the assessment would be done a second time and the group would be able to determine if there had been a change in the level of HIV awareness. An outcome of this project would be an actual decrease in the incidence of HIV. This is more complicated to determine and necessitates more time in order to allow the effects of the increased knowledge to affect the rate of HIV transmission.

Measuring the impact of a project is important. If some type of change cannot be measured, it is impossible to assess the efficacy of the project. Evaluation that allows some sort of measurement helps to assess

25. Shediac-Rizkallah and Bone, "Planning for Sustainability," 91.

26. Epstein et al., *Results That Matter*, 141.

how effective a project was vis-à-vis resources used and whether or not the methods should be replicated elsewhere.

THE DEVELOPMENT PROCESS

There is a process of actions, or steps, when doing a compassion ministry program that can serve as a guide and help to ensure that best practice is being used. While this process is flexible and can be tailored to meet the particular context where it is being used, understanding it and using it as guide can give order to any project and ensure that the above-mentioned competencies are addressed.

Community Mapping

The first step in any compassion ministry or development initiative should be to get to know the community or people group that you would like to work alongside. This is sometimes called community mapping. [27] Community mapping involves spending time in the community and with the people. As outsiders we cannot assume that we automatically know what is best for a particular community. Even though we might see issues that legitimately need to be addressed, these issues need to be agreed upon by those in the community. What we see as a priority might not be their priorities, and ultimately, it is their opinion that matters. If a compassion ministry project does not touch the priority felt needs of the people, then it is not centered on the people and will not encourage local participation and a sense of ownership. Community mapping will give the compassion ministry workers a chance to see the community and get to know the people.

Community mapping is a process of several steps that add up to a better understanding of the community and the context in which it operates. The first step is to gather objective, concrete information on the community. This is sometimes called a community profile. Information such as population, age distribution, housing, primary occupation and geographical situation is important. It can be helpful to actually create a physical map of the community, marking where people live, where businesses, schools, health facilities, water sources and other important landmarks are located.

As time is spent in the community, take note of the community leaders and stakeholders. A stakeholder is anyone of influence in the community. Sometimes there are formal stakeholders such as a mayor, doctor, or village

27. Dorfman, "Mapping Community Assets Workbook."

chief. There are also informal stakeholders, people who might not have a particular title or position, but who are well-respected and looked to for guidance and advice. It is important to identify all key stakeholders as their approval and involvement in the project is important for overall community acceptance. Taking the time to develop relationships with these key individuals is well worth the effort and will have a significant impact on the trajectory of the project.

Another part of community mapping is assessing and identifying local resources. Using local resources not only supports the local economy, but it also reaffirms to the community that they have valuable assets to be considered. Resources can range from financial to human, natural, intellectual/local knowledge, networking potentials and structures. While financial resources are important, often the most strategic resources are not financial.

When thinking about impoverished communities, it can be easy to assume that there are no resources. The fact that the community exists, however, is indicative of resources. If there were no resources, there would not be a community. The community life and ability to survive in a difficult place is in and of itself a valuable resource. Time should be taken to examine and undercover all local assets. This is where community participation begins. Encouraging the community members to reflect upon and discuss what resources they have locally can be an incredibly empowering experience as they realize the potential that is already in place.

Finally, when mapping out the community it is necessary to evaluate needs or issues that the people would like to address. At this point it is important to think about how to identify these needs. They should be issues that the community identifies, not those that the compassion ministry worker has decided upon. In some cultures, the word "needs" carries a lot of weight and asking people what their needs are can create very high expectations. There are many ways to word this. Questions such as "What obstacles are preventing your community from growth?", "What changes would you like to see in your community?", or "What things would you like to improve?" can help to target felt needs without creating unrealistic expectations. It is important to use wording that includes the community. Ask about "your community" or "What would you like to improve?" It is important that the community identifies their own needs and realizes that they are part of the solution. The community needs to not only be the ones to identify their most pressing needs, but they should also realize that they are a part of the solution.

Planning[28]

After getting to know the community and identifying stakeholders, resources and needs it is necessary to create a plan. Benjamin Franklin is reported to have said, "If you fail to plan, you plan to fail." Sometimes needs and the correct response to the needs are very obvious to an outsider and in an attempt to quickly meet the needs mistakes are made. Taking the time to plan an appropriate and successful response is very important. The process can be as important as the end goal. Planning needs to be done in collaboration with the community, usually represented by a smaller group made up of diverse stakeholders and community members. This group needs to be representative of the community as a whole, not just one group or demographic. This team will be responsible for deciding which needs to address first, how to address them and how to communicate decisions to the broader community while eliciting support for the project.

It is important to recognize that there are multiple possible responses to every problem. The team should think about all the possible responses and then decide which one is most appropriate and realistic for them to undertake.

For example, consider a small local church that is situated in a community that has a high prevalence of HIV/AIDS. What are the possible actions that this church could take to address HIV/AIDS?

- Build a clinic that provides free healthcare for those who are HIV positive
- Build a testing center and offer free counseling and testing
- Make regular home visits to those who are HIV positive in an effort to encourage them spiritually, emotionally and socially
- Seek training on HIV and start regular HIV/AIDS awareness and prevention programs

Any one of these actions could have a positive impact on the HIV situation in the community. However, to build and manage a clinic or testing center are actions that can be unrealistic. Many churches do not have the resources or the managerial capacity to undertake such a project. That said, any church regardless of size can make home visits and provide spiritual and social support. Everyone can show compassion and pray for those who are marginalized. Using the church as a base for HIV education and awareness campaigns is also something that would be very feasible for most

28. *Community Tool Box,* chapter 8.

churches and have a positive effect on the community. It is imperative that the community addresses an issue that is important to them and to choose a response that is within their capacity. Otherwise the logistics and obstacles of an expensive and complicated project become frustrating and the project risks being abandoned.

Once a priority need and response has been chosen, make goals and objectives. Goals are broad statements of what you would like to see at the end of the project and objectives are the actions, or steps, which need to be taken to achieve the goal.

A good objective is SMART goals:[29]

S—Specific

M—Measurable

A—Acceptable

R—Realistic

T—Time oriented

Taking the time to set appropriate goals and objectives will help the work to progress in the desired direction. They are the road map to your final destination.

For example, the local church mentioned earlier decided to start doing HIV awareness and education campaigns. Table 1 gives an example of a goal and SMART objectives that would be appropriate for this action.

Goal	To educate the church and community on HIV/AIDS
Objectives	1. Form an HIV/AIDS response committee with interested church members by May 1st.
	2. Committee members will attend an HIV/AIDS training seminar by June 1st.
	3. At the end of the seminar committee members will map out the church and community and decide where to do HIV/AIDS awareness and prevention.
	4. Starting July 1st, the committee will do 2 awareness and prevention campaigns per month, rotating between identified groups in the church and the community.
	5. After six months of awareness campaigns the committee will evaluate the impact of this action.

Table 1: SMART objectives for an HIV outreach

29. Centers for Disease Control, *Writing SMART Objectives.*

Notice that each objective in Table 1 is directly related to the goal. If each objective is carried out, there is a high probability that the goal will be reached.

The final step in the development process is evaluation.[30] There should always be a system of evaluation for all compassion ministry efforts. Evaluation is about learning. Through evaluation we learn what worked well and what did not so that the next time will be even more successful. Evaluation helps to identify the strengths and weaknesses of a program, determines if resources were used wisely and should, to some degree, measure the actual impact of the project. Typically, there are three areas of evaluation: process, goals/objectives, and impact.

Process evaluation refers to a time of reflecting about how the project was conceived, planned and executed. Did the process work well or do things need to be changed the next time? Did the team function well? Was the team representative of the community and effective in interfacing with the community? Were resources well managed?

Next evaluate your goals and objectives. If goals and objectives were well written during the planning phase, then they are easy to evaluate. The project either did or did not accomplish them. Finally evaluate the project's impact on the community. Did the project make a difference in the desire that was expressed in the goal?

Turning once again to the example of the local church HIV/AIDS education and awareness program, in evaluating the process, we are examining how the project was conceived, planned and managed.

- Did the process work?
- Was the church able to form an HIV committee made up of interested church members?
- Were the committee members able to find appropriate training?
- Did the training fit their needs?
- Did the committee adequately map out what groups or demographics they were going to target in the church and in the community?
- Did they have the necessary resources and were these resources used appropriately?

Evaluating the goals and objectives is probably the easiest form of evaluation. Did the church, and subsequently the committee, fulfill the goals and objectives that had been set?

---

30. Baker, et al., "An Evaluation Framework."

Finally, what was the impact of the project on the church and in the community? The original goal for this project was, according to table 1, "To educate the church and community on HIV/AIDS." Is the church more educated on HIV/AIDS? What about the community? The most effective way to evaluate impact is to do some sort of pre-program assessment. Before starting the HIV/AIDS education outreaches, conduct informal interviews with groups and individuals to assess their initial knowledge of the subject. Once the program has finished, talk to people again and see if they are able to verbalize increased knowledge of HIV/AIDS.

The community development process is often continual and circular, as shown in Figure 1.

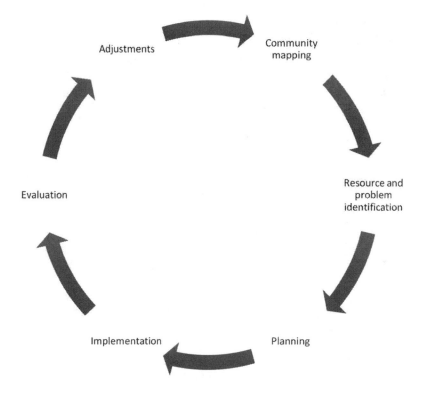

What would a compassion ministries project look like, if it contained the core competencies and followed the steps of the developmental process? For a missionary living overseas or a church wanting to help a local inner-city neighborhood, it would mean that first and foremost, time is spent in the community. Observing community life, traditions and interactions are ways of becoming familiar with the culture and community. Making relationships, listening to people's concerns and observing their successes and obstacles shed light on their daily struggles. Any action is decided upon and created with the input of community stakeholders, and with the understanding that it is for the community and by the community. For the most part, any project uses local resources and develops an action plan that is realistic and sustainable on a local level. At the end of the project, or at various points along the way, there is time to reflect and evaluate how things are progressing.

For a short-term team going overseas, these elements can be more challenging, but are still necessary if we want to make sure that best practice is followed. Teams should be in contact with the resident missionary or sponsor. Dialogue with the missionary can help give the team a picture of the community and how it works. Ideally the missionary would have already done the community mapping exercises, and community buy-in and involvement would be happening. This way the team is coming to work alongside an already involved local community who has a sense of ownership and excitement for the project. Sometimes this might mean changing the traditional methods that have been used. For teams going to an orphanage, for example, this often involves soccer camps, Bible lessons and enjoying spending time with the children. While these activities are not necessarily bad, perhaps other things could be done, or done differently, to build the capacity of the orphanage in a manner that continues long after the soccer camps have ended and the team has returned home. For example, a team could agree to help with the daily management of the orphanage for a week, giving the local, long-term management a chance to have more interaction and bonding time with the children. Alternately, the team could provide value-additive training for the local caregivers on subjects such as child development, child discipleship, play therapy or other pertinent topics that will enhance the long-term, local ministry of the orphanage.

Best Practice Program Models

There are some already constructed program templates that can be used by anyone, anywhere, to start a compassion ministries project. These programs use the basic steps to the developmental process and are designed around the key principles and competencies of best practice.

The first program is called *Community Health and Evangelism* (CHE). CHE is a program created by Stan Rowland, who had been associated with Medical Ambassadors International.[31] CHE takes the basic elements of best practice and combines them with appropriate Bible lessons to create a

31. Medical Ambassadors International, "*Community Health Evangelism Expanded.*"

Christian-based community development and disease prevention program that can be launched by a local church group or by a larger community interest group. CHE's emphasis is on empowering local groups and individuals through training trainers. Community participation, ownership, and sustainability are key elements of the CHE DNA.

CHE is formatted to be very user-friendly. While using foundational developmental principles and methods, its delivery format is an easily understood, well laid out program that simplifies the development process. One does not have to be a healthcare or development professional to successfully use the CHE program. Multiple times a year, in various locations all over the world, CHE training seminars are offered at low cost. These seminars train participants to become CHE trainers of trainers. CHE trainers learn how to train community health workers. These trained workers then go out into their community using skits, case studies and other participatory learning methods to teach basic health lessons and community development. There are successful CHE models in communities all over the world.

Another method is called Asset Based Community Development (ABCD). This model "considers local assets as the primary building blocks of sustainable community development. Building on the skills of local residents, the power of local associations, and the supportive functions of local institutions, asset-based community development draws upon existing community strengths to build stronger, more sustainable communities for the future"[32] ABCD emphasizes the need to view communities, no matter how impoverished, as places of life and potential rather than a bottomless pit of need. By focusing on community resources rather than problems, communities can realize their own potential and seek to focus on what they already have and how to maximize it.

Whatever the method, any compassion ministry project should seek to incorporate the core competencies of best practice while following the basic steps of the developmental process. These tools will help to guide a program towards effective, sustainable programs that can transform individuals and communities for Christ.

32. Asset-Based Community Development Institute.

PART 2

6

Compassion and Unreached People Groups

JEFF PALMER AND LYNDA HAUSFELD

IN RECENT YEARS, THERE has been an exciting awakening taking place regarding the need to send missionaries to unreached peoples. Just a few decades ago, and for various reasons, many missionaries around the world served in countries that were fairly easy to access. In many cases, Christians could serve openly as missionaries. A renewed emphasis on frontier missions and unreached people groups (UPGs), however, has changed much of this, and many Christian workers now have difficulty gaining access to the countries where the unreached reside.[1] As a result, a new term, "platform," has emerged to describe the way in which a person or team gains access to a particular area of the world, people group, or population segment. In its loosest definition, a platform describes anything that is done to give a person/team something to stand on in order for them to gain access to their target population.

Compassion-type ministries have become a common means of gaining access to restricted countries. These are platforms that can be for profit or non-profit but work toward addressing the basic needs of people such as food, water, shelter, gainful employment, and health care, among others.

---

1. For a helpful analysis of the emergence of the modern missions era and its renewed emphasis on frontier missions, see Johnson, "Analyzing the Frontier Missions Movement."

These types of ministries can address acute needs such as those resulting from natural or man-made disasters. More often they address chronic needs such as those resulting from poverty, hunger and underdevelopment.

Several organizations focus on compassion ministries through a local body of believers. They work exclusively through the local church to help empower and enhance local Kingdom capacities. Other organizations choose to prioritize their compassion ministries in more unreached and under-reached areas of the world where there is little or no Gospel presence or witness. Some do a mixture of both.

This chapter will look at human needs or compassion ministries from the perspective of the unreached and unengaged of the world. The general premise is that compassion ministries among unreached peoples should be understood fundamentally as Christ-centered concern for the whole person, their body as well as their soul.

THE UNIVERSAL COMPASSION OF GOD

The Biblical Perspective

Addressing the needs of people in the Bible in most cases is tied to care for fellow members of the house of Israel (in the Old Testament, see Deuteronomy, chapter 15) or those who claim to follow Jesus (in the New Testament, see Matthew, chapter 25). However, there are several scriptures and examples to support the idea that expressions of compassion can be and are an integral part to making God and his Kingdom known in a broader light to the gentiles or the nations.

A common theme throughout the Old Testament is God making his name known among the nations. This theme unfolds purposefully through Abraham and his descendants, and cannot be thwarted by Israel's unfaithfulness or shortcomings. God clearly states that even though he plans restoration for his people, Israel, that, "it is not for your sake that I will act, house of Israel, but for My holy name, which you profaned among the nations where you went. I will honor the holiness of My great name . . . The nations will know that I am *Yahweh*—when I demonstrate My holiness through you in their sight" (Ezek 36:22–23).[2]

The story of Joseph, the preservation of Israel in Egypt, and subsequent exodus of a new nation, is a testimony of God's goodness to his people and serves as a witness to the nations of his power, mercy and sovereignty.

---

2. Scripture quotations in this chapter are from HCSB version unless otherwise noted.

Joseph made it known to the leaders of Egypt that God was the source of his gifting (Gen 41:16). Pharaoh recognized God's Spirit in Joseph (Genesis 41:38). God's power was displayed through His mighty acts, the plagues. Through these multiple signs and wonders and God's word through his servants, the nation of Egypt was given opportunity to acknowledge and follow Him (Exod 7:1—11:10).

Naaman was the commander of Aram's army but he was a leper. Through the advice of his Israelite slave girl, he sought the help of Elisha, God's prophet in Israel. Naaman eventually followed Elisha's advice, was healed and said, "I know there's no God in the whole world except in Israel" (2 Kgs 5:15). Naaman asks for enough soil from Israel that he might build an altar because he no longer will offer a burnt sacrifice to any other God than the God of Israel.

In the waning days of the nation of Israel, God spoke through Micah the prophet and answered Micah's plea for restoration of Israel. God responded by saying that he will perform miracles in Israel, "as in the days of your exodus" in order that "Nations will see and be ashamed of all their power." Furthermore, "they will tremble in the presence of Yahweh our God; and they will stand in awe of You" (Micah 7:14–17).

In the New Testament, likewise, we see a concern for Israel and the emerging church as well. However, there is also concern for the nations, those who do not know God or know of the coming Messiah. God's healing and compassion extends to his people and to the nations to demonstrate his love and power and to, again, make his Name and glory known.

While the majority of Jesus's healing encounters were with Jewish people, we can see other instances of non-Jewish people receiving Christ's touch and demonstration of compassion. Jesus spent the bulk of his ministry life in Judea and Samaria, thus having the greatest natural contact with people of Jewish descent. He even remarked that he had come to "the lost sheep of the house of Israel." But even in that instance, because of the insistence of a broken hearted Canaanite (non-Jewish) mother and his great compassion, he instantaneously granted healing to the woman's daughter (Matt 15:21–28).

Interestingly, immediately afterward, Jesus goes up to a mountain and large crowds of the lame, blind, disabled, mute, and many others follow him. They are placed at his feet, and he heals them. The crowds are amazed to see the broken made whole. The scripture says, "And they gave glory to the God of Israel" (Matt 15:29–31).

In the story of the healing of a demon-possessed man from the region of the Gerasenes (Luke 8:26–39), the man experiences a miraculous healing and Jesus directly commands him to "Go back to your home, and tell all that God has done for you" (8:39). Christ demonstrates the power of God by proclaiming and instructing the healed person to give testimony to what God has done for him in what is possibly an unreached area.

The Strategic Perspective

Not only is it biblical to utilize proclamation and compassion ministries in an integrated way, it is also strategic from a missiological viewpoint. We see "signs and wonders" being done through the apostles in the early church that led to the adding of believers in their midst (Acts 2:19, 2:43, 3:1–10, 5:12). A paralyzed man (Aeneas) is healed by Peter and "all who lived in Lydda and Sharon saw him and turned to the Lord" (Acts 9:32–25). Paul and Silas, even though initially imprisoned over the act, saw the seeds of the gospel germinate in Philippi largely because of the miraculous healing of a demon-possessed slave girl (Acts 16:16–24). In fact, the Gospels frequently link Jesus' miracles to His compassion (Mark 1:41; 5:19; 6:34; 8:2; Matt 9:36; Matt 20:34; Luke 7:13).

Compassion has long been part of the church's missions effort.[3] Early Catholic missionaries established hospitals, social ministries such as feeding of the poor, and compassionate "charities" in poor and impoverished areas of the world. Pioneer evangelical mission work often went hand in hand with medical and health care ministries as well as others addressing the needs of target populations. While very few if any would have described this as an intentional strategy (i.e. utilizing compassion ministries for Gospel proclamation and kingdom expansion), they would have seen these ministries as a natural outflow of the Gospel.

The area of the world known as the 10/40 window has become a growing strategic focus of several mission agencies. Over seventy-five percent of the world's lost live in the window. [4] Despite renewed emphasis on the unreached, there remains a tremendous need for greater missionary presence in this area of the world. It is typically seen as highly resistant to the Gospel with cultural, physical, and governmental barriers. Particularly relevant to this study are the facts that (1) missionaries often serve in the 10/40 window

3. Crawley, *Global Mission*, 281.

4. In 1989, Christian mission strategist Luis Bush began to talk about a vast area of the world stretching from North Africa across Asia through China. As a defined area, it was reported to have the highest levels of socio-economic challenges while, at the same time, the least access to the Church, Christianity and Christian resources. Since this area was between ten and forty degrees latitude north of the equator, it became known as the 10/40 window; Luis Bush, "The 10/40 Window, Getting to the Core of the Core" (Paper presented to Lausanne II, Manila, July 1989).

through "creative access"—often involving some form of compassionate ministry, and (2) the 10/40 window also represents a major concentration of poverty and human need. Close to 80 percent of the poorest of the poor in the world live there.

The ABC's of Compassion among UPGs

While compassion ministries can never be salvific in the Christian sense, they do constitute an integral part of Christian missions. Charles Fielding wrote extensively how compassion ministries can be and are a strategic way to engage the unreached of the world. While his book focuses mainly on medical and health strategies, his observations can apply to broader compassion and human needs strategies. His focus was the simple and obvious things that compassion ministries can do as we seek to engage the unreached and unengaged. He calls these the "ABCs" of health care strategies which alludes to the time-tested "ABC's" of emergency assessment in a medical setting (Airway, Breathing, and Circulatory system). Fielding, however, applies and expands the ABCs in terms of missions to the unreached through compassion ministry.[5]

A—Access to unreached (and needy groups)

This is access in a way that allows us to go deep in relationship and gives an opportunity to gain a presence with an audience in need of help both physically and spiritually. It is biblically based and illustrated best in the life of Jesus and the life and journeys of the Apostle Paul and his colleagues.

B—Behind Closed Doors

This indicates deep access to relationships that allow the gospel to flow. It is access that allows us to find a safe and even inviting place in a person's life and their *oikos* (Greek for "home" our "household"). It gets us to the point in which Fielding describes the hosts as "leaning forward" ready to hear and share in someone's life story. "Behind closed doors" can be in a home, a tent, or even a public area. However, it is generally a place where we can meet the seeker and share the gospel without fear of others seeing and passing judgment. Fielding describes it as "intimate conversation."

---

5. Fielding, *Preach and Heal*, 60.

C—Care for the Needy (and Church Planting)

As we care for the needy with actions such as benevolent ministries, health care strategies, and hunger initiatives, we demonstrate the gospel in action. We also do not neglect the proclamation of the gospel as well. Rather, the two go hand-in-hand in holistic ministry.

D—Disciple Making

The basic command of the Great Commission is to make disciples. It is not simply to go. Anyone can go. The kingdom-minded development worker goes, ministers, *and* makes disciples. As Fielding says, "authentic disciples are the building blocks of church-planting movements."[6] Furthermore, it is interesting to note that the term "disciple" was by far the most common name given to those who were followers of Jesus Christ. Our goal is to minister physically and spiritually, to see the transformation of lives by the power of God's Spirit and then to see the newly emerging disciples taking the abundant life shared with them, both physical and spiritual, and share it with others.

E—Empowering the (Local) Church

The local church, as it begins to emerge, is empowered for ministry. The tasks of evangelism, discipleship, and compassion ministry must be instilled in the local community of believers that emerges. From the beginning, as people come to faith and begin to form into groups, they need to be taught and trained in the fact that they are now a part of the body with the same responsibilities and calling to reach the unreached by making Christ known in word and in deed.

COMPASSION AND UPGS: CASE STUDIES

Agriculture Production in South Asia

In one Gospel-resistant area of South Asia, a team consisting of local believers and expatriate counterparts were having a hard time gaining access and an audience to a large population segment of an unreached group. The target group was very strong in their local mixed-Hindu beliefs and could

6. Fielding, 80.

even be described as militant in their faith. The team had employed some traditional and proven methods of mass evangelism ranging from door to door surveys, public debate/sharing, etc. At every point, they were turned away, sometimes violently.

After several attempts at gaining access to homes and communities, the team decided they needed a different approach. They decided to "live out" the Christian life in some strategically selected communities. They utilized trained believer families to enter into the communities and begin farming projects such as vegetable gardening (for food and profit) as well as some animal husbandry projects (mainly swine raising).

At first it was slow. While the team members were from near-culture people groups, they were still technically outsiders and treated as such. People initially were cold and non-receptive to them and, at first, there was little opportunity for sharing of faith. The team was a bit discouraged.

Slowly, neighbors began noticing things about their "outsider" neighbors. They had productive gardens. They had nice animal projects. They had knowledge they were willing to share so that the whole community could benefit from what they knew and practiced.

The gardens and pigs led to community acceptance and improvement of lives. They also led to relationships and sharing of faith and the gospel. Within the first year, several of the initially resistant community members had become followers of Jesus (and better farmers!). Within a couple of years, there were several churches in the very communities that had been so guarded at the initial attempts of the team.

COMPASSION AND MUSLIM WOMEN

A very somber Algerian Jamila[7] paces up and down the aisles of a community center turned make-shift beauty salon. She walks and observes as kind women pamper the hands, feet, faces, and hearts of her Muslim friends with beauty services that they need but cannot often afford. Her own freshly manicured hand grips a crunched-up tissue, which she discreetly uses to dab away tears that trickle from overfilled eyes. Suddenly she begins to quiver and weep. She stops walking. With words that her staccato sobs all but bury, Jamila clamors: "Why are you doing these things for us? Where does such love come from?"

The event is a simple outreach in one of France's growing Muslim communities. Its organizer, Amina,[8] is a former Muslim, now Christ-follower,

7. "Jamila" is a protective alias.
8. "Amina" is a protective alias.

who understands first-hand the beauty needs Muslim women have as they transition from religiously restrictive geographies into more open ones and responds to this need. She helps them in their adjustments in ways that preserve honor and add value to their personal worth. Her community outreach strategy is quite simple. She rents time and space in a community center in a predominantly Muslim neighborhood and invites the area's women to an afternoon of tea and free beauty services. The women delivering those services are other like-hearted believers—some new disciples, and other mature believers from churches near and far—who hope to be part of Christ's redemptive work in the lives of unreached Muslim women. Amina and her teams pray that by addressing the personal beauty and self-worth needs of these economically, socially, politically and spiritually impoverished women, they might help them know their God-given value.

So, on this particular day, in this improvised salon setting, Amina walks over to Jamila, links arms with her, and lovingly escorts her to a more private spot where she can answer her pressing question. Amina forthrightly explains that the love being shown to the ladies this afternoon comes from Jesus. Jamila expresses interest in this love, and accepts Amina's invitation to spend some time together the next week to talk about it further.

This simple anecdote models how one woman's very deliberate compassion toward her Muslim sisters offers them hope for now and for generations to follow. By making Jesus' love central to everything that transpires, Amina and her teams transformationally touch the bodies and the souls of women. It is indeed a prototype of the limitless possibilities Christ gives the Church for effective, holistic *missio-Dei* presence among women who, since birth, have been dying from the lack of it.

Unreached Muslim woman are a critical need-based opportunity to show the love of Christ in practical ways. By expounding upon the anecdote already in process, this section will outline helpful best practices for biblical compassion in ministry to unreached Muslim women. Due to the Muslim woman's faith practice and Islamic modesty values, it is important to underscore that all one-on-one interactions with Muslims should remain gender-specific. This makes Christian women a vital key to God's will for Muslim women.

THE MUSLIM WOMAN: A GLOBAL NEED REALITY

She is Largely Unreached

The Muslim woman represents a need-reality that the church has capacity to address, but has perhaps unintentionally ignored. She is one of 750 million women; all marginalized by their religion into a system that diminishes their God-given worth and alienates them from truth. They comprise a tenth of the world's population, and without Jesus they are lost.

Most Muslim women reside in or migrate from the systemically re-stricted access regions of the 10/40 Window. This area is home to modern-day wealth dynasties that invest hugely in the propagation of Islam abroad while restricting their own people from access to other-faith beliefs and what Islamists perceive as Western legacies. Muslim women from these regions may be awash in wealth and privilege, but still be marginalized into personal poverties that would not be visible to them or the outside world. Whether they are poor or rich, Muslim women remain spiritually destitute, in need of biblical compassion.

The unreached Muslim woman who migrates from these Muslim ma-jority nations to freer contexts does not all of a sudden have access to the gospel's transformational work. For example, the migrant Muslim Somali woman who belongs to the unreached Oromo language/people group in her homeland remains as unreached in Minnesota as she has forever been in Somalia. A growing number of Oromo live in Minnesota, but still no one can represent Christ to her because language and culture barriers have iso-lated all of the Oromo from the gospel. Whether she is the Oromo woman in Somalia or the Oromo woman in Minnesota, she will perish unless bibli-cally compassionate Christ-followers cross cultural and linguistic barriers to reach her. This dynamic repeats itself globally. Wherever the unreached Muslim woman is, she represents millions like her who must rely on the church's compassion for very diverse poverty needs. At the heart of each need is the spiritual bleakness of Islam's hold upon her life.

She is Inherently Undervalued

Wherever Muslim women live, their core identities are held captive by a sixth-century religious revelation that ideally must transcend time and place. It tells them that they "have rights similar to the rights against them, according to what is equitable; but men have a degree (of advantage) over them" (Qur'an, Sura 2:28), and that they are religiously and intellectually deficient (Bukhari Hadith, 1.6.301).[9] The segregation of women in public life, which came into existence during Islam's early years, remains theologically central to Muslim codes for behavior; largely because, up to, through, and beyond medieval times, it was never sufficiently challenged.[10] These deeply ingrained practices continue to uphold Islam's modesty core values, which for the past fourteen centuries have been encased in the paradigm of Eastern shame/honor culture.

Shame/honor societies function in community, where the individual's identity rests in the strength of its group, and the group's identity rests in the propitious behavior of its individuals. In this culture, honor is key. The individual's driving life-value is to "maintain honor in the midst of a shameful and alienated world."[11] In Islam, the focus of honor is on morality and public righteousness.

Depending on how one views her, the Muslim woman becomes either the most vulnerable or the most valuable asset in this shame/honor paradigm. Her modest comportment reflects upon the men in her community, to whom Allah has commissioned her sustenance and protection "because Allah has given the one more [strength] than the other, and because they [men] support them [women] from their means" (Qur'an, Sura An-Nisa 4:34). Any impropriety on her part potentially shames her whole community, for which repercussions generally follow. Shame that cannot be hidden must be avenged or expunged.

Barbara Stowasser respectfully and realistically encapsulates the Muslim woman's time-honored role as follows: "In her traditional role as loving wife and mother, the woman fights a holy war for the sake of Islamic values where her conduct, domesticity, and dress are vital for the survival of the Islamic way of life. Religion, morality, and culture stand and fall with her."[12] She becomes the keeper of her community's honor.

Numerous Qur'an and hadith texts exalt the role of mothers. It is stereotypical to believe that all of Islam's women live their lives feeling marginalized by the roles society expects them to fulfill. Muslim women happily choose to honor these roles and the edicts that govern them. However, Christian women who experience the privilege of friendships with Muslim women know that Qur'anic and hadith texts also contain strong antithesis to their exalted status. A well-known Sahih al-Bukhari Hadith decries women's inherent intellectual and religious deficiencies and records

9. The hadith are collections of sayings of the Prophet Mohammed.

10. Stowasser, *Women in the Qur'an*, 8.

11. Müller, *Honor and Shame*, 51.

12. Stowasser, 7.

the Prophet Muhammad's sober reminder of having seen with his own eyes that the "majority of the dwellers of Hell-fire were you (women)" (Bukhari Hadith, 1.6.301). This overwhelms many Muslim women, and it keeps a great number of them in fear of failure and death.

Islam dictates that all Muslims, men and women, must earn their way to Paradise, Islam's heaven (Qur'an, Sura Al-Qar'iah 101:6–11). The unfortunate challenge every Muslim woman faces is that for at least one week of every month, the deficiency of her religion (menstruation) prohibits her from regular prayer, Ramadan's fasts, and an array of other good-deed rituals. She must find ways to make up for what she cannot do; she lives much of her life indebted to Islam's Judgment Day tally of her good deed credits. She knows that her hope for Paradise is challenged by the mere fact that she menstruates. Her religion devalues her by isolating her from its own reward.[13]

Conversely, biblical, transformative compassion, as modeled by Jesus, is "a natural, integral part of His earthly mission of redemption . . . integrated with all aspects of Jesus' great commission for evangelism, outreach, and discipleship in contextualized forms (Matt 28:19–20)."[14] Biblical compassion assures her of personal worth and offers her salvation.

She is Biblical Compassion's Great Opportunity

If Jesus were walking the earth today, he would feel at home with Muslim women,[15] and he wants his followers to experience the same comfort. Christ-like friendship is the manifestation of Christ's love for us, in that he left heaven to make his home with us (John 1:14), where he loves us completely (3:16) and models the mission he means for his people to live (13:33–35). Jesus says, "This is my commandment that you love one another as I have loved you" (15:12).

---

13. The oppression of women in Islam is a much debated topic as some within Islam claim that accusations of oppression are based on Western feminist ideologies; see for example, Lila Abu-Lughod, *Do Muslim Women Need Saving*, under "Introduction," n.p; Yet the fact remains, that several reform efforts have been undertaken by Islamic women themselves, highlighting the reality of this issue; see Lichter, *Muslim Women Reformers*. It is inconceivable that such reform efforts would even exist if various forms of oppression did not. Other defenders of Islam have sought to disentangle the oppression of women from the Qur'an by claiming that oppression can only be achieved by reading into the text what is not there; see Barlas, *"Believing Women in Islam."*

14. Grant, *Courageous Compassion*, location 516 of 3669, Kindle.

15. Loewen, *Woman to Woman*, 14–15.

Biblical compassion is the expression of God's love, modeled in Christ-like relationships. Christ-followers will serve Muslims best by committing to a 1 Corinthians 13 model, which gives basis for and credence to every compassionate deed and word, and leaves the miracles of salvation, signs, and wonders to the only One capable of working them.

Compassion provides a great place to start, because the Muslim woman has no concept of Christ's love. She believes that Jesus is a prophet, but he is not the Son of God. Although her Qur'an prolifically honors him for many of the things detailed in the New Testament, it removes Jesus from the cross (Qur'an, Sura 4:156–158) and negates humankind's need for a redeemer's compassion (Qur'an, Sura 101:6–11). It has created a vacuum that the Muslim woman might not know exists, but is tailor made for compassionate outreach.

Compassion is an attribute of Christ, who purposed to love his way to the cross, where his ultimate sacrifice authenticated every compassionate act along the way. Those acts were anticipated in Gen 3:15, with the Bible's first mention of a redeemer; who would come through the offspring of a very shamed Eve. God's promise in this passage was itself a sovereign act of compassion serving as proof of God's infinite, endless love for all, including women. God continued to reveal this hope in Matthew's cross-testamentary genealogy of Jesus,[16] where every woman mentioned wrestled with the issue of maintaining honor in dishonorable circumstances. They were foreigners; unlikely women who God deliberately grafted into this Messianic bloodline as part of his mission to bless the nations (including Muslim women). The substance of their narratives strikes the heart of most any Muslim woman's context, making it feasible for them to accept that Christ could indeed be the Savior, as Christians claim. The compelling nature of this story is the fact that it speaks to Muslim and Christian women alike, about the unfathomable breadth of God's love (Ps 103:17) for them, that he would so meticulously plan for the message with which he means to woo them to himself and to one another in loving friendship.

IN LAY-WOMEN'S TERMS

Christian women everywhere need to know how they can become involved in ministry to Muslim women. The only way Muslim women everywhere will have opportunity to experience the truth of Christ is if lay women everywhere band together with purpose and strategy for the sake of the

---

16. Matt 1:1–16, in reference to Tamar, Rahab, Ruth, Bathsheba, and Mary.

Muslims Jesus wants them to love. Enoch Wan's case study provides some foundations for best practice success:

- Commitment to disciplined daily prayer for Muslim women is non-negotiable. One must pray for guidance as one seeks opportunity for Christ-like friendships. Effective prayers will be those that are informed and focused on specific mosque communities, individuals, and needs. Prayer-walking in the neighborhoods, businesses, and schools where Muslim women have presence teaches the intercessor about the community she prays for and it blesses the Muslim women in it.

- Partnerships with like-minded friends and churches for shared prayer, worship, training, planning, practice, debriefs, and encouragement will undergird the capacity for relationships that will develop among Christian and Muslim women.

- Deliberate, love-driven pursuance of friendships with Muslim women by Christian women gives Muslim women their best hope for lasting transformation. Love that purposes to serve has capacity to relieve multiple poverties that indeed can draw Christian and Muslim friends closer to Jesus, together. It is often best to include another Christian friend in one's relationship with a Muslim woman, to help carry spiritual and physical challenges that may present themselves. If the Christian woman is married, it may be appropriate, after making initial acquaintance, that she suggest to her Muslim friend that they introduce spouses and pursue the friendship as couples.

- Sensitivity toward cultural and religious practices creates the safe places in which fruitful friendships flourish. The Christian woman who postures herself to learn will ask her Muslim friend to help her navigate cultural and religious differences. This will build strong scaffolding for friendships that are honorable and value-adding.

- Hospitality, which every Muslim regards as an act of righteousness and a reflection of morality, honorifically and affectionately regards the needs of a guest above one's own (Qur'an, Sura 59:9). Genuinely practiced, it creates space where Jesus can move in. Indeed, the best conversations Muslim and Christian women have will most likely take place in living rooms and kitchens.

- Whenever the opportunity avails itself, prayer and blessing, as an outpouring of biblical compassion, has the power to transform poverty to plenty and death to life. Muslims value and believe in prayer and blessing, and they respond to the God who sees them and calls them by name.[17]

God often uses the Christian woman's process of leaning on Christ for direction and learning about Muslim neighbors to enlarge the compassionate presence, which requires specific strategy and order. Amina's beauty outreaches began this way, and she took careful steps to give her vision every opportunity for success. The following simplified narrative can help guide other creative initiatives that God might purpose in the hearts of his daughters, for the Muslim women He also loves.

Need and Value-Based, Contextually Relevant Outreach

Amina's Muslim family immigrated to Paris, France, from a North African nation when she was very young. Her Muslim parents raised her to be Muslim, but through a friend, Amina met Jesus. Amina grew up knowing the important role beauty and beauty salons played in the lives of Muslim women. She also understood the conflict North African Muslim women experienced when they moved to France. Reconciling Islamic puristic beauty standards to a context of Parisian design and fashion proves difficult for many Muslim women who want to feel valued at home and in their community. Amina also cherished the value she had found in Christ, and she wanted it for her Muslim friends. God gave her a vision for a salon-type outreach. She wanted to provide a place of safety for Muslim women who needed help with basic beauty maintenance. Her contextually based beauty consults would add value to women whose enhanced self-confidence would track them for respectable status within family and the broader community. It would also open doors for relationship that could foster walks with God, who has fearfully and wonderfully created every Muslim woman (Ps 139:14).

Church-Anchored Vision and Process

Amina and her husband are church planters. Theirs was a contextual church entity, which they promoted as a center that featured worship, religious discourse, and ethnic fellowship. Every Friday night's event drew young French believers and unbelievers, as well as varied sects of Muslims from surrounding areas. It was a place where the gospel was proclaimed, and Muslims met Christ. Amina planned to draw collaborators from among the girls she had

17. Wan, *Diaspora Missiology*, 207.

led to Christ and discipled. It was not long before she had recruited an accountant, a make-up artist, and a trained hair stylist to help her dream and plan. Mature believers in the church were in place to lead seekers in Bible discovery groups and further progress into critical faith choices.

Sustainable Strategic Plan

Amina did not have much to invest in the salon and could not pay salaries. She needed the salon to make money, but she wanted to maintain its ministry ethos. With the help of a lawyer, who was also a former Muslim, she made plans to register the salon as an association. In France, this registration gave her the flexibility to offer services at prorated prices to accommodate low-income clients, and it cleared the way for her entrepreneurial staff to earn money from the services they rendered.

Amina performed an amateur market analysis. Had she not already been so connected in the community, she may have needed to invest more research into this component of her plans. With minimal up-front grant funding, she contracted a rental that would suit her needs and create a safe place for her workers and her female Muslim clients. She ordered products that her North African clients would recognize and appreciate. She made deliberate use of every bit of space in the small salon and decorated it in endearing, vintage spa fashion.

Community Favor

Amina's efforts with the salon and her personal contributions in the district, at large, fostered a great reputation with county authorities who, in turn, affirmed her work to others. They trusted and admired her for her philanthropy and for what she and her husband did to create community among the immigrants in that part of the city. They continue to support her efforts.

Perseverance through Challenge

As soon as the salon opened, it saw success; however, just a couple of months into operations, the apartment above the salon suffered severe leakage; the ceiling collapsed and the flooding destroyed the salon structure and furnishings. It took about twelve grueling months to re-open the salon. As of the end of 2015, the business was yielding a profit and had begun to fund and sustain salon outreaches into four conservative Muslim communities.

At the time of this writing, at least four Muslim women have professed faith in Christ. Many have experienced answers to their prayers.

If the world's 750 million Muslim women were to stand shoulder to shoulder in a line, that line would circumference the earth more than eleven times. The line of Christian women whose career mission is outreach to Muslim women would be less than 100 miles long.[18] This desolating statistic shouts a travesty to which the church must respond. An entire world of majority unreached Muslim women are dependent upon Christian women in the local church—globally—for the great hope that transformational, biblical compassion begs to facilitate.

The insurmountable task offers fresh opportunity as globalization ushers Muslim women from severely restrictive geographies to contexts of greater freedom, and as God increases compassion's access into hard-to-reach places. Acts 17:26 reminds the church that God orders the times and movements of peoples so that those who seek Jesus might find Him; so that those who languish in Hell's poverty might receive life at the hands of compassionate Christ-followers who know its source.

CONCLUSION

We as followers of Jesus Christ should naturally be compassionate people because our Savior is a compassionate God. Our compassion, which originates in his compassion, should not be segregated from all we do to make his name known among the nations. Rather it should be a natural part of our thought processes, strategies and methods as we strive to see the gospel preached to every nation.

In our world today, many of those who have never heard the gospel reside in places where missionaries have difficulty gaining access. Because of this, compassionate ministries serve as a key aspect of a biblical faith that opens doors for sustainable entry and engagement of the unreached and lesser-reached areas of the world. Being an integral part to Christian discipleship, compassion ministries allow us to both practice and model the compassionate and ethical demands of the gospel. As we engage in these ministries, we should do so in a way that embraces excellence. Our compassion ministries should not just be platforms in order for us to share the gospel. They should be excellent ministries that show the love of Christ and enhance our ability to make Christ known.

18. Conservative estimate based on figures drawn from Pew Research Center, Joshua Project, and Liberty University statistics, 2011. This figure is not scientific, but has been deemed reliable by authorities in the field; Say Hello, "About."

A ministry platform that is dishonest or that is merely a means to an end dishonors God. To say that we care for the needs of people when we really do not and have no plans to, can harm the ministry as well as others and thus the ability to proclaim the gospel. People are very attuned to manipulation and this is perhaps especially true among many UPGs. So, the need to think properly about our compassionate approach to UPGs is significant simply because our perceptions of what we do and why we do it are easily read by those we aim to reach.

At the same time, it is not enough to simply do compassion well. An individual or organization that does excellent work in health care, water, agriculture, literacy, etc., and yet fails to find a way to incorporate intentional Gospel proclamation, disciple making and church planting, woefully misses the mark.

Our heart and goal in missions should be to make Christ known in all that we say and do in both word and deed. Our goal should be to demonstrate practical expressions of compassion that are an outflow of a redeemed life, and that are ideally reproducible by local disciples. Those we try to reach should see our compassionate actions and come to the conclusion that this is an inherent part of our faith. In doing this, we foster Christ-centered compassion as a fundamental aspect of following Jesus. The rejection of "platform" language may not necessarily change what we do, but it should change how we think about those activities. Thinking rightly goes a long way toward fostering best practices.

7

Counterintuitive Missions in a McDonald's Age

Recovering the Apostolic, Incarnational Model to Integrating Gospel-As-Mission and Gospel-As-Deed

JEAN JOHNSON

"YOU CAN PUT YOUR bed in the hallway," said Savadthy. As a new missionary within the United States working among first-generation Cambodian refugees, my new home was with a Cambodian family of eight people living in a one-bedroom duplex. There was a bed in the kitchen for the oldest brother, and everyone else shared a room with curtains hanging from the ceiling to create a degree of privacy between beds. Every morning and every evening, family members walked by my bed in the hallway that connected the only bedroom to the kitchen and bathroom.

After the kids left for school, I would often hear the mother crying. I would cautiously pull back the curtain and sit on the side of her bed. I mostly listened as she emptied her heart of burden upon burden related to being a survivor of the Killing Fields, a widow, a refugee, and a mother trying to be the head of her household in a country not her own.

Eventually, I moved into an apartment building with about thirty Cambodian families. There I was . . . doing life . . . smack in the middle of these families. I would go from apartment to apartment or merely sit in the hallways with everyone else, practicing the language, eating popular Cambodian dishes, and sharing the gospel.

I remember the evening when the apartment manager asked me to serve as the third-floor captain after an incident in which a Cambodian child was raped by an outsider who snuck into the building. "The police aren't protecting us!" exclaimed the Cambodian manager. He went on to describe how the residents had decided to set up their own communal method of protection. I asked, "What does serving as the third-floor captain require?" Without hesitation, he said, "You will need to have a gun." I understood their frustration. I myself was robbed and manhandled in the foyer of the apartment building by two outsiders who snuck into the door right behind me. Unfortunately, there was no security system. Nonetheless, I told him I wasn't willing to carry a gun, but I would keep a watchful eye.

Being fresh out of college, I did not have the resources to live at a higher standard, and I chose to solicit just enough funding from local churches to live simply. This voluntarily chosen mode of life and ministry immediately created a degree of give-and-take between the Cambodians and myself. Doing daily life with Cambodians in their comfort zone enabled me to increasingly learn the worldview from the inside out, which is the best place to encourage transformation.

I was not doing anything I thought of as remarkable. I had studied cross-cultural communications at North Central University (formerly North Central Bible College). Upon graduation, I was willing and ready to start my Great Commission efforts among Cambodian refugees in St. Paul/ Minneapolis. I was taught to conduct cross-cultural missions in an incarnational way—live in the community, be in their homes, live at the level of the people, eat their food, and face their joys and challenges as an insider as much as possible.

I practiced this approach wholeheartedly. I did not know any other way until it was time to serve as a missionary overseas. After six years of living and serving among the Cambodians in my hometown, I was bound for Cambodia as a global missionary. I had in my mind that I would operate in the same manner as I had among the Cambodians in the USA. As I began to enter the landscape of contemporary foreign missions, however, I discovered that living close to and consistently with my primal message, the gospel,[1] was passé, and loving my neighbor as myself took on a whole new meaning. I began to hear words like NGOs, MOUs, English centers, schools, clinics, orphanages, rescue centers, development enterprise, fundraisers, donors, project managers, and building contractors. All these enti-

---

1. Hirsch, *The Forgotten Ways*, 20.

ties and roles, steeped in expertise, education, money, well-connectedness, and Americanism were meant to empower missionaries to include a social component in partnership with the gospel.

I indeed dabbled in some of these roles and strategies throughout my missions journey, but, in many ways, I have come full circle. I am more convinced than ever that cross-cultural workers need to ensure that both sides of the integral mission[2] equation—both gospel-as-word and gospel-as-deed—are owned by the local people, reproducible for the local people, and a grassroots expression of the local people.

Gospel-as-Word	+	Gospel-as-deed
Locally owned		Locally owned
Locally reproducible		Locally reproducible
A local grassroots expression		A local grassroots expression

As good as the outpouring of Western resources and finances may look from our headquarters in Chicago or Los Angeles, the reality on the ground often constitutes a mission enterprise that is impossible for local people to maintain or expand, thus creating dependency and stifling the reproduction of the indigenous church. We offer the Majority World methods that are beyond their ability to maintain, either through producing their own volunteers or by mobilizing their own local resources. Thus, we suck out the volunteers from the local churches and pay them salaries to achieve our agendas, and then we wonder why the local church does not do their part in loving their neighbors as themselves.

Over the course of sixteen years in Cambodia, I saw with my own eyes how Cambodians, slowly but surely, began to perceive that Christian success was based on money, status, ownership of property, buildings, and expensive gadgets, the ability to serve from a position of patron, and access to foreign donors, all of which has led to a worrisome degree of corruption, greed, maneuvering, competition, power grabs, materialism, and individualism in the Cambodian church. Wu Tein Tze referred to this type of behavior as an inherited psychology of dependence.[3] Can the church in its local context implement lasting transformation, which reflects justice, love, and the character of Jesus Christ, if it is steeped in the unintended consequences of Americanized missionary models?

2. "Integral mission" and "holistic mission" are used interchangeably throughout this paper to carry the meaning of integrating gospel proclamation and social demonstration.

3. Quoted in Swanson, "The Money Problem," 28.

Should this discourage America Christian's efforts overseas? All Christians have a mandate to share the gospel, but American Christians should be cautious about strategies that are culturally comfortable for them, and look for strategies that are easily reproducible by local Christians.

A young Christian professional spent several years in a South American country. She described how corruption runs through every level of the denomination to which she related. The churches worked hard to oust one of their most corrupt denominational leaders and then gave him a new position once they realized he was a major connection to the pipeline of foreign money. In another account, a Christian woman from England returned to her home country in Africa to offer her benevolent services. She described to me a woeful scene. The bishops and pastors—driven by the prosperity formula (give and you will receive blessings) and the need to pay dues to the national headquarters—collected three offerings per church service. The parishioners became so weary of giving the little they had that they cut their paper money into three pieces and then gave one piece per offering. The church had to assign elders to tape the money back together. Americanization of indigenous Christian leadership strategies is a major problem.

We are on a dangerous path of replacing a biblical, counterintuitive way of growing God's kingdom[4] with a Western intuitive way, thus making the fulfillment of the Great Commission utterly dependent on the worldview, purses, and purse strings of the West.

Erwin McManus says, "To reframe, we must first reflect; and to imagine, we must first examine."[5] The rest of this chapter, will reflect on and examine our Western intuitive ways and the contrasting ways of the kingdom with the hope that readers will strongly consider implementing and modeling biblical, counterintuitive ways of integrating gospel-as-word and gospel-as-deed in order to put growing God's kingdom into the hands of all the priesthood (1 Pet 2:5–9). Then, the essay will reframe and reimagine counterintuitive ways of integrating gospel-as-word and gospel-as-deed in the form of essential compassion, incarnational lifestyle, and holistic cooperative discipleship.

DO WE BUY OUR WAY IN?

A church from North America signed up to adopt a community in India via a reputable mission organization. They were excited about meeting spiritual and physical needs. This would be their second visit. They had already sent one team to bring finances and assist with starting a school and a youth

4. Smith, "CPMS," 28–31.
5. McManus, *An Unstoppable Force*, 12.

center. This time around they wanted to assess the projects and monitor the funding. Additionally, they planned to set up a makeshift health clinic, distribute food packages, hand out preloaded backpacks for the schoolchildren, hold a kids' club, and have evangelistic meetings in the evenings. This "integral package" of ministry was meant to empower the local believers to make headway into the community that they could not make on their own. This is a common picture today.

Church planters in India offered their perspective on the effect of this type of western volunteerism. "When we go to love and serve our own communities, we lose face because our local expressions of loving our neighbor are always inferior to the grand schemes of the foreign Christians in our midst." Basically, they were saying that Christians from affluent countries buy their way into communities, while indigenous church planters have to earn the right to be present. In this case, local believers could not reproduce the so-called integral approaches that were modeled by foreigners, and they came up short in the eyes of the community and in their own eyes. This kind of Western dominance, a common approach to mission today, usually results in three responses: Why bother? Let the missionaries do it! We need to start sending e-mails to organizations and churches in America and Europe to find partners to fund us.

Majority-World missionaries are on the rise. There were missionaries from the Majority World in Cambodia when I was there. It was an eye-opener when the Cambodian Christians stated that they tried harder and more often to connect with the missionaries from the West than those from the Majority World because Western connections gave them a better chance of financial gain. Sadly enough, this forced some of the Majority World missionaries to seek funding from the West so they could contend with the Western (and South Korean and Singaporean, etc.) missionary force. Scott Bessenecker asks this question: "Is there something about how the Protestant mission is shaped that makes it easier for white folk to enter and more difficult for others?"[6] Borrowing from Scott's question: "Is there something about how the Protestant mission is shaped that makes it easier for rich folk to enter and more difficult for others?" Western missionaries need to find ways to promote mission methods that are not solely dependent on the wealthy and well connected. This involves more than providing funds so local believers can do the mission work. In this case, the wealthy and well connected own the Great Commission. It was Jesus who said, "All authority in heaven and on earth has been given to me . . . And surely I am with you always, to the very end of the age" (Matt 28:18, 20, NIV).

6. Bessenecker, *Overturning Tables*, 21.

THE MCDONALDIZATION OF MISSIONS

In his book *The McDonaldization of Society*, sociologist George Ritzer claims that fast-food culture has been popularized in many sectors of society in the USA and is spreading from there to much of the world. In education, for example, Western education and classroom dynamics are being imported and copied all over the world. Ritzer shares four key aspects that characterize "McDonaldization:" efficiency, calculability, predictability, and control.

Efficiency is the ability to accomplish something with the fastest amount of time with the least amount of effort. Ritzer puts this concept in McDonaldization terms, the fastest way to move customers from hungry to full. In regard to *calculability*, the business or organization determines success by the quantity of the product delivered rather than the quality of the product. Sales trumps taste, so to speak. The costumer measures satisfaction in the same manner—the faster and cheaper, the better. Therefore, a characterization of McDonaldization is to judge success by speedy production rather than quality of the work or outcomes. *Predictability* celebrates standardized and uniformed services. This is why a customer can both recognize a McDonald's restaurant and know what to expect upon entering the business, no matter the location. Additionally, the workers perform their tasks with robotic consistency and predictability. The expectation is to reproduce the format, patterns, and experience everywhere. Finally, *control* enforces standardization and uniformity, especially using technology to ensure globalized efficiency, calculability, and predictability.[7]

Believe it or not, Ritzer claims there is also a counter-process he calls "de-McDonaldization." In this case, certain societies try to protect their localized and traditional values by denying McDonaldization. Recently, I have interviewed numerous missionaries-in-training regarding what they aim to do when they reach their cross-cultural destination. Their answers tend to line up with Ritzer's description of McDonaldization. The majority answer: teach English, start an anti–human trafficking NGO, or start an orphanage and/or school. This means they already have an efficient, calculable, standardized, and controlling strategy in mind.

Is it possible that Americans have McDonaldized global mission practices? Moreover, is it possible that McDonaldization is a form of neocolonialism? After all, top-down McDonaldization methods of global mission ignore the local worldview, localization, and traditional values. Is it possible that we are not so far removed from modern colonialist tendencies in the postmodern era? Richard Slimbach reminds us how the modern era

7. Ritzer, *The McDonaldization of Society*.

of missions materialized. He notes that in many ways, "missions" has gone hand-in-hand with Western Culture, and that man y missionaries have been blind to their own cultural captivity. Slimbach says, "Because Western missionaries were unaware of the pagan flaws in their own culture, the Gospel they took to distant lands carried a benevolent paternalism that was unprepared to recognize, appreciate, and build upon the resources of foreign cultures."[8]

Reflecting on Slimbach's statement, I am not so sure we are operating any differently in the twenty-first century. Perhaps we disguise our present-day paternalism with words like *poverty alleviation, compassion, holism, human flourishing, social justice, interdependence, global unity, and Christian expansion.* None of these concepts are negative in and of themselves, but if we really peel back the layers and examine practice, are we truly recognizing, appreciating, and building upon the resources of foreign cultures? If we are not, are we truly bringing the gospel in such a way that the local church can reproduce and multiply, making disciples of their own people in their own context? The mere fact that Christians from the West are going to the Rest *en masse* signifies that we do not and cannot leave much room for local contextualization. Steve Hyde, director of Words of Life Ministries, conveyed to a group of missionaries at a Mission Forum held in Cambodia in November 2014 that there are approximately 2500–3000 long-term foreign missionaries in Cambodia, as well as 80,000–100,0000 short-term mission team visitors per year—all those visitors per year in a country the size of Missouri. With that amount of foreign presence, how can a place like Cambodia take its rightful place in the Great Commission and avoid the inherited psychology of unhealthy dependence?

Mission practitioners have put a huge emphasis on the absolute necessity of holistic mission, stressing that every local church should be an expression of holistic ministry. Yet we often unknowingly try to implement holism in other nations by creating unnatural dichotomies within societies and communities.[9] This means that our "holistic" methods might actually be counterproductive to truly holistic impacts and outcomes! Buddhist temples and pagodas in Cambodian collective communities are an example. The temple is birthed from the inside out and forms the center of communal life, linking the sacred and the public. No Cambodian would claim that a pagoda is an alien structure among them. However, in Christian mission efforts, land is purchased and a handful of local people—often driven by outsiders and/

8. Richard Slimbach, "First Do No Harm."

9. *Holism* means seamlessly integrating gospel and deeds resulting in holistic outcomes—integrated and equal spiritual, social, and economic transformation.

or organized in conjunction with outsiders—plant a church in a community. Suddenly, there is an alternative, alien religious structure that divides the Christians from the rest of the community. In essence, they become a subculture enacting the sacred behind the walls of a church building. If they can build a big enough church structure, they create classrooms to separate out family members from their family units for age-group specific ministry in an effort to copy the individualistic Western church model. Additionally, it does not take long for new believers to learn from foreigners that "church hopping" is desirable—finding a church that accommodates to you rather than attending a church in your own community. So while the missionaries are encouraging local churches to holistically transform their communities, those churches are starting off on the wrong foot with social dichotomies and divisions that are a direct consequence of mission strategies.

Another concern is "the flaw of the excluded middle". Is excluding the middle of something counterproductive to holism? Paul Hiebert coined this term to refer to the way Westerners ignore the middle-level reality of the Majority World, supernatural, this-worldly beings and forces present and operating around us, because their reality is two-tiered/dualistic, dichotomizing the sacred/religious and the secular/scientific. Whether Western Christians admit it or not, we have moved many people throughout the world away from their middle view of reality, redeemed or otherwise, to a secular-scientific-materialistic worldview. In some ways we have led people further away from trusting God as the explanation for all of life and toward seeking science, technology, and development as the explanation (with God tucked in there somewhere). It would be quite sad if the Majority World joined Western Christians in their increasing conviction that the universe is a closed system, controlled by rules and laws of nature and science, in which God has minimal sovereignty.

Bryant Myers advises that we add gospel-as-sign (angels, prayer and visions, sacred space, and signs and wonders) to the holistic equation to make sure we redeem the middle for Christ rather than exclude it. Jerry Trousdale, author of *Miraculous Movements*, shares numerous accounts of how hundreds of thousands of Muslims are falling in love with Jesus through gospel-as-sign. Gospel-as-sign is a much needed part of the whole, However, in many parts of the world, many local people perceive that *gospel-as-deed*—delivered in Western modes and with Western money—is the key to so-called Christian success.

Is what we call holistic or integral really as holistic or integral as we think? If we want local churches who do not possess a Western worldview to integrate gospel–as–word, gospel–as–deed, and gospel–as–sign around the world, we need to get the West out of holism.

COUNTERINTUITIVE MISSIONS IN A MCDONALD'S AGE

We do not grasp how much of our Western worldview is entangled with our Christianity and how much of that we pass on through our McDonaldized mission paradigms. David Platt claims that "we have in many areas blindly and unknowingly embraced values and ideas that are common in our culture but are antithetical to the gospel [Jesus] taught."[10] Pursuit of what can be bought and quantified, equating money with ability, exalting entertainment and celebrity status, and viewing people as objects to market—have all co-opted our faith experiences.

The apostolic model presented in Scripture is quite different. Contrast bigger church crowds, larger church budgets, better church buildings, and impressive community projects with Terry Eagleton's statement: "[Jesus] is presented [in the gospels] as homeless, propertyless, peripatetic, socially marginal, disdain of kinfolk, without a trade or occupation, a friend of outcasts and pariahs, averse to material possessions, without fear for his own safety, a thorn in the side of the Establishment and a scourge of the rich and powerful."[11] Are we sure that we are not merely passing on to the world values and ideas that are antithetical to the gospel?

The church in the West faces a spiritual, theological, missional, and existential crisis.[12] If what we are doing in the West (and passing on to the rest) proves to fail in our own backyard in the long term, what will eventually happen to the rest of the world? For example, through social and economic enticements, Cambodians have converted from dedicated Folk Buddhists to lukewarm Christians; through a Western scientific-materialistic emphasis, Cambodians have converted from a deep spirituality to secularism; through promises of church and pastoral subsidies and empowerment, Cambodians have converted from a simplistic temple life and monkhood to clergy roles of position and power.

Once we have prototypes, formulas, systems, mechanisms, institutions, and technology to pass on to people, by default, we operate out of our own worldview and disregard others' worldview. Instead, we teach them English so they can learn our systems, and since language and worldview are inseparable, we convert them to our worldview. By the end of the day, the world perceives God as an American and thinks they must become American in order to relate to him. We need to keep asking ourselves how we can pass on the gospel and make disciples of all nations without passing

10. Platt, *Radical*, 19.
11. Eagleton, "Was Jesus Christ a Revolutionary?" 24.
12. Frost and Hirsch, *ReJesus*, 5.

on our values and ideas that are antithetical to the gospel. Perhaps essential compassion, incarnational compassion, and holistic cooperative discipleship are principles and practices that will empower us to offer counterintuitive missions in a McDonald's age.

PRACTICING ESSENTIAL COMPASSION

In Boise, Idaho, my sister introduced me to Charming Charlie's. Charming Charlie's is a store that makes and sells accessories, all conveniently arranged according to colors. Their online marketing wordage is "style it, snap it, share it." Basically, it is a store that sells frivolous accessories rather than essentials.

Charming Charlie's is a frighteningly accurate picture of some of our approaches to missions. The world is sorely in need of missionaries who model essential compassion without all the extra (and expensive) accessories. Compassion that requires complex structures, institutions, heavy centralized authority, projects, high education, and professionalism can be thought of as *accessory compassion*, which usually makes foreign money, donors, and power the engine. Conversely, *essential compassion* operates on the basis of compassion shown and centered in everyday life, relationships, and personal resources. Basically, you are the equipment:

> Jesus now called the Twelve and gave them authority and power to deal with all the demons and cure diseases. He commissioned them to preach the news of God's kingdom and heal the sick. He said, "Don't load yourselves up with equipment. Keep it simple; *you* are the equipment." (Luke 9:1–2, MSG)

In scripture, essential compassion was lived out by Jesus and the disciples on a daily basis. The mere fact that they were on the move constantly, partly because of persecution and partly because of strategy, speaks to this. Jesus did not allow people, institutionalism, or complex systems to prevent him from being light and nimble in his approach: "He left the next day for open country. But the crowds went looking and, when they found him, clung to him so he couldn't go on. He told them, 'Don't you realize that there are yet other villages where I have to tell the Message of God's kingdom, that this is the work God sent me to do?' Meanwhile he continued preaching in the meeting places of Galilee" (Luke 4:42–44, MSG).

Why is living out essential compassion so important in light of Jesus's Great Commission? Essential compassion is doable and reproducible for every disciple as a natural outflow of his or her everyday life. As I lived

and served in Cambodia as a missionary, I often came to what I refer to as
a compassion crossroads—a situation in which two roads intersected, and
depending on which road I chose, there would be different outcomes. For
example, I could be walking along in a village with local church planters
from that community, and we might encounter a man holding his extremely
sick daughter. Do I take the road of intervening with my missionary *accessories* to provide transportation to the best hospital and solicit donations from
my homeland to pay expensive ongoing medical bills, or do I take the road
of finding a way with the local church planters to show *essential* compassion
within their means and everyday context? If I intervene in a way that only
a well-funded missionary could do, I create future problems for the local
church planters, setting them up for failure. First, they cannot emulate my
mode of compassion. Second, the community regards them as hirelings of a
foreigner and her religion, or as a bridge to foreigners and potential perks,
rather than as neighbors and fellow Cambodians who knows, loves, and
serves Jesus.

When we model essential compassion, we inspire and empower local
people to discover and practice grassroots expressions of compassion, such
as we observe in Azab's life and church-planting ministry:

> Azab had moved to a distant village in hopes of telling others
> about the gospel of Jesus. He met a couple there named Ihmaad
> and Lina, who welcomed him to the village, and Azab thought
> for sure that he had found a family of peace. He was on the verge
> of staying with them and their children for an extended period
> of time when they asked the unexpected question: "Are you a
> follower of Jesus?" Azab told the truth, that he was committed
> to Jesus the Messiah, and immediately the entire family cooled
> in their welcome . . . And what happened next was definitely not
> encouraging.
>
> That same evening a cow went missing from the village . . .
> The people of the village began to suspect that Azab's presence in
> the community somehow caused this bad fortune to befall them
> . . . Suddenly, no one in the entire village would even speak to
> Azab. They did however, speak freely about him behind his back,
> referring to him as the "animal chaser." Early the next morning,
> Azab wandered into the bush and threw himself on the ground,
> weeping and crying out to God. Why was all this happening?
>
> Ihmaad and Lina permitted Azab to stay in their home,
> although their children did not refrain from making fun of the
> "animal chaser" over tea that evening. But in the course of con-
> versation, Ihmaad told Azab that he wanted to build a stable for
> his animals because the cows made him wealthy and deserved a

better place to stay, but he could not find a builder to construct it. Azab was experienced in carpentry and, seeing this as an opportunity to serve Ihmaad, he offered to build the stable . . . Azab had told him that he could quickly retrieve his carpentry tools in another town.

Within twenty-four hours, Azab had returned to the village with his tools, ready to work . . . During the time that Azab was building, the children of the village came to watch, so he began talking to them about respecting and obeying their parents. He began telling the children stories about God's creation, and the fall of mankind. It did not take long until some families noticed a change for the better in their children, and they discovered that Azab was sharing some wonderful stories with them.

About that time, Azab had to leave the village to stay in town for awhile, and during that time the people of the village realized that they, and especially their children, were missing the animal chaser. They wanted him back. So they started sending him gifts and inviting him to come back to the village.

He came as soon as he could. And when he returned, it was to a welcome reserved for dignitaries. The people wanted to hear more stories. They wanted to discover more about God . . . The first people to make Jesus the Lord of their lives were Ihmaad and Lina. The others followed rapidly . . . Today there are twelve churches in that Muslim area.[13]

Western missionaries should be careful about interrupting this "jars of clay" expression of gospel-as-word and gospel-as-deed with grandiose means of implementing integral mission. "But we have this treasure in jars of clay, to show that the surpassing power belongs to God and not to us" (2 Cor 4:7, ESV). Is it fair for Christians from wealthy nations to override local and grassroots expressions of integral mission by positioning ourselves as patrons, donors, and connections to donors back home?

To borrow Sidney J. W. Clark's evaluative question to test the soundness of our mission practices: "Can the work at any point of its development still be maintained by the people if it is left by the missionary?" Clark says, "If the answer is in the negative, then we have either planted a dead thing or a living thing badly."[14] Christians should consider being part of a movement of missionaries who implement and model biblical, counterintuitive ways of integrating Gospel-as-word, Gospel-as-sign, and Gospel-as-deed in order to put growing God's kingdom back into the hands of all the priesthood.

13. Trousdale, *Miraculous Movements*, 92.
14. Quoted in Swanson, "The Money Problem," 28.

INCARNATIONAL COMPASSION

Craig Greenfield, a former co-worker in Cambodia, wrote a pamphlet enti-tled *The Biblical Role of the Outsider*. In this pamphlet, Craig tells a personal story about his family. Craig and Nay and their child moved into the slums of Cambodia to both proclaim the gospel and demonstrate the love of God in practical ways. While they lived there, the moneymakers of society adver-tised that powdered milk would make kids smarter and stronger. Mothers who did not have access to clean drinking water mixed the powdered milk with contaminated water, causing severe diarrhea and all the complications that accompany it. Educators, nongovernment organizations, and the gov-ernment conducted a massive campaign to reverse the false perception that powdered milk was better than breast-feeding. These campaigns produced minimal results.

During these campaigns, Nay had her second child while living in the slums. The Cambodian mothers watched Nay intently as she breastfed her baby, and they took notice as her baby grew strong and healthy without powdered milk. As a result, the mothers in the area started to breast-feed their babies and experience the benefits as well. Nay accomplished in a few months what years of campaigns could not. Craig summarizes the key to this transformation: "Through the simple, prophetic act of incarnational motherhood, we accomplished in our slum what poster campaigns, visiting educators, and government campaigns had been unable to accomplish—transformation." Craig and Nay offered an example of integral mission in a simple, grassroots, and reproducible way.

PUTTING IT ALL TOGETHER IN A PRACTICAL SENSE

Western intuitive ways of doing missions are not necessarily best. There are truly holistic, incarnational, and apostolic alternatives available to us. The rest of this chapter will highlight the concepts we have been exploring and introduce practical guidelines to put the concepts into practice.

End Vision

If we are to foster truly reproducible, indigenous churches, we must always start with an end vision and measure all strategies and answer all questions in accordance with that end vision. An example of an end vision might be: launch a movement of disciples reproducing disciples to the 4th +

generation,[15] disciples who readily live out the gospel-as-word, gospel-as-sign, and gospel-as-deed among their neighbors. For the rest of our discussion, let's use this as our working end vision.

END VISION BIBLE VERSES

It is important that all end visions are rooted in Scripture and can be readily passed on. Below are key Bible verses that drive our working end vision and allow people to pass it on.

Disciples Making Disciples

"Then Jesus came to them and said, 'All authority in heaven and on earth has been given to me. Therefore go and make disciples of all nations, baptizing them in the name of the Father and of the Son and of the Holy Spirit, and teaching them to obey everything I have commanded you. And surely I am with you always, to the very end of the age'" (Matthew 28:18–20, NIV).

Gospel-as-Word

"For I am not ashamed of the Gospel, because it is the power of God that brings salvation to everyone who believes: first to the Jew, then to the Gentile" (Romans 1:16, NIV).

Gospel-as-Sign

"Heal the sick who are there and tell them, 'The kingdom of God has come near to you'" (Luke 10:9, NIV).

Gospel-as-Deed

"What good is it, my brothers and sisters, if someone claims to have faith but has no deeds? Can such faith save them? Suppose a brother or a sister

15. The 4th + generation means that disciple groups and churches reproduce more disciple groups and churches to the fourth generation and beyond. Disciple Making Movements (DMMs) and Church Planting Movements (CPMs) practitioners have discovered that an effort needs to multiply to four generations to become a sustainable movement. DMMs and CPMs are missions strategies popularized by David Garrison's book, Church Planting Movements.

is without clothes and daily food. If one of you says to them, 'Go in peace; keep warm and well fed,' but does nothing about their physical needs, what good is it? In the same way, faith by itself, if it is not accompanied by action, is dead" (James 2:14–15, NIV).

Among Neighbors (Your Circle of Influence)

"The next day Peter started out with them, and some of the believers from Joppa went along. The following day he arrived in Caesarea. Cornelius was expecting them and had called together his relatives and close friends" (Acts 10:23–24, NIV).

4th + Generation of Disciples

"And the things you have heard me say in the presence of many witnesses entrust to reliable people who will also be qualified to teach others" (2 Timothy 2:2, NIV).

THREE VITAL INGREDIENTS FOR THE END VISION IN THREE VITAL FORMS

Gospel-as-Word +	Gospel-as-sign +	Gospel-as-deed
Locally owned	Locally owned	Locally owned
Locally reproducible	Locally reproducible	Locally reproducible
A local grassroots expression	A local grassroots expression	A local grassroots expression

Locally Owned

Fundamentally, local ownership is a frame of mind backed up with action. It is a mind-set that says, we are responsible, we desire to be responsible, and we will be responsible for the gospel-as-word, gospel-as-sign, and gospel-as-deed in our communities. Esther Mwaura Muiru of Groots, Kenya, offers an example of local ownership and grassroots solutions: "Community members are taking up the challenge by sustaining life and giving love—providing home-based care and visitation. Moreover, they are providing hours of their time without compensation and donating their own scarce resources . . . as good neighbors and caring people, they have responded to the inhumane gap in access to care and support in poor communities."[16] Longevity, sacrifice, self-determination, dignity, and loving others are just a few of the outcomes of local ownership.

Local ownership is cultivated from the first day of any effort when local people dream about, wrestle with, pray over, and conceive ideas, sacrifice for those ideas, and put those ideas into action. It is nearly impossible to convert missionary ownership to local ownership; it needs to be birthed within the local people from the foundation.

In practice, the cross-cultural worker must first set aside preconceived plans and ideas (avoid a *bring it—teach it* model)[17] and instead become a catalyst for helping local people birth creative ideas and put those ideas into practice (practice a *find it—encourage it* model).[18]

Locally Reproducible

Most recently, church-planting movement and disciple-making movement practitioners have deemed a movement sustainable if it multiplies to the 4th + generation. In other words, if a movement effort ceases at the 1st, 2nd, or 3rd generation, it has not perpetuated as a movement. Those of us who are passionate about compassion may want to take note of this type of sustainability if we desire to experience a movement of local Christ followers who love God mightily and their neighbors as themselves to the fourth generation and beyond. If multiplication is part of the end vision, then we need to make sure that every component of the holistic equation—gospel-as-word, gospel-as-sign, and gospel-as-deed—is readily reproducible by everyone, not just some.[19]

For example, if through our rhetoric and practices we give people the illusion that the gospel-as-deed is for development workers only, then we cut out the majority of Christ followers from the gospel-as-deed process. Furthermore, if the gospel-as-deed becomes dependent on outside funding, professionalism, expertise, complicated projects, or weighty content,

16. Olson et al., "Raising Community Awareness and Inspiring Action," 7.

17. Ethnomusicologists use the terms "bring it—teach it" and "find it—encourage it" to facilitate creativity.

18. Schrag, "Ethnoartistic Cocreation in the Kingdom of God," 51.

19. "Everyone, not just some" is a phrase consistently used by Ying Kai, the creator of T4T; see "What is T4T."

disciples making disciples who integrate loving their neighbors as themselves will struggle to see fruit beyond the first generation.

This thinking applies to all components: gospel-as-word, gospel-as-sign, and gospel-as-deed. For example, if a Christ follower relies on a healing crusade, which requires stages, tents, buildings, professional-type healers, permits, etc., to bring the gospel-as-sign to a community, he or she will send an unintentional message that integral mission and discipleship is just for some, not all because of its utter non-reproducible nature. The apostle Paul taught the principle of "willingness and means" (2 Cor 8:11–12). This means that local people are required to love their neighbor according to their willingness and means, not the missionary's willingness and means. Remember, Jesus sent the disciples out to emulate him. Thus he trained with reproducibility in mind.

For the most part, people will do what you do, not what you say. For example, if you teach on group Discovery Bible Studies (DBS)[20] in a lecture, classroom style, your modeling will be incoherent with what you want people to reproduce. Modeling and reproducibility are inseparable. Therefore, in the case of DBS, you would teach using the DBS method. Either our modeling will lead to reproducibility or it will inhibit it. Both the missionary and the local disciples are responsible to see that local reproducibility is built in from the start.

Local Grassroots Expression

There is a strong and healthy push among missionaries today to plant the gospel on the foundation of Christ while allowing the local people to discover local grassroots expressions of faith, church, worship, etc. If this is the case, should not this be true for gospel-as-deed as well? If the aim is for integral mission and discipleship to produce fruit to the 4th + generation, then should we not work strategically to ensure that we facilitate local people to discover, identify, and practice grassroots expressions of integral discipleship among their neighbors in conjunction with Scripture and the leading of the Holy Spirit?

---

20. Discovery Bible Study is a simple, reproducible inductive approach to Bible study that focuses on discipleship and transformation.

DAY 1 ACTIVITIES FOR THE MISSIONARY

For teachers, "Day 1 Affects Day 100."[21] What we do in the very beginning will set the course for or against our end vision in the near and far future. As a matter of fact, our end vision will also determine our effectiveness. For instance, if our end vision is to penetrate the arts and entertainment sphere of society, we will most likely create a movie or two and lead a few people in the industry to Christ. However, if our end vision is to launch a movement of disciples making disciples in the arts community to the 4th + generation, we will most likely see hundreds of disciples, churches, and leaders raised up in the arts community.

An end vision provides the answers to any questions you might have. Let's say the question is, "What method should I use to teach the Bible?" Your answer should not be, "I love preparing sermon outlines and presenting the content." Rather, your answer should be: "What will it take to launch a movement of disciples making disciples to the 4th + generation, who readily live out the gospel-as-word, gospel-as-sign, and gospel-as-deed among their neighbors?" With this goal in mind, I would lean toward Discovery Bible Studies (DBS), which produce local ownership and reproducibility as well as protect against commentary trapped in an outsider's cultural baggage (thus encouraging local grassroots expressions). Below are examples of Day 1 activities for missionaries that accelerate rather than inhibit our hypothetical end vision.

End Vision: launch a movement of disciples reproducing disciples to the 4th + generation, disciples who readily live out the gospel-as-word, gospel-as-sign, and gospel-as-deed among their neighbors.[22] The following is an example of what an end vision might look like:

---

21. Johnson, *We Are Not The Hero*, 64.

22. Day 1 Activities for the Missionary table is prepared from the premise that the missionary is launching and modeling components of the integral disciple-making movement for the first generation.

Day 1 Activities	Strategic Questions	Examples
Incarnation-alize[A]	How should I live and conduct myself in order to accelerate the end vision? ** Keep in mind relational, communicatory, and strategic accelerators or inhibitors to the end vision as it relates to lifestyle choices.	When participating with local people, I will use the same transportation modes and level of technology that they use. I will not set the pace when it comes to transportation, tech-nology, or equipment. If and when these tools become their norm and are reproducible for that segment of people, then I will follow suit.
Deculturalize[B] your repre-sentation of the gospel-as-word, gospel-as-sign, and gospel-as-deed.	How will I minimize my own cultural ways of representing the gospel-as-word (Jesus, church, evangelism, etc.), gospel-as-sign (praying for the sick, fasting, etc.), and gospel-as-deed (compassion, justice, etc.) in order to accelerate the end vision? **Westerners struggle to know how to deculturalize social ac-tion/word-as-deed.	I will not conceptualize or start a compassion ministry or church, but rather I will model essential compassion and essential discipleship while facilitating local people to identify, own, and practice their own expressions of the gospel-as-word, gospel-as-sign, and gospel-as-deed.
Contextualize the gospel-as-word, gospel-as-sign, and gospel-as-deed.	How will I encourage local people to identify and practice locally reproducible, lo-cally interdependent, and local grassroots expressions of the gospel-as-word, gospel-as-sign, and gospel-as-deed in order to accelerate the end vision?	I will ask local Christ follow-ers how they want to obey Christ among their network of relationships according to the Scriptures, the guidance of the Holy Spirit, and their local culture. **Insiders are more equipped to decipher what forms of the culture are life giving, God honoring and beneficial for the movement.

[A.] I coined the word "incarnationalize" to coincide with deculturalize and contextualize.

[B.] David Watson regularly uses the word "deculturalize" in his Disciple-Making Movements (DMM) trainings. Watson, "Church Planting Essentials."

Day 1 Activities	Strategic Questions	Examples
Balance integral mission.	How will I seamlessly integrate the gospel-as-word, gospel-as-sign, and gospel-as-deed in order to accelerate the end vision? **As Westerners, we have a tendency to make word-as-deed more high-profile and important than the other components due to our worldview, and we tend to run and model these projects based on Western rationality.	I will not start a nonreproducible project for creative access purposes, as this will serve one good purpose (my access) and generate one bad outcome (stifling local people from owning and expressing integral mission and discipleship). Perhaps I will have to discover a creative access means that puts the creative access role behind the scenes of my low-profile efforts to launch a movement.
Emphasize obedience.	How will I encourage obedience as the main drive and outcome of integral mission in order to accelerate the end vision? **Avoid promoting Gospel-as-deed as an evangelism technique or as a social action program. Rather, teach and promote Gospel-as-deed as part of the discipleship process and as the privilege and duty of every disciple.	I will start every Bible study and every disciple-multiplication group meeting with the question: "How did you obey Christ?" And I will end every Bible study and every disciple-multiplication group meeting with the question: "How will you obey Christ?"
Build in reciprocity and sharing.	How will I build in group/communal reciprocity and sharing in order to accelerate the end vision?	I will stay clear of "meeting needs" or suggesting we "meet needs." Rather, from the second or third disciple-multiplication group meeting of the movement, I will teach reciprocity and mutual sharing from the Scriptures and pose the question: "How can you help one another and your community based on your willingness and means?" This question will be a part of every disciple-multiplication group.

Day 1 Activities	Strategic Questions	Examples
Build in accountability.	How will I build in group accountability in order to accelerate the end vision?	At the beginning of every disciple-multiplication group meeting, I will check in with people using these accountability questions: "How did you live out the gospel-as-word, gospel-as-sign, and gospel-as-deed? What did you do and what happened? Is there anything you might want to do differently?" At the end of meeting, I will facilitate the disciple-makers to set action plans at the end of our time together. This will become a habitual practice of the movement.
Cast Vision	How will I cast vision in order to accelerate the end vision?	I will include vision casting at every disciple-multiplication group meeting with real-life accounts or Bible stories of disciples making disciples through the gospel-as-word, gospel-as-sign, and gospel-as-deed.

Jesus conveyed to the teacher of the law the following two commandments as most important: "'Love the Lord your God with all your heart and with all your soul and with all your mind and with all your strength.' The second is this: 'Love your neighbor as yourself'" (Mark 12:29–31). Jonathan Martin writes, "If a church or ministry starts dependent on western money—western money will eventually end it."[23] In light of Martin's comment, is it not possible that if integral mission—loving God and loving others—starts dependent on Western money, professionalism, nonessentials, and extra-biblical requirements, then all those things will eventually end it?

If your end vision happens to be "launch a movement of disciples reproducing disciples to the 4th + generation, disciples who readily live out the gospel-as-word, gospel-as-sign, and gospel-as-deed among their neighbors," then I encourage you to accelerate this end vision from Day 1 (the beginning) so that on Day 100 (the future) you will experience integral mission and integral outcomes to the fourth and fifth generations and beyond.

23. Martin, *Giving Wisely?* 118.

An outstanding example of an all-inclusive process for disciple-making movements is T4T, developed by Ying Kai. Furthermore, one can weave gospel-as-word, gospel-as-sign, and gospel-as-deed into the Three Thirds Process of T4T.[24]

If we start a compassion project or church, that is what we will most likely get—a project or two or a church or two. On the other hand, if we launch and cultivate an integral disciple-making movement, that is what we will most likely get—multiple generations of disciples and churches living out the gospel-as-word, the gospel-as-sign, and the gospel-as-deed.

CONCLUSION

Loving your neighbor as yourself is Jesus's command and way of life. Mission should be integral. John, who learned from being with Jesus day in and day out, declared as much: "This is how we know what love is: Jesus Christ laid down his life for us. And we ought to lay down our lives for our brothers and sisters. If anyone has material possessions and sees a brother or sister in need but has no pity on them, how can the love of God be in that person? Dear children, let us not love with words or speech but with actions and in truth" (1 John 3:16–18).

It is also clear that local communities of Christ have both the privilege and the mandate to readily and naturally love their neighbors as an outflow of their own lives. Paul instructs children and grandchildren to be the first in line to care for widows. The local church is then second in line to care for the widows who truly have no family (1 Tim 5:3–4). According to Paul, benevolence starts from the grassroots up.

While working one day, I overheard a CBN news piece on the church in Cuba. In the piece, Jason Carlisle with International Mission Board (IMB) expressed that Cuba has planted fifteen thousand churches in the last twenty years and has established a missionary movement, which includes sending missionaries to other countries. One particular group in Cuba had developed a self-sustaining mission training center that is supported by an adjacent farm. After one year of training, the students are sent to an unreached people group.

Jason Carlisle expressed about why Cuba is effective in mission work. Cuban Christians learned to be a church under harsh limitations and scarcity. This taught the Cuban church to use simple, reproducible church-planting

---

24. The Three Thirds Process of T4T is a way to implement every reproducible-meeting, which includes seven parts that lead to multiplication: pastoral care, worship, accountability, vision casting, new lesson, practice, sets goals and pray. "What is T4T."

methods and few resources. Today, the Cubans' light-and-nimble lifestyle and methods allow them to readily integrate into communities and plant churches exponentially. Carlisle invited the American church to learn from Cuban Christ followers. [25]

Integral mission is biblical and important. Missionaries need to step back from trying to make the Majority World show compassion based on our Western abilities and our imperfect worldview and encourage them to eagerly offer the gospel-as-word, gospel-as-sign, and gospel-as-deed based on the best version of themselves through Christ's empowerment.

Is it possible to return to apostolic missions? Is the aim to make disciples who love God and love others according to the best versions of themselves? Will missionaries leave the paternalism, prototypes, protocols, institutions, schemes, and McDonaldization at home? Maybe it is time to start a movement that spreads counterintuitive ways of growing God's kingdom in God's way. Missionaries should continue praying for insight and keep the conversation going.

25. Sells, "In the Midst of Hardships."

8

In Pursuit of Holistic Economic Development[1]

Brian Fikkert

A missionary stands in the front of the church gathering and shares her vision for her ministry in rural Kenya: "I want to be able to help the Masai girls far in the interior regions. The Masai fathers do not want to invest in their daughters' education because their daughters will be lost to other families when they get married. I want to teach the girls living in the interior regions, so that I can empower them to be just like us."

What would it mean to be "just like them?" All of the women in this church gathering—*including the missionary*—are Masai, a semi-nomadic tribe in East Africa. Their ears strain under the weight of their heavy earrings. In fact, their entire bodies seem to strain under the weight of their difficult lives. Masai women are viewed as property by their husbands, relegating them to a second-class social status. They are subjected to backbreaking work, female genital mutilation, polygamy, and low levels of education. Indeed, the strain of this reality is evident on the faces of all the women gathered in this small church in rural Kenya.

But there is hope in their faces as well, hope that has come from the church's ministry, a ministry that the women run themselves: a *microfinance ministry*. Lacking access to formal banking services, these women have

1. Portions of this chapter have been taken from the following two publications: Corbett and Fikkert, *When Helping Hurts*; Fikkert and Mask, *From Dependence to Dignity*. Used by permission.

always struggled to save and to borrow, except possibly from loan sharks who charge them exorbitant interest rates. As a result, they have had a hard time accumulating the money they so desperately need to start small businesses, to pay school fees, to purchase medicine, and to respond to other opportunities and needs.

Microfinance addresses these problems by providing poor people with access to the financial services that they lack—savings, loans, insurance, and money transfers—in the hope of helping them to improve their economic situation and to get out of poverty. In the past several decades the microfinance movement has experienced explosive growth, becoming one of the leading strategies for alleviating poverty in the Global South. As a result, in 2006 the Nobel Peace Prize was awarded to Muhammed Yunus, the founder of the microfinance movement, and to the Grameen Bank of Bangladesh that he founded.

In the case of the Masai church, the women are engaging in a simple— but powerful—form of microfinance, a savings and credit association that has enabled the women to save and lend *their own money* to one another. No loan capital from outsiders is needed. In other words, this is a very poor church using its own spiritual, human, financial, and technical resources to restore oppressed women and then to send them out as missionaries to other oppressed women.

Savings and loan services can do all of that? No, not on their own, but this savings and credit association does far more than provide beneficial financial services. Group meetings consist of Bible study, prayer, singing, and fellowship, providing these "second class citizens" with a profound encounter with the ultimate solution to all of our needs: Jesus Christ.

Indeed, the women share how God has used the savings and credit association to bless their lives in multiple ways. Despite being born into an inferior social status, each of these Masai ladies now resemble the woman described in Proverbs 31, whose hard work, entrepreneurship, and faith resulted in praise from her children and her husband. They hold their heads high as they describe how the association has provided them with the capital and the dignity they need to start and expand their own small businesses and to meet a variety of economic needs. This is ministry—powerful, holistic, restorative, microfinance ministry.

One lady testifies, "I bought a cow with my loan of 20,000 Kenya Shillings (approximately $300 U.S.) and then sold it. I got good profit! When I finished this loan, I took another loan of 20,000. I am so happy. This has really uplifted me. I have now started another business of selling practice tests to students to help them prepare for the national exams. With the profits I am able to pay the school fees for my children."

Another lady shares, "I am a pure Masai. Some Masai women look at all my business activities and wonder if I am a pure Masai. They do not believe that a Masai woman can do all these things. But I am a pure Masai."

How do the Masai men view the empowerment of these women? One lady, who became a cattle trader as a result of the microfinance ministry, beams as she states, "Because we are born-again Christians, the Lord has helped this group of ladies. My husband is very proud of me. The Masai men don't think we women can do anything. But because I have been working so hard, my husband sees that I am a very important person." Another woman states, "As a result of this group, my husband is proud of me. Even my children are proud. I am doing business and paying school fees for my children. I am even paying the tuition for my husband to get more education. All the family members are happy."

Masai outside the church are taking note. Seeing the improved economic and social status of these ladies, unbelievers are asking if they can join this microfinance ministry. The women anticipate that after these unbelievers join the savings and credit association, they will eventually become Christians and join their church. Now the ladies are sending out one of their own as a missionary to other Masai girls far in the interior regions, so that those girls can be "just like them," namely, restored image bearers who are seeking to restore others.

LOCAL CHURCHES, LOCAL RESOURCES, LASTING CHANGE

This is more than just an inspiring story; it represents a key feature of what is needed for the church of Jesus Christ to advance the Great Commission in the 21st Century: indigenous churches *using their own gifts*—spiritual, human, financial, and technical—to pursue *holistic economic development*, proclaiming and demonstrating the gospel by enabling poor people to glorify God through sustaining work.

As the center of Christianity moves from the West to the Global South (Africa, Asia, and Latin America), grinding poverty is on the front doorstep—and in the front pews—of the church of Jesus Christ on a daily basis. As historian Philip Jenkins notes, the typical Christian in the world in the 21st Century is not a businessperson attending a mega-church in an American suburb but a poor woman in a slum in Sao Paulo, Brazil or in a village in Nigeria[2] . . . or a poor Masai woman in rural Kenya. Similarly, missiologist Andrew Walls states that the church of the 21st Century will be a "church

2. Jenkins, *The Next Christendom*, 1–2.

of the poor. Christianity will be mainly the religion of rather poor and very poor people with few gifts to bring except the gospel itself. And the heartlands of the Church will include some of the poorest countries on earth."[3]

The Great Commission has been given to the church, and in the 21st Century this church will largely consist of very poor people bringing the gospel to other very poor people. Hence, these churches comprised of poor people need strategies *that they can use* to pursue *integral mission,* i.e. the proclamation and demonstration of the good news of the kingdom of God.[4] The Masai church's microfinance ministry is one such strategy.

Of course, there are times when it can be helpful to bring in outside resources and expertise. Indeed, God has blessed the global body of Christ with an abundance of resources, and He delights when those resources are shared. At the same time, an improper use of outside resources can undermine the use of local gifts, prevent long-run sustainability, hinder replication, and create unhealthy dependencies. In particular, it is often extremely difficult to use outside resources in a way that empowers materially poor churches to use economic development to pursue integral mission.[5] Therein lies the significance of the Masai church's microfinance ministry. Outside resources were used to equip a very poor church to use its own resources to bring economic development that is holistic, restorative, and replicable.

This chapter describes the key issues and options for churches and missionaries that want to use microfinance ministries to foster holistic economic development in the Global South. It also briefly discusses an associated strategy: business as missions. Before delving into those topics, it is necessary to lay a proper foundation by considering the goal of holistic economic development.

WHAT IS THE GOAL?

This is a chapter about "economic development," a term which conjures up images of factories, roads, and dams being built in order to spur macroeconomic growth and lift a country out of poverty. Indeed, macroeconomic growth has contributed to unprecedented reductions in material poverty in the past quarter century. Since 1990, the number of people living on less than $1.90 per day—the World Bank's global poverty line—has declined by

3. Walls, "Demographics, Power, and the Gospel," 6.

4. See The Lausanne Movement, *The Capetown Commitment* Part 1, Section 10.B.

5. For an elaboration of these ideas, see Fikkert and Mask, *From Dependence to Dignity.*

more than half, falling from 1.95 billion in 1990 to 896 million in 2012.[6] These incredible reductions in poverty were not primarily due to Christian organizations dispensing malaria nets and drilling wells—as important as those activities are—but rather to rapid macroeconomic growth resulting from the adoption of Western-style, market-based institutions and policies.[7] In fact, many global leaders believe that—should such economic growth continue—it will be possible to lift the entire world above the $1.90 poverty line by the year 2030.[8]

While these massive reductions in material poverty should be celebrated, there are reasons for concern as well. Western-style economic growth and the institutions, policies, and practices that undergird it are rooted in a materialistic understanding of human beings and of human flourishing. As a result, Western culture's unprecedented economic growth is accompanied by self-centered individualism, increased isolation, social fragmentation, environmental degradation, and mushrooming rates of mental illness.[9] Surely, there is something more to human flourishing than simply increasing people's material prosperity.

As described in the book *From Dependence to Dignity: How to Alleviate Poverty Through Church-Centered Microfinance* by Brian Fikkert and Russell Mask,[10] the Triune God is a relational being. Hence, as His image bearers, human beings are created for relationship, with God, self, others, and the rest of creation. When human beings experience these relationships in the way that God designed them to be experienced, we experience human flourishing. Unfortunately, the fall of humanity into sin has broken these four relationships for every human being. For some, this brokenness bubbles up into material poverty, while for others it is present in other ways, including the self-centered materialism that is enslaving the West. The good news of the gospel is that Jesus Christ is reconciling all things (Col 1:15–20), so that those who are "in Christ" have the hope of being restored to full human flourishing, enabling them to once again enjoy a proper relationship with God, self, others, and the rest of creation.

Hence, the goal is not to turn the Global South into the West, for both are profoundly broken. Rather, the goal is to help both the Global South and the West to look more like the New Jerusalem. In this light, the focus of

---

6. United Nations, *The Millenium Development Goals Report* 2015, 4.

7. Bluhm, et al., *Poor Trends*; Kraay, "When is Growth Pro-Poor?" 198–227.

8. United Nations, "Sustainable Development Goals."

9. See Fikkert, "How Do We Flourish? The Image of God and Homo Economicus," 46–58.

10. See also Corbett and Fikkert, *When Helping Hurts.*

this chapter is on "holistic economic development"—restoring poor people to a proper relationship with the rest of creation—which is not the same as simply increasing their material prosperity. From a biblical perspective, there are at least four dimensions to a proper relationship to creation:

1. As stewards over the creation, human beings are called to preserve and protect it, caring for the environment for its own sake and for the sake of future generations.

2. As image bearers, humans are called to reflect their Creator by working to unpack and develop the potentialities that He has placed in the creation. Work is not simply a necessary evil that must be endured in order to acquire more material things. Rather, work is an act of worship, and glorifying God through work is central to human flourishing.

3. The fruits of our work should be sufficient to sustain ourselves and our families. In a fallen world this is not guaranteed, so holistic development seeks creative ways to enable people to earn a living wage.

4. The relationship to creation is not isolated from the other relationships. Rather, we should walk in communion with God and with others as we work to steward God's world. Such communion roots the purpose of work in service to God and to neighbor, thereby preventing either the work or the output from becoming idols in and of themselves. Furthermore, such communion keeps work in its proper balance, preventing it from crowding out all of the other aspects of life that contribute to human flourishing: family, church, school, community, etc.

Unfortunately, in most countries in the Global South, there are simply not enough jobs to enable people to fulfill their callings as workers. This is where holistic economic development steps in, seeking to create opportunities for people to work in ways that are consistent with a proper relationship to creation. In particular, how can microfinance be used to pursue holistic economic development?

THE MICROFINANCE REVOLUTION

In 1976, a virtually unknown economics professor was visiting a village in rural Bangladesh during a devastating famine. There he encountered Sufiya, a very poor woman who was struggling to support her family by weaving bamboo stools. Sufiya was trapped. She needed to borrow twenty-two cents per day to buy materials, but banks would not lend to her because she did not have acceptable collateral and her desired loan size was too small. As a result, Sufiya was forced to borrow from loan sharks, whose exorbitant rates of interest left her with only two cents of profit at the end of a twelve-hour workday. Sufiya's neighbors expressed similar frustration, facing interest rates ranging from 10 percent per week (520 percent per year) to 10 percent per day (3,650 percent) per year. The professor reached into his pocket and lent Sufiya and forty-one of her neighbors a *total* of twenty-seven dollars. To the amazement of observers, the loans were fully repaid on time.[11] Contrary to the received wisdom, it was possible to lend money to very poor people and get it paid back!

Forty years later, that economics professor, Dr. Muhammad Yunus, is a Nobel laureate, and the Grameen Bank, which he established to provide credit to the poorest people of Bangladesh, has 8.5 million poor borrowers who have repaid over 98 percent of their loans, enabling Grameen's money to be lent and re-lent to poor people over and over again.[12] Moreover, Dr. Yunus's work spawned the global microfinance movement, which has now provided microloans to over 200 million people worldwide.[13]

What is the secret? Grameen showed that by placing clients in borrowing groups of their own choosing and then requiring the group members to guarantee each other's loans, it was possible to obtain high repayment rates from poor people.[14] Moreover, Grameen showed that it was feasible to generate sufficient interest income from these loans to cover its operating costs and to maintain the value of its loan portfolio.

The response of the donor community to Yunus' invention was understandably euphoric. Rather than give money away for, say, a community health project that requires ongoing subsidies, donors saw the opportunity to give money that would be recycled perpetually as microcredit programs lent and re-lent their loan funds. As a result, microfinance institutions (MFIs) sprung up all over the Global South, lending money from donors and investors to poor people, collecting the money back, and then lending it out again. In the process, many poor people have been able to access capital at lower interest rates than they would have otherwise.

---

11. Yunus, *Banker to the Poor.*

12. Grameen Bank, "Grameen Bank Monthly Update."

13. Reed, *Mapping Pathways out of Poverty*, 1.

14. Both theoretical and empirical research is ongoing about the importance of groups in general and of the joint-liability incentive structure that characterized the original Grameen methodology, with some doubting that the joint-liability feature is essential. See Karlan and Appel, *More Than Good*, 109–141; Carpenter, "Moral Hazard, Peer Monitoring, and Microcredit;" Hermes and Lensink, "The Empirics of Microfinance," 1–10.

What makes MFIs work? There are many technical issues, but a key factor is that borrowers must have a strong economic incentive to repay their loans. MFIs offer such incentives through both carrots and sticks. The carrot is that if Joe repays his loan he will be eligible for a bigger loan in the future. The stick is that if Joe fails to repay his loan, neither Joe nor the other members of Joe's borrowing group can get any more loans. This approach creates an incentive for the group members to monitor Joe to make sure that he repays.

The only way for MFIs to be able to provide proper repayment incentives is if the borrowers believe that the MFI will be able to provide loans over the long haul. For example, if the borrowers believe that the MFI is running out of loan capital and that no more loans will be available in the future, the borrowers will not have the economic incentive to repay their current loans. And of course, the failure to repay their current loans will then cause the MFI to run out of loan capital. The expectation becomes self-fulfilling. *MFIs must be financially sustainable in order for poor people to have an economic incentive to repay their loans.*

THE LIMITS OF MFIS' MICROCREDIT-FOR-MICROENTERPRISES APPROACH

The original vision for microfinance was a "microcredit-for-microenterprises" approach in which MFIs provided loans to enable poor people to start or expand their own small businesses so that they could get out of poverty. Indeed, well-functioning MFIs are very good at quickly injecting capital into microenterprises and should be seen as a tremendous asset in low-income communities.

However, MFIs also have some shortcomings that should be noted:

- *Difficulties in providing savings services:* Research has found that many poor people would rather save than borrow. This is particularly true for the "extreme or destitute poor," whose income is well below the poverty line (see Figure 1 below).[15] Such people are particularly vulnerable, making savings very attractive to them, since saving is less risky than borrowing. Unfortunately, MFIs have historically focused on lending money and have not provided options for poor people to

---

15. The poverty line is the level of income that divides the "poor" from the "non-poor." The international poverty line that is commonly used is $1.90 U.S. dollar per day.

save. While this is changing in some places, many MFIs are still pro-
hibited by government regulations from holding people's savings.[16]

- *Failure to reach the very poor:* It is difficult to find MFIs that can provide loans of less than $40, and many cannot even provide loans that
  small.[17] Unfortunately, the "extreme and destitute" poor in Figure 1
  typically cannot handle loans this large, usually desiring loans in the
  $5–$12 range. Loan sizes that are too large and the absence of savings
  services make MFIs incapable of ministering to those who are very
  poor. Hence MFIs are better able to help the "moderate poor" or "near
  poor," whose incomes levels are just below or just above the poverty
  line, respectively.[18]

- *Failure to reach the rural poor:* It is much cheaper to lend money in
  areas with high population density because transportation costs per
  client are lower; hence, MFIs struggle to reach the rural poor, who
  account for 70–75 percent of the total poor in the Global South.[19]

- *Exclusive focus on businesses:* Poor people need lump sums of money—
  amounts of money that are in excess of their daily income—for a range
  of things: business capital, household improvements, emergencies,
  consumption smoothing, and life cycle events such as weddings and
  funerals. MFIs have tended to focus narrowly on finance for business,
  which is the reason that the MFIs' services are sometimes referred to
  as "microenterprise development." In reality, poor households actually
  need finance for many aspects of their lives, requiring a range of savings, loans, insurance, and money transfer services, all of which fall
  under the broader category of "microfinance."

- *Lack of evangelism and discipleship activities:* The pressure to become
  financially sustainable is pushing many MFIs to reduce costs by cutting out all services other than loans and other financial products.
  Unfortunately, this trend has sometimes caused the MFIs operated

16. Sometimes MFIs claim to offer savings services when in reality the MFIs are
requiring borrowers to place money on deposit with the MFI as collateral for loans.
These "savings" are typically not accessible by the MFI clients until their loans are repaid, making this money useless in alleviating emergencies

17. As mentioned earlier, financial sustainability is essential for MFIs. It is cheaper
for MFIs to lend, say $100 to one person than $10 to ten different people. Hence, in an
effort to achieve financial sustainability, MFIs' loan sizes tend to creep upwards.

18. While the number of MFIs' clients continues to grow, in recent years the
number of clients whose incomes fall below the poverty line of $1.90 US per day has
declined. See Reed, *Mapping Pathways*, 1.

19. Ravallion, et al., *New Evidence.*

by Christian relief and development organizations to reduce their evangelism and discipleship activities. Loans alone, however, cannot reconcile people to God, self, others, and the rest of creation. "Faith comes by hearing," not through borrowing money.

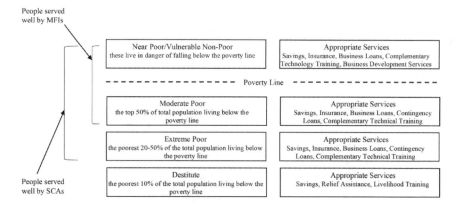

Figure 2:
Microfinance-Related Services Desired by Households of Different Poverty Levels[20]

In retrospect, it is also becoming clear that it was too much to expect MFIs' "microcredit-for-microenterprises" strategy to get most borrowers onto a fast-moving, "upward escalator" out of poverty.[21] A lack of access to capital is not the only thing holding poor people back, so it is unreasonable to expect that microloans could unleash waves of latent entrepreneurial talent.

As mentioned earlier, most economists believe that a necessary condition for widespread poverty alleviation—in the purely material sense of raising incomes above the poverty line—is macroeconomic growth driven by increases in agricultural productivity and mass industrialization,[22] with China being the most recent example. It is through rising agricultural output and small, medium, and large-scale enterprises—not microenterprises—that the Global South can create enough jobs to achieve widespread reductions in material poverty.

20. Adapted from Cohen, *The Impact of Microfinance*, 1.

21. Recent empirical research has found that MFIs' loans do not appear to have any impact on standard measures of material poverty in the first 11–22 months. For a discussion of these studies, see Fikkert and Mask, *From Dependence to Dignity*.

22. See Easterly, *The Elusive Quest for Growth*.

In the absence of such jobs, poor people are often forced to become self-employed via their own microenterprises. Being an "entrepreneur by force," however, is fundamentally different from being truly gifted with the skills to start and expand a business that can lift one's family out of poverty and create jobs for others. Simply put, most people in the world are not entrepreneurs and are better suited to working in jobs created by the relatively small number of people who are. Hence, eradicating poverty will take something more than business loans to "microentrepreneurs." In this sense, it is becoming clear that the "microcredit-for-microenterprises" strategy is not the silver bullet that many have assumed.

However, none of this is meant to suggest that microfinance is useless. Rather, microfinance is both so much more and so much less than the "microcredit-for-microenterprises" story suggests. It is *less*, because it is unlikely that the vast majority of the world's poor will achieve a substantial increase in their incomes through loans to microenterprises. It is *more*, because researchers and practitioners are discovering that poor households need a vast range of financial services—including many types of loans, savings, insurance, and money transfer services—and they are experimenting with innovative ways to address those needs. Seen in this light, microfinance has the potential to impact poor households in more ways—albeit in more subtle ways—and on a larger scale than the simple "microcredit-for-microenterprises" story suggests.

THE VAST POTENTIAL OF THE "MICROFINANCE-FOR-HOUSEHOLDS" APPROACH

In order to understand the untapped potential for microfinance, it is helpful to start by focusing on poor *households* rather than on just the *microenterprises* that some of those households own. In the path-breaking book *Portfolios of the Poor: How the World's Poor Live on $2 a Day*,[23] a team of researchers interviewed poor households at least twice per month for a full year, enabling them to create "financial diaries" that sought to document every penny that flowed in and out of their sample of 250 households from Bangladesh, India, and South Africa.

The picture that emerges in *Portfolios of the Poor* is of poor households that are intensely engaged—every day—in using a wide range of activities to enable them to manage their money. The reason for this is that in addition to being *small*, the incomes of poor households are highly *irregular* and *unpredictable*. One day a household earns $5.00 US, and the next it earns

23. Collins, et al., *Portfolios of the Poor.*

$0.05 US. The children need to eat every day, not just on days when there is enough income. When there is a medical emergency, money is needed to buy the medicine immediately. There is no time to wait for the household's microenterprise to have a good sales day.

In order to manage their *small, irregular,* and *unpredictable* incomes, poor households are intensely engaged in using a variety of creative tools to provide them with cash when they need it. Whereas wealthy people around the world use stocks, bonds, and checking accounts to manage their finances, the financial portfolios of poor households include such things as hiding money in a sock, making a deposit into a savings and credit association, pawning jewelry at the local shop, and investing in various kinds of livestock. *Portfolios of the Poor* argues that despite their very low incomes— indeed *because* they have very low incomes—poor people are more *actively* engaged in day-to-day financial management than the rest of the world. It is this finding that provides the opportunity for microfinance to address far more issues than the "microcredit-for-microenterprise" story led the world to believe.

Indeed, poor households have a host of needs for *convenient, flexible, and reliable financial services.*[24] In the past several decades, microfinance researchers have been able to summarize these financial service needs into the following categories:[25]

1. *Consumption Smoothing*: On days when a household's income is low, the family members still need to eat. Hence, poor households are constantly involved in saving and borrowing just to put food on the table each day.

2. *Business Investments*: Due to few employment opportunities, many poor households are forced to operate their own microenterprises or to farm small plots of land. They need financial services to provide capital for start-up, day-to-day operations, and business expansion.

3. *Household Investments:* Poor households need financial services to enable them to save or borrow for relatively large expenditures such as repairing a leaky roof, buying a cooking pot, or paying school fees for their children. Although these expenditures may sound less exciting than business investment, they are crucial for the family's health and survival. In particular, keeping children in school is absolutely essential for the family's long-run economic health.

24. Ibid., 153.
25. Ibid.; Rutherford, *The Poor and Their Money.*

4. *Life-Cycle Needs:* Weddings, funerals, and other significant milestones can consume a very high percentage of a family's annual income. Savings and loan services can help to pay for these events, as can insurance products such as life insurance and burial insurance.

5. *Emergencies:* Unexpected events can put an enormous strain on poor families. In particular, health emergencies are one of the leading reasons that families fall into a financial crisis.[26] Hence, in addition to being able to save and borrow, multiple forms of insurance to help with emergencies are vitally needed throughout the Global South.

Within each of these five categories, there is a need to develop a vast range of financial services. For example, just in the category of emergencies, there is a need for many forms of insurance including medical, crop, accident, unemployment, property, disability, etc. This is where the opportunities for microfinance ministry are nearly limitless. The poorest people on the planet have a financial service needs that the "microcredit-for-microenterprise" strategy has only begun to address, a felt need that some of the poorest churches on the planet are already addressing in profound ways, as we saw in the case of the Masai church at the start of this chapter.

RECALIBRATING EXPECTATIONS

As mentioned earlier, recent research is suggesting that, contrary to the expectations created by the "microfinance-for-microenterprises" story, it is unlikely that microfinance will get most poor households on the fast-moving, "upward escalator" out of poverty. Rather, as illustrated in Figure 3 below, we need to shift our expectations about the impact of microfinance. The "microcredit-for-microenterprises" story led the world to believe that loans to poor microentrepreneurs would quickly raise their incomes, lifting them out of poverty as shown in the upper dotted curve. For a small fraction of the world's poor, this may be true. For most people, however, microfinance will likely yield the lower dotted curve, reducing the overall fluctuations in their consumption so that life becomes a bit more stable, providing the possibility that, over a long period of time, the family may experience an increase in its income, if not in this generation, then in the next.

26. Krishna, *One Illness Away*; Collins et al., *Portfolios of the Poor*, 68.

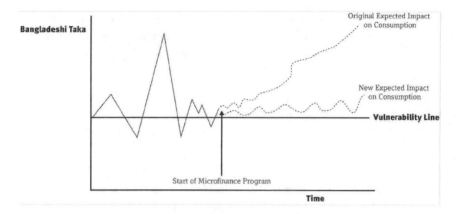

Figure 3: Revised Expectations of Impacts of Microfinance

Although stabilizing a family's consumption seems less exciting than increasing it, the effects may be more profound than first meets the eye. Falling below the vulnerability line can expose the family to malnutrition, sickness, and even death. Children are typically withdrawn from school at these moments, putting their future at risk and increasing their exposure to human trafficking in the present. In addition, with death less imminent, it becomes possible for the household to catch its breath, to have a bit more peace of mind, to dare to think about the future, and maybe even to acquire a small dose of one of the most powerful antidotes to human suffering: hope.

Moreover, the methodologies employed in gospel-centered *microfinance ministries* allow for even more powerful effects. As discussed earlier, holistic economic development seeks to restore people's foundational relationships with God, self, others, and the rest of creation. By intentionally incorporating evangelism and discipleship, church-centered microfinance ministries are able to address all four of these relationships, thereby having more profound effects than immediately meets the eye. Although much more research needs to be done to determine the exact causes, magnitudes, extent, and longevity of the impacts being reported from the frontlines, the numerous testimonies from poor people are too powerful to ignore: God is clearly using microfinance ministries to bear witness to the transformative power of His kingdom all over the Global South.

HOLISTIC ECONOMIC DEVELOPMENT OPTIONS FOR CHURCHES AND MISSIONARIES

With all of this background in mind, this section explores the answers to the following questions:

- How can missionaries and churches in the Global South use microfinance as part of integral mission?
- What can be done beyond microfinance to pursue holistic economic development?
- What is the role of outsiders, particularly those from wealthy nations?

Option 1: The Provider Model of Microfinance

Many missionaries, churches, and small ministries in the Global South pursue the "Provider Model" in which they try to emulate the Grameen Bank by providing business loans to poor people. Usually, the money for the loans comes from some outside donor such as a Christian foundation, NGO, or wealthy church.

Unfortunately, missionaries and churches are particularly ill-suited to provide loans for two reasons. First, they do not have the technical, managerial, and financial resources to achieve the necessary scale to make their loan program financially sustainable. As discussed earlier, program sustainability is a prerequisite for borrowers to be willing to repay their loans. In order to achieve such sustainability, MFIs lend out a large amount of money to earn sufficient interest revenues to cover their operational costs. In most contexts, this requires MFIs to have thousands or tens of thousands of clients, a number which is simply beyond the capacity of most missionaries and churches.[27] Second, missionaries and churches find it very difficult to balance their culture of grace with the discipline needed to enforce loan repayment. How many missionaries or pastors would be willing to enforce loan repayment—e.g. by confiscating collateral—from a widow with five children who failed to repay her loan? If the missionary or pastor will not enforce loan repayment from this widow, other borrowers will believe that they do not have to repay their loans, and the program will fail. Lending money and collecting it back is a tough line of work.

27. In the absence of financial sustainability, small loan programs often rely on relational capital to encourage loan repayment, which can put strain on those relationships. For a further discussion of this issue, see chapter 10 of Fikkert and Mask, *From Dependence to Dignity*.

Many readers will not accept this message and will believe that they can successfully pursue the Provider Model. The landscape is covered with the emptied coffers of failed loan programs started by well-meaning missionaries, churches, and small ministries. Do not try the Provider Model!

Option 2: The Promotion Model of Microfinance

The story of the Masai church at the start of this chapter is an example of the Promotion Model, an approach to microfinance in which a church or missionary helps a group of poor people to start and operate their own savings and credit association (SCA), which can be thought of as a simple credit union that is owned and operated by the members themselves. Unlike the Provider Model, group members in SCAs save and lend *their own money*, which they tend to treat with more care than money donated by outsiders. Moreover, the SCA members manage the group themselves, keeping records, collecting savings deposits, lending and collecting loans, etc.

The role of the indigenous church or missionary in this model is simply to promote the group by facilitating its formation. The church or missionary does not manage the group or handle the money. Rather, the church or missionary empowers the poor to do this for themselves, equipping them to create and manage a system for saving and borrowing the lump sums of money that they need for their households. In addition, the group meetings provide an excellent context for evangelism and discipleship activities that may be offered by the missionary, the church, or by the group members themselves.

Promoting SCAs has proven to be a highly effective and strategic intervention for indigenous churches and missionaries in the Global South for the following reasons:

- SCAs are simple to facilitate, can work on a small scale, and do not require the churches or missionaries to lend and collect money.
- In addition to providing loans, SCAs offer a way for poor people to save and even to earn interest on their savings.
- SCAs can work in both urban and rural areas.
- Loan sizes in the $5–$12 range are entirely feasible, as are loan sizes amounting to hundreds of dollars; hence, SCAs can minister to multiple levels of poverty, including the extreme poor.
- Savings withdrawals and loans from SCAs can be used for the full range of households' needs, not just financing business investments.

In other words, SCAs are consistent with the "microfinance-for-households" approach.

- Because SCAs are indigenous to many countries in the Global South and rely on local savings and know-how, they are a strategy in which even very poor churches can *use their own gifts*—spiritual, human, financial, and technical—to pursue holistic economic development.[28]

- SCAs can be promoted using highly participatory methods, allowing group members to make their own policies rather than prescribing such policies for them. This affirms the dignity and capacity of the members and allows them to tailor the group to meet their own particular situation.[29]

- The fact that SCAs can originate from the ministries of churches and missionaries makes it relatively easy to maintain evangelism and discipleship activities.

There are numerous examples of individual churches and missionaries promoting SCAs on a small scale, but large-scale programs are also possible. For example, using a demand-driven distribution structure, the Chalmers Center for Economic Development at Covenant College[30] has helped churches in West Africa to promote SCAs to over 40,000 members.[31] Worldwide, HOPE International has equipped churches to promote SCAs to almost 400,000 people.[32]

What are the downsides of promoting SCAs? Two problems stand out. First, poor people sometimes struggle to manage their groups well, to keep accurate records, and to enforce discipline. Many MFIs perform better in all of these functions. Second, SCAs do not mobilize large amounts of loan capital as quickly as MFIs do. Group members can grow impatient with the process of saving money for loan capital, particularly if they have businesses that can handle larger loan sizes. Nevertheless, the Promotion Model is a very viable alternative that churches and missionaries can use to pursue integral mission for all ranges of poverty in the Global South.

28. SCAs are consistent with "asset-based" development. See Corbett and Fikkert, *When Helping Hurts,* chapter 5.

29. When SCA members participate in the design, execution, and evaluation of the SCA, it is consistent with a "learning process" rather than "blueprint" approach. See Corbett and Fikkert, *When Helping Hurts,* chapter 6.

30. See The Chalmers Center.

31. The countries currently include Benin, Burkina Faso, Ghana, Mali, and Togo. For a discussion of this demand-driven distribution system, see chapter 13 in Fikkert and Mask, *From Dependence to Dignity.*

32. HOPE International, *HOPE International Annual Report* 2015.

Option 3: The Partnership Model of Microfinance

As mentioned earlier, the need to be financially sustainable is making it difficult for Christian MFIs to maintain evangelism and discipleship activities. At the same time, missionaries and churches in the Global South are ill-equipped to become loan providers. When both MFIs and churches/missionaries have a holistic vision, they can join hands in ministry, with each party providing a component of what is needed for holistic economic development.

During the savage civil war in Liberia, a Christian MFI sought to minister to those suffering from the carnage. The MFI provided loan services and then actively partnered with local churches, soliciting their help in ministering to the spiritual needs of borrowers. The MFI loan group meetings were intentionally held in or near local churches in order to make it easier for the churches to be able to minister to these groups. Pastors and church staff played significant roles in leading Bible studies at group meetings, visiting and counseling individual group members, and reminding borrowers of their need to repay their loans as a matter of integrity. The pastors expressed a great deal of "ownership of these groups," seeing them as an integral part of their churches' ministries.

The comprehensive impacts of this partnership were quite amazing. The civil war victims were able to generate enough income from their businesses to avoid starvation. As one borrower explained, "Before [the microfinance program], I prayed to God to take my life because I didn't want to suffer any more. My children were malnourished and complained of headaches. When they were hungry, they frowned and couldn't smile. (Now) we always have something to eat."[33] There was also evidence of improvements in borrowers' educational investments, healthcare, sense of dignity and responsibility, inter-tribal relationships, and spiritual maturity.

The pastors expressed joy over the way that this partnership has strengthened their churches. The MFI borrowers who were church members used their increased skills, confidence, spiritual maturity, and incomes to advance the full range of their churches' ministries. As one pastor stated, "Every week during our church's testimony time I hear praises and expressions of gratitude to God for [this microfinance ministry]."[34]

The Partnership Model can be a powerful approach as long as the MFIs' financial series are a good fit for the target population.[35] The MFIs can

33. As quoted in Larson, "A Leap of Faith for Church-Centered Microfinance," 10.

34. Ibid., 13.

35. As mentioned earlier, this would typically require a target population whose income category is "moderate" poor or above (see Figure 1) and which desires loans for business rather than the other household financial service needs.

provide the financial services such as lending money and monitoring repayment. The churches and missionaries can offer a range of complementary services that MFIs typically cannot provide, such as evangelism and discipleship, individual counseling, emergency assistance, and the additional training described in Option 4.

Option 4: The Complementary Training Model

The microfinance movement is based on the premise that a lack of access to capital is the primary constraint facing poor entrepreneurs, not a lack of knowledge or skills concerning small business management. Moreover, many doubt that business training can be effective in overcoming whatever knowledge or skills are lacking. For these reasons, relatively little effort has been made to offer business training to poor entrepreneurs.

However, some are now questioning the standard microfinance approach, arguing that poverty is multifaceted and cannot be overcome through capital alone. Indeed, there is a growing body of evidence suggesting that complementing financial services with appropriate training topics and methodologies can improve the businesses and lives of poor people.[36]

The Chalmers Center has integrated biblical worldview messages into technical curricula that were originally developed by a highly-respected, non-sectarian, NGO. In addition to training poor people in basic principles of small business management, household financial literacy, and healthcare topics (malaria, HIV/AIDS, diarrhea), the worldview messages apply a biblical understanding of the four, key relationships to the lies of Traditional Religion by emphasizing the themes of dignity, stewardship, and discipline.

While these curricula are suitable for many Christian ministry contexts, they are specifically designed to be used in SCA group meetings, thereby augmenting the holistic nature of the Promotion Model. Furthermore, churches and missionaries pursuing the Partnership Model could provide this complementary training to MFI client groups, resulting in a more holistic approach to poverty alleviation than the MFIs can offer on their own.

Readers who would like to learn more about Options 1–4 are encouraged to read *From Dependence to Dignity: How to Alleviate Poverty Through Church-Centered Microfinance*. Readers can also access the Chalmers Center's curricula for using the Promotion Model, the Partnership Model, and the Complementary Training Model from the Center's website.[37]

36. Karlan and Valdivia, *Teaching Entrepreneurship: Impact of Business Training on Microfinance Clients and Institutions*; Sebatad and Cohen *Financial Education for the Poor*; Gray, et al., *Microfinance against Malaria*.

37. www.chalmers.org/our-work/intl-savings-group-training/get-resources.

Option 5: Business as Missions

Another economic development strategy that has gained some popularity in the past two decades is called business as missions (BAM). BAM finds its roots in the ministries of Paul, Aquila, and Priscilla, who used tent making as a means of supporting their missionary work. Today, BAM takes on many forms, but its defining feature is that the church or missionary owns and operates a legitimate, for-profit business that they use as a vehicle for ministry.[38] In contrast, "microfinance-for-microenterprises" and the small business training described in Option 4 above focus on helping poor people to own and operate their own microenterprises.

BAM offers an opportunity for business people to participate in the missions movement by using their entrepreneurial ability, managerial talent, and financial resources for cross-cultural ministry. BAM enterprises are typically small-to-medium-scale businesses, employing anywhere from a dozen to a thousand workers.

While BAM can be used for a variety of reasons, such as gaining access to a closed country, providing the income needed for a ministry, or offering a natural context for developing relationships, a number of missionaries are using BAM as a means of poverty alleviation. Given that one of the primary problems in the Global South is a lack of employment opportunities, it makes sense to start and operate businesses that can directly provide jobs for poor people. By intentionally developing relationships with employees, suppliers, and customers, opportunities for evangelism and discipleship abound.

While BAM is as old as the New Testament, there has been very little systematic research concerning its effectiveness as a poverty alleviation strategy for the twenty-first century; hence, it is difficult to compare its pros and cons to microfinance and microenterprise development. However, a few observations are possible:

- BAM is likely to impact *directly* fewer poor people per ministry dollar than the Promotion, Partnership, or Complementary Training models. BAM enterprises are more sophisticated than microenterprises, requiring greater technical expertise and larger amounts of capital per employee than in microenterprises. This is not to say that the "kingdom bang for the buck" is necessarily less in BAM. Jesus only had twelve disciples, and they changed the world! One does have to ask, however, whether BAM has advantages that justify its added expense per poor person directly impacted.

38. See Yamamori and Eldred, *On Kingdom Business*; Rundle and Steffen, *Great Commission Companies*.

- It is likely that the increase in incomes for BAM employees are greater than for those ministered to by microfinance initiatives. Compared to microenterprises, BAM enterprises bring greater enhancement to workers' productivity through improved technology and larger amounts of capital. Hence, while fewer people are directly impacted in BAM, those who are impacted are likely to experience a far greater increase in their incomes than in microfinance.

- BAM is not for everyone. Many churches and missionaries are not good at running businesses in a highly-competitive, global economy. The Promotion, Partnership, and Complementary Training Models are all much simpler to pursue than BAM, thereby reducing the risk of harm.

- Churches and missionaries pursuing BAM need to be careful to avoid dependency-creating subsidies. For example, when missionaries operating businesses in the Global South transport and market handcrafts to churches in North America, they create a dangerous situation. When the missionary retires, it might be impossible for the business to pay for the management, transportation, and marketing services that the missionary was providing. As a result, the business may fail, and poor employees may be left with nothing. BAM enterprises must be real businesses, covering *all* of their costs, both explicit and implicit.

- As in the Partnership Model of microfinance (see Option 3 above), it will usually take high degrees of intentionality to relate the more sophisticated BAM initiatives to the ministry of the local church. It is not easy for outside business people, with access to vast amounts of capital and expertise, to work with poor churches in such a way that the gifts of those churches are recognized and mobilized for integral mission. For more information and training on BAM, the Business as Mission website is a clearinghouse for educational resources, organizations, and conferences.[39]

THE ROLE OF OUTSIDERS

Thus far the chapter has focused on how missionaries and indigenous churches in the Global South can minister to poor people as they seek to advance the Great Commission. It is absolutely imperative to recognize that these missionaries and churches are the primary embodiment of Jesus

39. "Business as Mission."

Christ in those contexts, so outsiders must accept a backstage, supporting role, allowing indigenous churches and missionaries to be on center stage. In particular, note that missionaries and indigenous churches are fully capable of implementing the Promotion, Partnership, and Complementary Training Models.

What then is the appropriate role of outsiders? Here are some suggestions:

- Financially subsidize the training of missionaries and indigenous churches so that they can implement the Promotion, Partnership, and Complementary Training Models. Do not pay all the costs of this training, however, as people usually place greater value on things that they have paid something to receive.[40]

- Become a trainer of trainers. Although missionaries and indigenous churches are better positioned for frontline ministry than outsiders, the missionaries and indigenous churches need people to train them in Options 2–4 described in this chapter. Towards that end, explore the training and resources available from the Chalmers Center.

- Provide funds for MFIs to add evangelism and discipleship components to their programs. If a MFI is already financially sustainable, do not donate money for loan capital, since a financially sustainable MFI can raise such funds on international capital markets.

- Consider investing financial and human resources in support of a BAM enterprise.

- Become an advocate for holistic economic development by finding organizations that share your vision and by supporting those organizations through prayers, networking, and financial assistance.

CONCLUSION

As always, the advancement of the Great Commission in the 21st Century requires the church to proclaim and demonstrate the good news of the kingdom

---

40. For more on the topic of distributing training and curricula well, see chapter 13 in Fikkert and Mask, *From Dependence to Dignity*. A number of Christian organizations are involved in training churches to use microfinance, including the Chalmers Center (www.chalmers.org), Five Talents International (www.fivetalents.org), HOPE International (www.hopeinternational.org), Tearfund (www.tearfund.org), Saddleback Church PEACE Plan (www.saddleback.com), and World Relief (www.worldrelief.org).

of God to the poor.[41] At the heart of the kingdom is reconciliation, restoring people to what they were created to be: image bearers who glorify God through sustaining work. Designing holistic economic development strategies to bring such restoration is always difficult, but the challenge is even greater when the primary vehicle for implementing such strategies is itself very poor, namely churches in the Global South. As the story of the Masai church illustrates, God is full of surprises. He is currently enabling some of the poorest churches on the planet to use their own resources to restore people to dignity, worth, and capacity. We would do well to join His work.

---

41. Isa 58:1–10; Luke 4:14–21; 7:18–23; and Gal 2:1–10. See also chapter 1 of Corbett and Fikkert, *When Helping Hurts.*

9

The Church's Response to Injustice

JoAnn Butrin, Suzanne Hurst,
Brandy Tuesday Wilson, and Jerry Ireland

Throughout Scripture God calls his covenant people to be champions of justice and defenders of the weak (e.g., Ps 82:3; 106:3; Prov 21:3). Because injustice is rampant in the world, it is not possible to address every issue related to this topic. Therefore, this essay will focus on three issues that missionaries are likely to encounter, namely (1) war and genocide, (2) human trafficking, and (3) justice for women. The guidelines provided in this chapter though could be applied broadly to a number of injustice issues.

PART I: WAR AND GENOCIDE

"We sang hymns in good feeling with our Tutsi brothers and sisters, our voices blending in chorus," recalls a Rwandan man named Adalbert. This was the Saturday of Easter week. The next day, the Tutsi's from that choir had already fled and after Sunday morning mass, the Hutus changed from their church clothes, took up clubs and machetes and pursued and slaughtered the very Tutsi's with whom they had sung in harmony the day before. Thus began, in 1994, the Rwandan genocide in one of the most Christianized nations of Africa.[1]

1. Katongole and Wilson-Hartgrove, *Mirror to the Church*, under chapter 2, section "Church Related."

Genocide describes efforts to wipe out an entire group of people. Most scholars agree that the twentieth century has seen at least six genocides but the most notable was the Jewish Holocaust in which, over the course of seven years (1938 to 1945), at least six million Jews were killed along with gypsies, homosexuals and Nazi resisters. The world at that time, cried, "never again" and the UN adopted a Convention on the Prevention and Punishment of the Crime of Genocide, which is also when the term "genocide" was adopted. Yet, following the United States' war in Vietnam, two million Cambodians died at the hands of Pol Pot's Khmer Rouge. In 1992, Serbian leader Slobodan Milosovic led a genocide against Muslims in Bosnia, resulting in 200,000 deaths. And in the Spring of 1994, 800,000 Rwandans were slaughtered by an opposing tribe in one hundred days.

War, as opposed to genocide, normally has a military/political goal in view that makes one side a competitor to the other, with both being able to strategize and fight to win. In genocide, the enemy is not a competitor that must be conquered, but, in the mind of the perpetrator, the enemy is a sinister force behind society's ills that must be utterly destroyed. The victim rarely has opportunity to fight back and is ill equipped to do more than run or hide to survive.

There are conflicts, such as that of the Democratic Republic of Congo (DRC), which could be termed both war and genocide. Since 1996, DRC has been embroiled in violence that has claimed the lives of as many as 5.4 million people. It has been called the world's bloodiest war since World War II. It is termed "war" because there are deep-seated military and political goals, disputes over land and natural resources, and outside nations joining in the conflict for political gain. The conflict could also be considered genocide because of the systematic efforts to eliminate entire groups of people. It is thought that close to three million people have been displaced during this conflict that has resulted in famine, disease, and extreme poverty for much of the population of North East DRC. Plus, infant and child mortality rates are extremely high as a result of widespread famine and malnutrition.

Syria also falls into the category of both war and genocide. The crisis in Syria began in early 2011 when Syrian President Bashar al-Assad began a brutal crackdown on growing peaceful protests throughout the country. With the use of tanks, attack helicopters, artillery against protesters, and the torture and execution of children, protests spread and opposition groups took up arms.

The attacks and counter-attacks escalated into a full-fledged civil war between the Assad regime with allied militias and an array of opposition groups. The spread of the Islamist extremist group, Islamic State of Iraq and Syria (ISIS) into Syria has added another dangerous element increasing atrocities and threatening genocide against the Yazidi and other minority groups.[2] At the writing of this chapter, hundreds of thousands of refugees are flooding into Europe, seeking asylum from the conflict, violence, and mass destruction in Syria.

There are smaller wars and genocides taking place in many countries of the world for various reasons. However, whether war or genocide, the most common striking element is that of "suffering." The loss of lives, loved ones, security, homes, and countries are natural outcomes of either of these conflicts with psychological shock and trauma, fear, grief, and sheer terror characteristic of individuals caught in the ravages of war or genocide. In the midst of such tremendous suffering, people are often desperate for "supernatural help" and longing to hold on to some type of spiritual anchor.

THE ROLE OF THE CHURCH IN WAR AND GENOCIDE

I (JoAnn) have personally been at the scene of the Rwandan crisis as a million refugees poured into what was then Zaire, now Democratic Republic of Congo (DRC). I was also in Albania during the Kosovo genocide, attending to the refugees piled into warehouses. In both cases, the church was visibly absent on the front lines of responders. I recall sitting with church leaders in Goma, Zaire trying to come up with a strategy for outreach. Given the long-term border conflicts with Rwanda and the poor relationships between the Hutu's who had come to live in Zaire, there was not a great enthusiasm for outreach and a general sense of "letting the foreign NGO's take the lead." In Albania, the church was young and uncertain about direct outreach, but did offer their facilities for refugee-related activities.

Yet as I tended to and talked with refugees in both situations, I did note amidst the dismay and sadness and overall trauma, an immediate positive response to being asked if they would like prayer. Often, the prayer would be accompanied by tears and then a show of gratitude for the spiritual care offered.

In most accounts of the Rwandan genocide, there is a great deal of analysis focusing on how a nation claiming to be 85 percent Christian could succumb to such evil and atrocious acts against each other. Not only did the church not rise to assist and shelter, but in many cases, aided the perpetrators. There are many churches that are now memorials to the multiple deaths that happened inside their walls.

A Cardinal of the Catholic Church, representing the pope, was sent to Rwanda to talk with church leaders about the genocide. He asked whether

2. United to End Genocide, under "Syria Backgrounder."

the blood of tribalism is deeper than the waters of baptism and the leaders replied, "yes it is."[3] One could conclude from these experiences that "identity" can be formed and shaped by historical and political forces and cannot be assumed to be "remade" by simply a verbal declaration of faith. This is not unique to Rwanda, but could be asked in any geopolitical context—does Christianity make a difference in the way people live their lives? What difference does the gospel make when nations go to war? What difference does church membership make when governments call upon their people to engage in unjust actions?

Romans 12:2 speaks of not conforming to the world, but being transformed "by the renewing of our minds." When Christ enters one's life, a transformation process begins that is deeply personal. As individuals grow closer in their relationship and walk with the Lord, former identities will begin to be overtaken by kingdom identities and our actions will be shaped by being a follower of Jesus. The label of Christian becomes internalized through our new identity in Him and gives us a different lens with which to view the world. It brings freedom from the identities that held us captive and gives us a more Christ-like view of the things that divide us as human beings. Human behavior ought to be radically "different" when Christ is truly our Lord.

So how can the church proclaim an identity-changing gospel that will lead people to a transformation of the way they see themselves and the world in which they live? I submit that as the gospel is preached, it needs also to be lived. The church is, can be, and should be the open arms into which the sufferers of war, genocide, violence and conflict fall. In John 1:14 we read, "the word became flesh and made his dwelling among us." Jesus announced and established a new political order which Scripture defines as the kingdom of God. It is a reality into which Jesus invites us now and into which the church invites others. Through the power of the Holy Spirit the church is able to stand and assume a new identity.[4] The church is not "of the world" but enters into the world of pain, suffering, and need. It does not do this from a position of assumed authority, but motivated by a true desire to know and understand the experience of those who are in need.

Sometimes missionaries and Western aid responders can be surprised at the church's lack of response to these crises. In many parts of the world the church is reluctant to be involved in government and politics. Westerners can have a hard time understanding this, as advocacy, lending support

3. Hebblethwaite, "In Rwanda, 'Blood Is Thicker Than Water,'" under chapter 1, section "Facing the Contradictions."

4. Katongole and Wilson-Hartgrove, under chapter 5, "Postures of Christian Social Engagement," section "Is There Another Way."

to government-funded social programs, and who we choose to vote for are often considered important actions that reflect our Christian values. However, in many parts of the world being aligned with the government or other politics can be detrimental, even dangerous, to the church. Governments that are corrupt, that claim democracy but monitor who votes for whom and respond accordingly, create an atmosphere of fear and political withdrawal. Yet there are times when the church can be involved without making a political statement, simply by reaching out to the suffering and marginalized. The Bible is adamant about the need to show compassion to the poor and suffering, often specifically mentioning orphans, widows and aliens (e.g., Deut 16:14; 24:17; Isa 1:17). Churches, who for years have deliberately distanced themselves from politics, can suddenly find themselves in the middle of a situation in which there is so much pain and suffering that they cannot, in good Christian conscience, ignore what is happening around them. In these cases, churches can struggle with how to respond after years of self-isolation. At the same time, the church members themselves are often affected by the situation. It can be difficult to find the balance of caring for their own that are affected by the crisis, and also reaching outside of their own walls.

Missionaries, faith-based organizations and Westerners who arrive wanting to help during a crisis need to be aware of these dynamics. Taking the time to dialogue with church leaders and assess the needs within the church, even on a very basic level, conveys to local churches that they are understood, yet important in the response. When appropriate, responses should allow for the church to remain as politically neutral as possible while empowering local believers to minister to those who are affected. Sometimes, such as in the case of widespread acts of atrocity against the population, neutrality does not work and churches need help and support in standing up against evil.

Though the failure of the church has been demonstrated in the Rwandan genocide, there are many stories of brave individuals who denied tribal boundaries and who cried out against the horrors, risking life and freedom to be the light of Christ in that very dark story. There are many churches in this present day that are reaching out to refugees, to the displaced, to those deeply marginalized, and those affected by war and conflict. They are living out the gospel that they proclaim and many are turning to faith in Jesus Christ because of the love radiating from the believing Church.

As Christian outsiders responding to these events, it is important to work with local churches when possible. When thinking about responses during these extreme times, it is easy to jump right to the well-publicized actions of food distribution, clinics and health care. Small acts, however, can also have a big impact. Local churches must be involved in designing the response, as they know the local culture and have more on the ground knowledge and resources. Each situation is different and each church will have a different ability to respond. The important thing is that the response fits the capacity of that church. The response should be planned carefully so that the church can be actively involved in its implementation, and has components that they can continue to carry out, even after Western aid organizations have moved on. All responses should be aimed at alleviating suffering while demonstrating the love of Christ and involving and promoting the local church.

An example of this happened in the DRC. During one of the more turbulent times in Eastern Congo there were many internally displaced persons (IDPs). As these people fled the war, they descended upon a town in Eastern Congo. This small town, with few resources, was quickly overrun by the IDP's and living conditions were miserable. A local Assemblies of God church wanted to help. While they did not have a lot of resources, they decided to do what they could. All church members were asked to donate two pieces of clothing to give to the IDPs. An offering was taken up and with it basic gardening tools were bought. Because the local church did all of this, they knew where to go for the best prices and were able to make their small offering go a long way. The church worked with one group of IDP's, giving them the donated clothing, helping them to start gardens and holding church services specifically designed to minister to these traumatized individuals. Somehow word got out that this small church was doing great things in the midst of the crisis. A wealthy Congolese businessman, who was a Christian and who lived over 1,000 miles away in the capital city of Kinshasa heard about it. He promptly arranged to fly an entire truckload of supplies to the church to help in the effort. When asked what motivated him to do such a generous thing he replied that he heard about the plight of the IDP's in the news and it touched him. He was so far away and did not know how to respond. When he heard about the local church's ministry, he knew that he could work through them and have a part in ministering to these people. This is a great example of the power of the local church. Sensitized through godly leadership and preaching they knew they needed to do something. They created a plan that fit their resources and capacity. God blessed their plan and other Congolese were motivated to take action when they heard about the work.

Some practical wisdom for churches ready and willing to minister to victims of conflict, war and genocide are:

1. The church needs to be prepared to face the reality of a hostile environment. Often churches are not well prepared for resistance, and persecution. The church must hear what God is saying and what society is saying and know how to bridge the gap between them.

2. As the church enters into the experience of the victims, assumptions should not be made as to what is needed, beyond immediate physical requirements for food, water and shelter. Simply walk the journey in love and kindness, allowing the Holy Spirit to minister through actions and words.

3. Do not hesitate to ask victims if prayer is desired and inquire about their spiritual situation. Many are hungry to grasp on to something real and beyond themselves.

4. Find ways to follow-up or pass the person on to another community of faith so that any seed planted can continue to be watered, even if the person is transient and moving on.

5. Realize that trauma is there, even if it is not visible. Allow time for people to tell their stories if they wish to. Give children the opportunity to draw pictures of their experience. Involve those with psychological skills if available to help the person work through the trauma.

6. Be patient and do not give up. Dealing with victims of tragedy is a long and hard process. Not everyone is eager or grateful for the help of the church, nor its message.

7. Remember the words of Mother Teresa who was known to say, "we can do no great things, only small things with great love."

PART II: HUMAN TRAFFICKING

Human trafficking and sexual exploitation are not new problems in our sin-depraved world. The deep disregard for humankind that leads to trafficking was evident only a few short generations after the Garden of Eden. Greed, lust, perversion, and the cravings for power were so pervasive that Genesis 6:5–6 says, "The Lord observed the extent of human wickedness on the earth, and he saw that everything they thought or imagined was consistently and totally evil. So the Lord was sorry he had ever made them and put them on the earth. It broke his heart."[5] In the judgment that followed—The

---

5. All scripture in this section on human trafficking is from the *New Living Translation* unless otherwise noted.

Flood—all mankind except Noah and his family were destroyed. This did not end mankind's thirst for abuse and exploitation.

As God's covenant people, we are called upon to defend those who are the victims of human depravity, and trafficked persons certainly fit that description. Scripture says, "Open your mouth for the mute, for the rights of all the unfortunate. Open your mouth, judge righteously, and defend the rights of the afflicted and needy" (Prov 31:8–9, NASB).

THE SCOPE OF HUMAN TRAFFICKING

The Organization of the High Commissioner for Human Rights gives the following definition to describe the two forms of human trafficking or trafficking in persons:

> 'Trafficking in persons' shall mean the recruitment, transportation, transfer, harboring, or receipt of persons, by means of threat or use of force or other forms of coercion, of abduction, of fraud, of deception, of the abuse of power or of a position of vulnerability or of the giving or receiving of payments or benefits to achieve the consent of the person having control over another person, for the purpose of exploitation.
>
> Exploitation shall include, at a minimum, the exploitation or the prostitution of others or other form of sexual exploitation, forced labor or services, slavery or practices similar to slavery servitude or the removal of organs.[6]

The statistics concerning human trafficking are staggering and increase yearly. Presently, the most reliable sources are from 2010 to 2012.

- The International Labor Organization reports, "21 million people are now victims of forced labor. According to new ILO estimates, three out of every 1,000 people worldwide are trapped in jobs into which they were coerced or deceived and which they cannot leave."[7]

- "Of those exploited by individuals or enterprises, 4.5 million are victims of forced sexual exploitation."[8]

6. "Protocol to Prevent, Suppress and Punish Trafficking in Persons, Especially Women and Children, Supplementing the United Nations Convention Against Transitional Organized Crime."

7. International Labor Organization of the United Nations, "21 Million People Are Now Victims of Forced Labour, ILO Says."

8. International Labor Organization of the United Nations, "Forced Labour, Human Trafficking and Slavery."

- Victims of 152 different citizenships have been identified in 124 countries across the world.

- At least 510 trafficking flows have been detected.

- Some 72 percent of convicted traffickers are men, and 28 per cent are women.

- 49 percent of detected victims are adult women.

- 33 percent of detected victims are children.[9]

- The ILO "estimates that there are 20.9 million victims of human trafficking worldwide, 5.5 million of those are children, 14.2 million of those are victims of labor exploitation."

Sex trafficking is big business today, netting millions of dollars. A 2011 FBI report labels sex trafficking as "the most common form of modern-day slavery." Plus, "it is the fastest-growing business of organized crime and the third-largest criminal enterprise in the world."[10] Children are often sold to traffickers for very little money, while others are simply kidnapped. In their desire for a better life, many women and men are tricked into sex and/or labor bondage through a perpetrator's lies of a good job or an education. Always for the trafficker, the goal is money, power, and control.

CONFLICTING VIEWS OF HUMAN LIFE

Human beings do not come with price tags, but the one true God establishes that we are of inestimable worth by bestowing an innate dignity and worthiness to each person. The Psalmist paints a beautiful picture of how God views us in Psalm 139:13–15: "You made all the delicate, inner parts of my body and knit me together in my mother's womb. Thank you for making me so wonderfully complex! Your workmanship is marvelous—how well I know it . . . You saw me before I was born." The Creator of all participated in the pre-birth development of each person. He adores and desires each person with the purest form of love. Human beings are His creation and are not disposable.

Not everyone views God's creation as He does. The values of those in human trafficking are in direct contrast to the character and nature of God. They strip away personhood and lay claim to the physical body as well as the emotional, psychological, and spiritual part of the victim.

9. United Nations Office on Drugs and Crime, "Global Report on Trafficking in Persons 2014."

10. Federal Bureau of Investigation, "Human Sex Trafficking."

Sadly, traffickers reduce their victims to a commodity. Her worth is valued only as long as she can add to the man's or woman's coffers or provide sexual services. Through manipulation, coercion, and force, the trafficker controls every action of the victim's life while distorting and destroying the very fibers of the victim's soul. As the humanity of trafficked persons is stripped away, they become commodities—disposable items like coffee, tea, and cacao that are intended to be traded, sold, and bought.

Lili's Story[11]

Lili began her life as a trafficked young woman after being abducted and taken to a hotel room where she was held for several days without food or water. Men paid to rape her. Her abductor/captor used this time to prepare her for what he had in store for her future. When Lili refused to be touched by the men who paid to rape her, she was beaten and often raped by her captor. During this process, Lili's will and heart were shattered. Breaking Lili's sense of self, her sense of humanity, and her sense of freedom was her captor's intended goal. The trafficker distorted and destroyed the very fibers of the Lili's soul.

Anna's Story

While in Buenos Aires, Argentina, I worked with Anna, a lovely, young woman with a broken heart and a traumatized body and soul. When she was six years old, her mother wanted to provide a better life for her and was willing to go anywhere to make money so that Anna could have a different, more meaningful life. Under the guise of lucrative house help, Anna's mother was lured to Buenos Aires. Unknowingly, she was being trafficked. Anna's mother ended up in a hostel in Buenos Aires, not in a fancy, upper-class home as a helper. Four years passed. Anna felt unloved and could not remember what it felt like to love herself.

When she was 10 years old, Anna received a letter from her mother. She was excited because her mother had purchased a ticket for her to visit Buenos Aires. She was sure her life would change. As the day approached for Anna to leave the Dominican Republic, she could not stop thinking and talking about what it would be like to see her mother and hug her. It would be wonderful for her mother to hold her in her arms like she remembered.

---

11. The names of the prostituted women have been changed to protect their identity.

When the day finally arrived, Anna did not know to say a long and forever goodbye to her grandmother with whom she had lived since her mother left. After a long flight, Anna passed through the passport checks and through the sliding doors that led to her mother's arms. Those arms were not waiting in love and eagerness to hold a valued daughter. Her mother was looking forward to closing a deal with her pimp and then boarding a flight back to the Dominican Republic, leaving her young daughter in the hands of the man who had trafficked her to Argentina four years earlier.

Anna's mother kissed her on the top of her head and took her hand and placed it in the hand of the man who would rape, traumatize, and sell her for many years. Her mother exchanged her for a two-week holiday in the Dominican Republic, her home country. Anna was the insurance policy that her mother would return.

When I met Anna, she did not talk, not even to her mother who did return to Buenos Aires. She trusted no one. She felt worthless and would not allow anyone to get close enough to be a friend. The one person Anna needed to believe in and depend on had betrayed her. She could not allow that to happen again.

It took months of increasing presence in the area of Anna's hostel before she spoke to me. Her first words to me were, "How do you know my name?" Anna and I became friends. Soon we were having long conversations about wholeness and restored dignity that only comes from Christ. On a street corner not far from her hostel where I had erected easels, we became friends as we painted on the canvases. This broken young woman needed someone to listen, to be trustworthy, to walk with her in this life she could not leave.

THE CHURCH'S RESPONSE

Scores of individuals want to change the face of modern-day slavery. They want to step into red-light districts and take women off the streets and out of brothels. Dreams and fantasies of rescuing those in bondage influence the creation of NGOs and independent missionaries who have the best of intentions but lack the proper knowledge and understanding of the women they want to serve.

Ministry opportunities among trafficked communities are difficult and reveal a worker's strengths and failures emotionally and spiritually. Walking day or night through streets where human bodies are for sale or rent can challenge the faith of even the most mature Christian.

While ministering in Argentina, a 21-year-old Bible college student interviewed with me for an internship to work in human trafficking and prostitution. During our discussion she informed me her interest was in hugging, rescuing, and giving women a better life outside the red-light districts. She was convinced she could personally save several women during her eight-week internship. She had not researched the human trafficking problem and did not understand the women or the dangers on the streets. She had no idea that hugging a prostituted woman would anger the woman's owner and could result in her own death. An internship in Buenos Aires that summer would have been a disaster for her and the ministry.

Understanding the mind-set of the trafficking community is essential. God created humankind for community and fellowship with Him and with each other. Sometimes we are born into a life-long community; other times our community develops with people who are in similar situations, life stages, work settings, or the same church or small group. We see this in brothels, apartments, hostels, and on streets where trafficked and prostituted women are together and form familial–type communities.

Interdependence for survival and life-sustaining community develop in the midst of their daily horror. Snatching a woman from her support group only harms her further. The woman needs and deserves to be humanized, and this process takes time. Her personhood deserves to be examined in an unbiased method since she did not choose to sell or have her body sold for sex.

The worker needs to examine her intentions, expectations, and reasons for her desire to help. Has she invested her life to build presence and a consistency of Christ-centered compassion in the prostituted woman's life? Will the women trust the worker? Can the woman leave her current situation? If she can leave, has a plan been developed for her recovery? With what community will she connect? "Relationships and trust must be established before effective rescue can occur. Rescuing an individual without providing them the opportunity to develop practical skills for working and living, as well as an opportunity to heal, will potentially make them vulnerable to being trafficked again or to voluntarily return to the life into which they were trafficked."[12]

MISCONCEPTIONS

For many people within the church, the word *prostitution* conjures images of loose or sex-craved women who stand along street corners to lure helpless,

12. Butrin, "Taking a Stand Against Human Trafficking."

sex-deprived men into their webs. But women become prostituted for many reasons. In my experience as a missionary, a woman does not wake up one day and decide she wants to sell her body for money.

> Women become involved in prostitution for a variety of reasons such as homelessness, child sexual abuse, mental ill health, trauma, previous sexual violence, drug and alcohol misuse, money pressures and poverty. These factors, which serve to lead or force women into prostitution, should not be mistaken for the cause of prostitution itself, which is the demand from men to buy sex. If men were not prepared to buy sex, then prostitution would not work as a survival behavior.[13]

We must be careful to judge those who are enslaved. One former prostituted woman said, "I thought it was my free choice, but as I've matured, I've realized that it wasn't a 'free' choice. It was a choice made by a mind damaged by childhood abuse."[14]

Ivana's Story

During my time in Argentina, I developed a friendship with Ivana. She recounted stories to me of her childhood and growing up in a sexually and physically dysfunctional home. The men and boys in her family raped and molested her until her early teen years. The abuse Ivana suffered led her to believe she was only valuable and only existed for sex. As a young adult, Ivana realized she needed to pay rent and utilities and buy food. The salary from her regular job was not enough to cover everything after her boyfriend moved out, so she decided to stand on Esmerelda Street in downtown Buenos Aires for a few days until she had enough money to catch up financially. The first two nights some men bought her; others left her alone. On the third night, a bouncer from down the street took her by the arm and dragged her to a bar. The owner of this particular bar also owned all of the women on Esmerelda Street. In his mind, Ivana was stealing money from him by standing on his street. Ivana's freedom ended that night.

Erika Rist, a legal theorist and writer on women's issues says, "While the notion of choice is ethically, academically, socio-culturally, and in other ways problematic, most people enter the sex trade due to a lack of choices and are exploited because of their need to sell sex to survive."[15]

13. *Prostitution: Money and Power.*
14. Soul Destruction, "Voices of Prostitution Survivors."
15. Rist, "When Humans Become Commodities."

Myrlla's Story

Myrlla longed for acceptance. Some of her first memories involved her grandfather's betrayal of her body. He passed her from his hands to his friends' hands who paid to sexually abuse her. Myrlla felt like a commodity, and she was. Those she needed to trust and depend on betrayed her in every way. Two decades later when I met Myrlla, she appeared reserved, shy, and untrusting. The community in which she was born did not value her. If they could not see her value and worth, how could she expect anyone else to see those things in her? How could Myrlla trust anyone to respect her body?

The New Testament says that Jesus came to seek and save those who are lost (Luke 19:10). Jesus not only engaged the marginalized, including the sexually marginalized, he also clearly directed his followers to show that same love (See Luke 7:35–50; 10:25–37; Luke 15:11–32,). "Jesus' practice of compassion was a natural integral part of his earthly missions of redemption—not a separate initiative."[16] Jesus showed that prostituted women deserve dignity and a voice. Today's trafficked woman deserves dignity, recognition, humanity, and life simply because she exists and is created in the image of God.

SHARING LIFE WITH VICTIMS OF TRAFFICKING

When well-meaning Christians enter red light districts or areas known for sexual exploitation, often the focus is not on restoration and redemption of the soul, but rather on the perceived sin of the prostitutes. Scripture indeed calls willfully defiling one's body a sin, for the body is God's temple (1 Cor 6:19–20). Willfully engaging in sexual exploitation, however, is very different from being forced to do so against one's will. It is vital that the church make this distinction.

Sharing life with a trafficked woman requires the willingness to enter her world. Perhaps that is over a cup of coffee at a nearby café, or accepting the invitation to visit with her fellow prostituted prisoners in their location. Listen to her story. What does she want to tell you? By listening, you show her that she has value, that her words are important. Trafficking and prostitution strips a woman of her dignity and the very essence of her humanity. In Buenos Aires, we found that we could use mobile art stations—complete with easels, canvas and various art supplies set up on the street as women were changing shifts—worked as a point of initial connection and way to build presence in the community.

16. Grant, *Courageous* Compassion, 26.

Our purpose for engaging should be to make Jesus Christ known among the community where we serve and to live life as Jesus lived. His life exemplified grace, compassion, mercy, hope, healing, and freedom. We must not only limit our services to *church times*, where the body of Christ is gathered for corporate worship, but we must also live outside the walls of the building. We are called to engage with our neighbors while investing in both key players in the community and in the weakest among them.

WHERE DO WE GO FROM HERE?

As mentioned in previous chapters, "best practice" refers to research-based methods that constitute widely accepted, preferred ways doing things. Best practice in human trafficking consists of the following:

- Prevention is the most important intervention and the primary focus of any anti-trafficking effort.

- The dignity and rights of the victim are preserved in any outreach or intervention.

- Multi-sector cooperation is more effective than ministry in isolation.

- Assessment of who is doing what, how it is being done, and how cooperation can be established is essential.

- Raid-type rescue should not be done. This usually causes repeated trauma to victims.

- The safety and privacy of the survivors should be of utmost importance.

- Media, photos, and other forms of promotion or reporting should protect the identity and dignity of the victims and should be used rarely or with great caution.

- Nongovernmental organizations, churches, and individuals should not play a lead role in a raid or rescue as they lack the authority and government backing to carry out such efforts. Caregivers must not attempt to rescue a trafficked victim without the intervention and help of law enforcement officials.

- Rescuing prostitute women without providing them the opportunity to develop practical skills for working and living, as well as an opportunity to heal, will potentially make them vulnerable to being trafficked again or to voluntarily return to the life in which they were trafficked.

- Relationships and trust must be established before effective rescue can occur.

- Victims' needs are paramount to donor/benefactor needs.[17]

As participants in God's redemptive plan, we must seek to follow the example of Christ and allow compassion to become a natural, integral part of our lives. We need to explore and employ practices that best serve the women to whom we feel called. We must remember the women we serve are not commodities, or products. Our job is not to move women from the streets to a place we deem safe. Rather, we must invest in their lives through building relationships, observing the assets within their reach, and encouraging them to make decisions about their future.

A prostituted woman thinks she has no right or opportunity to make choices, but she does. Those choices might not be based on geographical movement. Perhaps her pimp or owner decides where her physical body must be, but she needs to know she can decide what happens to her heart, her soul, and her mind. Freedom is not always geographical or physical. When a worker invests time and compassion, the prostituted woman begins to understand her worth and that her value comes only from being created in God's image. She then grasps that her inherent value does not depend on what happens to her body and her soul has an opportunity to breathe. Then she can begin to imagine life and freedom outside of the trauma and entrapment of her body.

PART III: JUSTICE FOR WOMEN

The inferior way in which women are viewed in many cultures of the world has set up a series of injustices against women that are tragic to contemplate and overwhelming in scope. These include Female Genital Mutilation (or FGM, also known as female circumcision), rape, spousal and widow abuse, widow neglect, and lack of basic human rights. How should the church respond to these issues? What does the Bible say about the value and role of women? What does it mean for the church to be salt and light in places where women are mistreated and undervalued in often systematic ways?

Women: A Biblical Perspective

There can be no doubt that the Bible has sometimes been wrongly used to justify the subjugation and abuse of women, just as it has been wrongly used to justify slavery. Yet, when we pay careful attention to the Bible's teaching on the value and role of women, we discover that both Judaism

17. Butrin, "Taking a Stand Against Human Trafficking," n.p.

and Christianity elevated the role and status of women far beyond cultural norms.

One of the clearest examples of Christianity rejecting cultural norms regarding women and honoring them in ways far above what was common can be found in the story of Jesus' appearance to women after His resurrection. All four Gospels report that the women were the first to discover and report to the other disciples that Jesus' tomb was empty. This is quite remarkable, given that in the first century women's testimony was not highly regarded. For example, Josephus, the first-century Jewish historian wrote:

> Put not trust in a single witness, but let there be three or at the least two, whose evidence shall be accredited by their past lives. From women let no evidence be accepted, because of the levity and temerity of their sex; neither let slaves bear witness because of the baseness of their soul, since whether from cupidity or fear it is like[ly?] that they will not attest to the truth.[18]

Even in Scripture we see that the disciples were inclined not to trust the report that the women gave. "When they heard that He was alive they refused to believe it" (Mark 16:11). In a world in which a women's place in society was only slightly better than slaves, Jesus chose to make his first resurrection appearances to women. In doing so, he attributed to them an honor and status unheard of in that day.

Going against cultural norms was in fact a common feature of Jesus' treatment of women. Nowhere is this more pronounced than in his encounter with the Samaritan woman at the well in John 4. Here he not only spoke to and taught a woman, but set aside religious constraints ignoring the boundaries that were normally observed between Jews and Samaritans. Jesus also refused to let the moral perceptions of others be a hindrance to Him reaching out to a woman who was broken and in need of God's redemptive grace.

Not only did Jesus invite women to follow him, but he also consistently displayed great compassion for women in need. In Luke 13 we read about a woman who was severely crippled, and whom Jesus healed. Luke, interestingly, attributes her condition to the work of Satan (13:11). This is important because it reveals not only Jesus' approach to physical and spiritual suffering, but provides insight into the relationship between the kingdom of God and injustice. As Joel Green explains, "Because Luke has presented Jesus as the divine agent of salvation in whose ministry the kingdom of God is made present and in whose ministry the domain of Satan is rolled back, Luke's depiction of this woman's illness prepares us for a redemptive

18. Josephus, *Antiq.*, IV:219.

encounter of startling proportions."[19] Jesus' ministry to her signals God's agency in healing and in making visible the plight of those who are often socially invisible.[20]

These examples represent a small sample of the occasions in which Jesus demonstrated compassion toward women. Jesus' actions can be described as recognizing a cultural deficiency regarding the treatment of women, and taking steps to move closer toward a more kingdom-oriented ethic.[21] This is what William Webb refers to as a "redemptive movement hermeneutic." In Scripture we do not always get the highest ideal that God desires for his people, but rather we get evidence that through progressive revelation God is moving his covenant people closer to his intended goal. The challenge for God's people then is to recognize this movement and continue it by reflecting on ways our own culture fails to meet God's standards. As Webb explains:

> Scripture provides the direction toward the divine destination, but its literal, isolated words are not always the destination itself. Sometimes God's instructions are simply designed to get his flock moving. Rather than laying out the entire journey, some texts simply outline the first major steps along with way.[22]

The challenge then for every culture is to evaluate our own cultural norms against the ethical standards of God's kingdom, in which "there is neither slave nor free . . . male nor female" (Gal 3:28; NASB95). This does not mean that gender differences are erased, but that Christ incorporates us into the one body of Christ where all are equally valued. We become a community that celebrates the unique ways in which God made us while being drawn together by the Holy Spirit in unity, fellowship, and mutual concern.

Widows

In the patriarchal era of the Old Testament, the safety and security of women often depended on their being married. When a woman married she was incorporated into the household of her husband and father-in-law, so that even if her husband died she retained a place in the family. Because of this, a woman was often not considered a widow unless she had lost both her husband and father-in-law and thereby had no male protector. To be without a

19. Green, *The Gospel of Luke*, 521.
20. Ibid.
21. See chapter 2.
22. Webb, *Slaves, Women and Homosexuals*, chapter 2, under "Theological Rational."

protector was to be destitute. In several cases when the Old Testament refers to the plight of widows, it is because God himself has taken on the role of protector and advocate "calling on the larger Hebrew community to look after them (see Exod 22:22; Deut 10:18; 14:29; 16:11)."[23]

The New Testament paints a picture in which the community's care for widows seeks not only their survival, but also that they become productive members of society. In Acts 6 a controversy arises over the care of widows, and the disciples appoint members of the community to oversee this need. What is important to recognize here is that the church recognized both the need to address this problem and the need to safeguard the apostles' role in preaching and worship. As important as compassionate ministries are in the church, they can never stand in the place of proclamation. Identifying members of the community who have gifts of mercy and service helps ensure this does not happen. In Acts 9 we read about a disciple named Tabitha, who "appears to employ a group of widows in her tailor shop. Rather than receiving handouts, they are contributing members of the believing community, not dependent on a male head of household."[24]

As modern missions churches respond to the needs of widows, these same concerns should be our guide. God's people should endeavor to provide and protect vulnerable widows. This should also be done in a way that empowers widows to become less dependent and active, contributing members of the Christian community as was modeled in the ministry of Tabitha.

Justice for Widows

Widow abuse is a common occurrence in many parts of the world. In many places, their basic human rights are overlooked or ignored. As one UN publication observes:

> It can be said that there is no group more affected by the sin of omission than widows. They are painfully absent from the statistics of many developing countries, and they are rarely mentioned in the multitude of reports on women's poverty, development, health or human rights published in the last twenty-five years. Growing evidence of their vulnerability, both socio-economic and psychological . . . now challenges many conventional views and assumptions about this "invisible" group of women.[25]

23. Finger, "Widows," 836.
24. Finger, "Widows," 837.
25. UN, "Widowhood: Invisible women, secluded or excluded," 2.

The suffering endured by widows is often unimaginable, as seen in this story told by Janet Walsh:

> The case of Emily Owino, a widow Human Rights Watch interviewed in western Kenya, is a classic example. Shortly after her husband died, Owino's in-laws took all her possessions—including farm equipment, livestock, household goods, and clothing. The in-laws insisted that she be "cleansed" by having sex with a social outcast as a condition of staying in her home. They paid a herdsman the equivalent of US $6 to have sex with Owino, against her will and without a condom. She recalled, "I tried to refuse, but my in-laws said I must be cleansed or they'd beat me and chase me out of my home. They said they had bought me [with the dowry], and therefore I had no voice in that home." The in-laws eventually forced her out of her home anyway. Owino tried to get help from an elder and the village chief, but they asked for bribes that she could not pay. She and her children were homeless until someone offered her a small, leaky shack. No longer able to afford school fees, her children dropped out of school.[26]

It is unthinkable that churches and individual Christians would do nothing in response to this. Yet in many places, that is exactly the case. I know of places in Africa where pastors and churches have chosen not to address these practices, even though they are rampant even among church goers. One is left to wonder what does it mean for Scripture to say that God is "a judge for the widows" (Ps 68:5; NASB95) when God's people stand idly by and let such atrocities take place? What does it mean when the people of God are commanded to "rescue the weak and needy" (Ps 82:3; NASB95)? Surely it means that the church must take a counter–cultural stand against those who abuse widows.

What might be included in a church's response to the needs of widows? First, one might follow the pattern of Acts (6:1–6), and designate a deacon or leader in the church to oversee their care. This might include weekly or monthly visits, especially during the first year of widowhood, as this is the time when grief and loneliness are often highest. It might also encourage widows within the church to form networks of care and support for each other.[27] In order for any church-based ministry to widows to succeed, though, the pastor must be intentional about supporting the program.[28]

26. Walsh, "Women's Property Rights Violations and HIV/AIDS in Africa," 190.

27. Teterud, *Caring for Widows*, 97.

28. Ibid, 104.

FEMALE GENITAL MUTILATION

According to the World Health Organization, Female Genital Mutilation (FGM) affects about 200 million girls from about 30 countries, mostly in Africa. Victims usually range in age from toddlers up to age 15. The practice constitutes a basic human rights violation. Those who practice it believe that it will prevent premarital intercourse and keep a girl marriageable. FGM causes numerous health problems and has absolutely no health benefits whatsoever.[29] As Faiza Mohamed explains:

> It is a practice that translates into the partial or total removal of the clitoris (clitoridectomy), the removal of the entire clitoris and the cutting of the labia minora (excision), or in its most extreme form the removal of all external genitalia and the stitching together of the two sides of the vulva (infibulation). The cutting is done generally without anesthetic and those who survive it experience lifelong health consequences including chronic infection, severe pain during menstruation, sexual intercourse and childbirth, and psychological trauma.[30]

The Church in Response to FGM

What can churches do in response to what is clearly a form of abuse? Samuel Kunhiyop proposes several things. First, the church should approach those who practice FGM with respect. This may sound odd, given the severity of the practice. The Bible commands us to be kind to everyone, even those who might be described as evil. We are in fact to model our own kindness on the kindness of God, who is merciful to all (Luke 6:35; Rom 11:22). Plus, as Kunhiyop says, most who perform FGM do so for what they believe are good reasons. However much we may disagree, being unkind to those who engage in this practice will not help bring about change. Second, churches need to become knowledgeable about the issue. Local practices and ethnic distinctions need to be studied and understood before they can be effectively addressed. Third, change must be community driven and come from within. Passing legislation often has little effect as laws are easily skirted. Fourth, community-driven change means education. This requires identifying the positive cultural values that may be inherent in the practice, such as wanting a bright future for one's child, and retaining and recasting that value within

29. World Health Organization, "Female Genital Mutilation."
30. Mohamed, "Putting an End to Female Genital Mutilation," 114.

a biblical framework while discarding the harmful practices. Fifth, this then requires the introduction of substitute practices. Often female circumcision takes place within the context of child initiation rites. Kunhiyop gives the example of a community in Kenya that transitioned from FGM to a ceremony called "Ntanira Na Mugambo or circumcision through words."[31] Kunhiyop argues that these initiation ceremonies can be recast to pass on Christian values and virtues. Finally, believers can push for legislation. Usually this can only be done after local community leaders, tribal chiefs, and local people have accepted the idea. Trying to force legislation without doing the grassroots work first is almost always counterproductive.[32]

JUSTICE AND MISSIO DEI

At this point, I (Jerry) wish to reflect on not only justice for women, but the issue of justice broadly within a missions context. Throughout this chapter we have tried to carefully articulate ways that churches and local believers can respond to these and other issues of injustice. We have not yet looked in much detail at what this looks like from the missions side of the equation. It is to that question that we now turn.

The question is not whether the people of God should be concerned about issues of justice. The Bible is clear that they should. Over and over again the Bible admonishes the faithful to not "distort" or "pervert" justice (Deut 16:19; 24:17), and contrasts justice with wickedness (Job 34:12). Likewise, Paul says, "the kingdom of God is not eating and drinking, but righteousness and peace and joy in the Holy Spirit" (Rom 14:17).[33] What does this mean for missionaries? Considering not only the material presented in this chapter, but also the theological and missiological foundations presented in chapters two and three, I propose two things that missionaries can do to support local churches: empowering through discipleship, and resourcing.

Justice and Discipleship

Perhaps the most enduring thing a missionary can do when it comes to stemming the tide of injustice is to focus on discipleship. This would involve

31. Kunhiyop, *African Christian Ethics*, 300.

32. Ibid., 298–301.

33. It is best to understand Paul's use of righteousness here not in the sense of justification, but in ethical and relational terms, as Moo has pointed out; Moo, *The Epistle to the Romans*, 857.

discipling followers of Christ in such a way that the moral and ethical demands of the gospel are underscored. By doing this, believers are positioned
to stop injustices before they begin. They become equipped to critique their
culture through the gospel and, within a scriptural framework, to describe
the reasons for standing against all forms of injustice. The first step in addressing injustice must always start with the church, for it is the church that
is called to be salt and light in the community. This means that the church is
to be a radiant expression of the kingdom of God in the community. When
believers begin to live according to the ethical and just demands of Jesus,
the King of Righteousness (Isa 32:1), they point to a better future open to all
who would come and submit to the Lordship of Jesus.

Discipling for justice could take the form of a preaching series or Sunday
school classes on Jesus' Sermon on the Mount. Or it might involve a home
group or Bible study that looks at the parable of the Good Samaritan or the
many passages in Scripture that refer to justice and righteousness. The goal
would be to get people to think both biblically and practically about these
passages. What does it mean to be salt and light in *this* neighborhood? What
are some concrete ways in which we can love our neighbors and stand against
injustice? What members of our community are victims of injustice, and how
can we help? What does justice for widows and victims of FGM look like?
One of the goals in discipleship is that local believers would embody a "surpassing righteousness" (Matt 5:20), that they would become the front line of
defense in their families, in their work places, in their schools, and wherever
injustice is found.

Apart from discipling local believers to understand and practice justice from a biblical perspective, missionaries run the risk of being perceived
as outsiders who come in try to impose their own cultural norms on others.
Only when change comes from within does it have true staying power. This
is why discipleship is vital. Insiders can speak to their own culture in a way
that outsiders cannot. By intentionally making concern for justice a part of
the discipleship process we go a long way toward empowering local people
to address the issues that directly affect them. Leymah Gbowee was awarded
the Nobel Peace Prize in 2011 for her work toward ending the civil war in
Liberia primarily through the empowerment of women. Gbowee observes
that local people have insight and skills that outsiders can never have, or
possibly even comprehend. She writes:

> Organizations like the UN do a lot of good . . . but there are
> certain basic realities they never seem to grasp . . . Maybe the
> most important truth that eludes these organizations is that it is
> insulting when outsiders come in and tell a traumatized people

what it will take for them to heal. You cannot go to another country and make a plan for it. The cultural context is so different from what you know that you will not understand much of what you see. I would never come to the US and claim to understand what's going on, even in the African American culture. People who live through a terrible conflict may be hungry and desperate, but they are not stupid. They often have very good ideas about how peace can evolve, and they need to be asked.

That includes women. Most especially women. When it comes to preventing conflict or building peace, there's a way in which women are the experts . . . we know our communities. We know our history. We know the people. We know how to talk to an ex-combatant and get his cooperation, because we know where he comes from. To outsiders like the UN, these soldiers were a problem to be managed. But they were our children.[34]

When missionaries come in and set themselves up as the resident experts on issues of injustice faced by local people, we inevitably trample on the unique insights that only local people, and especially women, bring. If we are to ever escape our paternalistic inclinations as missionaries, we must begin by placing a premium on the wisdom inherent in local communities. No one knows a community better than the women who live there and have raised their children there.

Resourcing for Long-term Results

Discipling for justice will likely require that missionaries and missions agencies devote personnel and resources to developing curriculum and other educational materials to aid local churches in this task. This presents an obvious challenge for missionaries when it comes to fundraising. It is much easier to raise money to "rescue victims of trafficking" than it is to raise money for a Sunday school curriculum aimed at discipling believers. We must become adept at conveying long-term effectiveness to our support base and convincing them that settling for short-term solutions often amounts to a waste of time and resources.

Resourcing requires expertise. While missionaries may be less skilled in cultural knowledge than local people, there are nonetheless skills that we can bring that will make a valuable contribution. These might include theological and biblical knowledge, since books and other resources for theological training are often in short supply. Missionaries can also provide

34. Gbowee, *Mighty Be Our Powers*, 171–172; cited in Sider, *Nonviolent Action*, 114.

expertise in development and public health. This might take the form of training on the medical implications of FGM, or the physical and psychological health hazards related to widow abuse. It may involve pedagogical training aimed at helping local people teach more effectively. Many in the majority world know only rote memorization when it comes to education because that is what they have seen modeled. They can often benefit greatly by being introduced to more interactive approaches to education. The bottom line is that a missionary is not automatically qualified to address issues of injustice simply because they are a missionary. Without some level of expertise, missionaries can easily do more damage than good.

CONCLUSION

When discipleship does not take place and missionaries function as the primary agents working for justice in a cross-cultural context, we inevitably convey the notion that standing against injustice is the prerogative of cultural outsiders. This has disastrous results in that it diminishes the overall effectiveness of the church, because that which should be a concern of every believer is reduced to the concerns of just a handful of specialists. This is not to say that every believer should be involved first-hand in addressing human trafficking or directly providing for the needs of widows. Every believer should be concerned about these things and support those who are directly involved. Every believer should have a basic understanding of what justice means from a biblical perspective and what that means for God's people. All Christians should endeavor to serve the cause of justice in their community in a way equal to their understanding and competency. Most people have no idea where to begin. For this reason, curricula aimed at helping disciples address issues of injustice are indispensable. Discipleship is most effective precisely because it empowers people to be the gathered people of God in their community and to demonstrate solidarity with those who suffer injustices in a way that only comes through constant proximity. As Pope Francis has said, "I see clearly that the thing the church needs most today is the ability to heal wounds and to warm the hearts of the faithful; it needs nearness, proximity. I see the church as a field hospital after battle."[35]

35. Spadaro, S. J., "Francis: A Big Heart Open to God," 1.

10

Orphans and Vulnerable Children

Jerry M. Ireland

When my wife and began our missionary assignment to Zambia in 2007, we had no plans to become involved in youth ministry. Yet, as we traveled from church to church preaching, we began to notice a disturbing trend. Many of the churches we visited were filled with children and teens, often more than double the number of the adult congregation. Yet in church after church, very little attention was being given to discipling these young people. In fact, we once asked a group of teenagers who were gathered for their weekly Sunday school class what sort of things they normally discussed. They told us, "you know, normal stuff—like is it ok to braid your hair when you go to church." We could hardly believe our ears. As disturbing as this was, we were even more shocked when the national director of youth ministry for this denomination told us later that there was no need to try to disciple teens, and that they should just organize youth choirs and have competitions. In his view, this was all that was necessary and all that was possible when it came to youth.

Sadly, this reality is repeated throughout the world and across the age spectrum from toddlers to teens. Many churches in the majority world simply do not have the resources to effectively disciple the children that come. Some, as we have just seen, may lack a vision for what is possible when it comes to discipling children. Missionaries also bear responsibility for not giving adequate attention to reaching children. As Bryant Myers says, "the situation of children and youth in the world is a significant blind spot in

Christian missions."[1] Yet a simple fact remains: the local church is the best hope for reaching children in a community and for being a source of healing and wholeness in children's lives. Not only that, but children and youth are a vital part of the body of Christ and have a great deal to offer the church through the spiritual gifts they bring. In this chapter we will describe ways in which missionaries can foster effective compassionate outreach to children and youth by building the capacity of local churches.

CHILDREN AND YOUTH: A BIBLICAL PERSPECTIVE

Several important themes in the Old Testament provide insight into how the people of God should view children. First, children are frequently portrayed as a blessing and gift. In Psalm 127:3, for example, we read, "Behold, children are a heritage from the LORD, the fruit of the womb a reward" (see also Ps 113:9, 128:3–4; Isa 8:18).[2] Second, the Old Testament also emphasizes parents' responsibility to teach their children and admonishes children to obey (Exod 20:12; Prov 1:8). The author of Deuteronomy instructs God's people to not only guard the works of God which they have seen and heard, but to also "make them known to [their] sons and [their] grandsons" (Deut 4:9). Third, "adults had special responsibility to provide not only for their own children but also for orphans, including the orphans of foreigners (Exod 22:22; Deut 10:18; 24:17; Isa 1:17; 10:2; Jer 22:3)."[3]

Perhaps no image in Scripture affirms the value of children more than that of God himself becoming a child. Even before the advent of Jesus, the New Testament addresses the responsibility of parents toward their children. In the announcement of the ministry of John the Baptist, an angel tells his father Zechariah that "he will turn many of the children of Israel to the Lord their God, and he will go before him in the spirit and power of Elijah, to turn the hearts of the fathers to the children, and the disobedient to the wisdom of the just" (Luke 1:17). Not only will John turn people to God, but he will also turn fathers to their children. It is noteworthy that here fathers and children are contrasted with the disobedient and just, indicating that many (most?) fathers had been grossly negligent in caring for their children. As Joel Green has observed, it is well documented that sexual abuse and severe disciplining of children were commonplace in the Greco-Roman

1. Myers, "State of the World's Children," 98.

2. All Scripture references in this chapter are from the English Standard Version Bible unless otherwise noted.

3. Miles, "Children," 135.

world.[4] Turning the hearts of the people toward God required turning the people away from this abusive behavior. The proper worship of God could not take place in an ethical vacuum, and chief among God's concerns was the proper treatment of children.

At one point in Jesus' ministry, his disciples rebuked those who were trying to bring their children to Jesus to receive a blessing. Jesus responded with both indignation and a poignant object lesson on the kingdom of God. In Mark's Gospel we read that "when Jesus saw it, he was indignant and said to them, "Let the children come to me; do not hinder them, for to such belongs the kingdom of God" (10:13). Jesus went on to tell those gathered that if they wanted to enter the kingdom of God they too had to become like little children. Jesus then took the children in his arms and blessed them (10:16). The importance of this biblical story should not be overlooked both as it relates to children and to discipleship in general. In our ministry in Africa, we have often encountered pastors who, not unlike the disciples, literally chased children away from their churches on Sunday morning, considering them nothing more than a nuisance. Yet Jesus taught that not only are we to welcome children and bless them, but that children also have something to teach us about humility and depending on God. The way children depend entirely on their parents and joyfully receive from them the things they need models for us how we should approach God.

A few years ago I attended a children's ministry training conducted by a missionary colleague in Zambia. After my friend taught on Jesus' rebuke of the disciples in Mark 10, one pastor came forward, knelt down, and asked for prayer for forgiveness because he had been guilty of not welcoming children into his church. I was deeply moved by this pastor's humility, and I cannot think of a more powerful embodiment of Jesus' instruction about becoming child-like in order to enter the kingdom. Missionaries too would be well-served in approaching issues related to children with a good dose of child-like humility.

Children have potential to be used by God, as is evident in the Old Testament stories of Joseph, Samuel, and David all having experienced a divine call at a young age (Genesis 37; 1 Sam 3:1–14; 1 Sam 16:12). More importantly, all children are created in the image of God and thereby worthy of love, care, and dignity (Gen 1:26–27; Gen 9:6). Thus, "even a disabled child or an unborn child is recognized as having inherent worth."[5]

4. Green, *The Gospel of Luke*, 77.
5. Fox, "Eating the Flesh of Our Sons and Daughters," 501.

The Importance of Children and Youth

According to Bryant Myers, children are a vital and yet often neglected aspect of modern missions strategies. As a corrective to this, he provides three primary reasons why children are important in the way we think about and conduct Christian missions. First, children constitute the largest demographic in the majority world, where one out of two people is under the age of nineteen. Second, most people come to faith between the ages of four and fourteen, giving rise to the term "4/14 window."[6] Third, 78 percent of children and youth are from non-Christian homes and therefore have limited access to the gospel.[7] These factors should compel us to develop missions strategies that include a vision for reaching and ministering to the needs of children.

The Challenges Facing Children and Youth

The children and youth of the world also should be a concern to Christians because of the tremendous adversity they face. Due to issues such as high child mortality rates, urbanization, neglect, abuse, sexual exploitation, and child labor, many children around the world suffer extreme deprivation. This is especially true of girls.[8] According to the World Health Organization (WHO), sixteen thousand children under the age of five die every day, most of preventable causes.[9] One in four children around the world suffer stunted growth due to lack of proper nutrition.[10] According to UNICEF, 150 million children worldwide are engaged in child labor.[11] The prospects for a bright future for many children around the world are simply nonexistent unless someone intervenes. The crucial question though for missionaries and missions agencies is how: How can we formulate a missions strategy that responds to the needs and challenges facing children, *and* stay true to our calling to strengthen and plant indigenous churches?

6. See data in Myers, "State of the World's Children," 99; Kennedy, "The 4/14 Window," 53.

7. Myers, "State of the World's Children," 99.

8. Ibid., 99–100.

9. See World Health Organization, "Global Health Observatory Data: Child Health."

10. World Food Programme, "Hunger Statistics," accessed May 30, 2016, https://www.wfp.org/hunger/stats.

11. UNICEF, "Child Protection: Current Status + Progress."

THE ROLE OF THE FAMILY

We cannot begin to formulate a biblical understanding of how missionaries should engage in ministry to children and teens apart from understanding the role of the family in scripture. In the Bible, the family exists as the most fundamental, God-ordained building block of society. Paul says that the very concept of family itself (Gr. *patria*) derives its name and existence from God the Father (Gr. *Pater*). "For this reason I bow my knees before the Father (*Pater*), from whom every family (*patria*) in heaven and on earth is named" (Eph 3:14–15).[12] This means that God's own concern and care for his children tells us something about how we should care for our children. Even the church in the New Testament is described as a "household of faith" (Gal 6:10) and the "household of God" (Eph 2:19). In the Old Testament, the household was the very epicenter of life. It "was the center not only of economic production but also of teaching, religious life, moral instruction, and protection."[13] When the New Testament speaks of the church as a "household," it is likely that all of these Old Testament characteristics are in view. Both the biological family and the spiritual family then are vital to the growth and flourishing of children.

For missionaries, the importance of this cannot be overstated. Whatever strategies or approaches we take to evangelize and care for children, we must endeavor to strengthen a child's biological family whenever possible and incorporate them into a family of faith. Studies have shown that children tend to take on the religious beliefs of their parents.[14] Plus, what a child believes by the age of thirteen, they are likely to believe for the rest of their lives.[15] Because of this, every effort should be made by missionaries working with children to keep families together and to preserve or strengthen the bonds between children and their parents.

ORPHANS

As we have already noted, the Bible is anything but silent on the issue of orphan care. To say that God is "Father to the fatherless" (Ps 68:5) means that God has a special concern for orphans. In Deuteronomy, God instructed Israel to incorporate into its farming practices the care of, among others, orphans (Deut 24:19, 21). Mistreatment of orphans incurs God's wrath (Deut

12. Kline, "Family," 238.
13. Miles, "Family," 300.
14. Myers, "State of the World's Children," 99.
15. Barna, "Research Shows."

27:19). God's people are to defend orphans in their pursuit of justice (Isa 1:17). James describes true religion as caring for orphans and widows, and keeping one's self pure (Jas 1:27).

In all of these it is important to observe that God has a special role for the people of God in the care of needy and vulnerable children. Missionaries should work to strengthen this capacity in local churches and avoid being the primary care givers. This is necessary both to guard the forward momentum of missions, and also because local churches are integral parts of the communities in which they reside. They know the children who are in need in their community often by name, and have watched them grow up. In many cases, the needy children may be part of the extended families of some church members. Thus local churches can enter into the lives of children in their community in a way that no outsider can.

What is an Orphan?

According to UNICEF, there are 132 million children in the world that fit the definition of "orphan." Among these, "the vast majority of orphans are living with a surviving parent, grandparent, or other family member."[16] Many from the West find this surprising because of the tendency to define orphans as those who have lost both parents. It was especially the global AIDS crisis though that give rise to the need for some clarification. Now, children are referred to as either "double orphans"—having lost both parents, and "single orphans"—having lost only a single parent. Furthermore:

> this difference in terminology can have concrete implications for policies and programming for children. For example, UNICEF's 'orphan' statistic might be interpreted to mean that globally there are 132 million children in need of a new family, shelter, or care. This misunderstanding may then lead to responses that focus on providing care for individual children rather than supporting the families and communities that care for orphans and are in need of support.[17]

Sadly, misconceptions about the realities of orphans and the ability of local communities and extended families to provide care has given rise to a phenomenon known as "AIDS Orphan Tourism."[18] In this trend, a definition of "orphan" is generated solely in order to illicit outside support,

16. UNICEF, "Orphans."
17. Ibid.
18. Richter and Norman, "AIDS Orphan Tourism," 217–229.

often meaning that someone from the global North travels to the global South to provide care in an institutional setting. Often these institutions, or orphanages, ignore the power and presence of local communities and extended families in caring for orphans. Not only that, but many times they exacerbate the challenges faced by orphans because they contribute to the cycle of "attachment and abandonment," owing to the short-term nature of these volunteer efforts. In other words, one of a developing child's greatest needs is stability when it comes to the care they receive. Yet, AIDS orphan tourism fosters exactly the opposite through a ministry model that ensures a non-stop revolving door of individuals in and out of a child's life.[19]

In addition, the very existence of an orphanage itself may encourage local parents and extended family members to abandon a child in hopes that the child will receive better care than the family can provide. We might recall that in 2010, ten American missionaries were arrested for taking "orphans" out of Haiti following the earthquake there. As it turned out, many of the children's parents gave their children to the missionaries, after the missionaries had promised to provide the children with a better life.[20] Steve Roa's assessment is right on target. He says

> The problem with the institutional approach is that it gradually begins to isolate young people from their communities, creating a sub-culture with an inevitable identity crisis. Ironically, Americans have done away with orphanages in their own country because of the many problems they create. Yet we unquestionably continue to use this problematic model around the world![21]

The most effective means of helping orphans include group homes and strategies aimed at supporting extended families. A key concept in all of these is to ensure that children are raised with close ties to their own culture and not made outcasts in their own country.

Child Sponsorship

In addition to orphanages, child sponsorship has emerged as a sometimes controversial approach to the needs of children in the developing world. Though recognized as an enormously successful way to raise money, the practice has not been without its critics. In 2009, the sponsors of between

19. Ibid.
20. Cable News Network, "US Missionaries Charged with Kidnapping in Haiti."
21. Steve Roa, "Community-Based Care," 21.

eight and twelve million children gave over $3 billion.[22] However, does the ability to generate funds translate into what is best for the child and into good missions strategy?

Among the core criticisms of child sponsorship are some of the issues already mentioned such as the potential to do damage to family units for the same reasons we have just discussed. Indeed, it may be true that the child sponsorship program can provide better care than the child's family. This should force us to ask whether it is possible to become involved in helping needy children in ways that support the family structure rather than threaten it. Sadly, some attempts to do just that have failed because donors "wanted that one to one relationship with the kid."[23] In other words, the desires of the donor took precedence over the needs of the family and over the needs of the child. It was the donors' wishes that ultimately drove strategy and this is an ever-present danger when finances are the driving force.

Child sponsorship must also contend with the tendency toward what has been called "pornography of poverty," or simply "poverty porn," referring to the exploitation of poor children for marketing purposes "where people are portrayed as helpless, passive objects."[24] Images of fly-ridden children with distended bellies are commonplace. As Coulter says, "The wide-eyed child, smiling or starving, is the most powerful fundraiser for aid agencies."[25] The crucial question is whether such practices take into account the privacy and dignity of the child and whether they embody a Christ-like concern for others? It seems to me that such practices amount to taking advantage of suffering children. Sometimes this concern is explained away saying that these types of images allow us to raise funds and ultimately help more children in need. Exploitation for a good cause is still exploitation. The children in these photos are not given an opportunity to say whether they approve of the practice or not.

Others have pointed out that child sponsorship amounts to poor stewardship. In the mid 1980's some were claiming that the money spent sponsoring one child could provide life-saving immunizations for 31 children.[26] Finally, it must be admitted that many approaches to child sponsorship only treat symptoms when what is needed is a solution that addresses root causes.

None of this is to say that child sponsorship is inherently problematic or even *necessarily* detrimental. Indeed, many organizations involved in

---

22. Watson and Clarke, "Introduction to Key Issues in Child Sponsorship," 1.

23. Moore, "The Myth of the Needy Child," 17.

24. Watson, et al., "Issues in Historic Child Sponsorship," 87.

25. Paddy Coulter, "Pretty as a Picture."

26. Brad Watson, et al., "Issues in Historic Child Sponsorship," 85.

child sponsorship have, in response to the above criticisms, began developing more community-based models. Also, one widely cited study has shown that child sponsorship can be an effective means of generating hope for a child, and that sponsored children tend to fair better in life than their non-sponsored contemporaries.[27] A great deal more research though is needed. Even despite some of the concerns expressed above, it may be best to see organizations engaged in child sponsorship as "ethical organizations, committed to child poverty reduction as they continue to grapple with complex issues."[28] Problems are sure to arise, though, to the degree that organizations are either unwilling or uninterested in grappling with these complexities.

Beyond all of these issues though, we must ask how child sponsorship fits within the indigenous principles laid out in chapter three, whether or not they are the best means of supporting families, and how they comport with the fundamental notions of best practices in development described in chapter five. From a missional perspective, the question of whether or not child sponsorship "works" cannot be settled simply by pragmatism. For something to "work" as a missions strategy, there must be evidence of both efficacy *and* fidelity to *missio Dei*. This means that even if child sponsorship produces favorable outcomes in the life of children, it may be an activity more suited for NGOs, who have no mandate to plant churches, than it is for denominational missions organizations who have precisely that mandate. This is because any program that is built on ongoing and necessary outside funding cannot possibly contribute to the indigeneity of local churches, given that self-support constitutes one of three foundational indigenous principles. This also means that partnerships between NGOs and missions organizations should be forged in such a way as to not impede the forward momentum of missions.

MISSIONS STRATEGIES FOR CHILDREN AND YOUTH

What does it mean to engage in children's ministry in ways that uphold the indigenous church principles of self-support, propagation, and governance? In this section we will look at three keys necessary to ensure that what we do in compassionate missions regarding children amounts to more than a quick fix. By focusing on three things, contextualization, cooperation, and empowerment, we can not only serve the world's children in ways faithful to the gospel, but we can help ensure that our work will long outlast our presence.

27. Wydick, et al., "Does International Child Sponsorship Work?" 393–436; Wydick, "Want to Change the World: Sponsor a Child," 20–25.

28. Watson and Clarke, "Introduction," 1.

Contextualization

Effective children's ministry requires, as Bryant Myers has observed, that we rethink what it means to contextualize the gospel.[29] Not only do we have to contextualize the gospel itself for children in ways that they can understand and relate to, but our gospel deeds must also be contextualized and relevant to the challenges faced by local people in local communities. Contextualization "means articulating biblical faith using vernacular terms and engaging local issues."[30] Contextualization is crucial to any effective missions strategy whether the focus is establishing Bible schools or responding to the needs of children. Apart from contextualization, the gospel will always be seen as something foreign to the local culture. Plus, without it, missionaries themselves risk operating in an over-under relationship with those they serve. If the gospel is seen as more at home in the missionary's culture than in the local culture, then this often is because we have imposed our own cultural encumbrances upon the gospel. The Bible warns against doing this very thing (Rev 22:18).

Branson, Missouri is a small town in the Ozarks, about forty-five minutes south of Springfield. It is also home to an almost endless run of shows and dinner theaters ranging from kitschy to captivating. Mostly, Branson is pure Americana. Shows regularly feature a rendition of the Star-Spangled Banner and performers often are clad in outfits modeled on Old Glory. For the American Midwest, it all seems quite appropriate. I was dumbstruck, though, when I recently heard that a missionary was quite literally transporting a Branson show to Lomé, Togo in West Africa, in an effort to reach African children—especially those in the 4/14 window. I currently live in Lomé, but have previously lived not far from Branson, in Springfield. I can say with some authority that culturally these two places could not be further apart. Exactly what message are we sending when we present the gospel wrapped not only in a foreign language but also cultural forms that have limited appeal even within the sending culture? In doing so are we not diminishing the culture of those we seek to help and subtly claiming that our cultural norms can tell the gospel story better than theirs? Contextualization requires that we trust the ability of the Holy Spirit to convey biblical truth in culturally relevant ways.

29. Myers, "State of the World's Children," 101.
30. Gener, "Contextualization," 192.

Cooperation

Our efforts in compassion must be cognizant of the needs and cultural practices of those we serve or we will inevitably waste resources, time, and accomplish little of lasting significance. Therefore, closely related to the concept of contextualization is cooperation—or, involving those we would help as equal partners. We cannot engage in compassionate missions in indigenous ways without inviting those we would serve to sit at the table and have an equal voice in developing a response.

Steve Roa tells the story of a short-term missions team that went to Northern Uganda to work with an orphanage. Upon arrival, the team members were appalled to discover that the children were using a hole in the ground for a toilet. But after raising funds and installing modern flush toilets, they discovered that the children refused to sit on them, and instead stood on them. Their rational was that "squatting is much more sanitary than sitting on a seat where everyone else has sat!"[31]

In another example, a child in West Africa received a box of assorted gifts as part of a child sponsorship program. After sending in his picture, the child received an assortment of colored pencils, stickers, and a letter. The child's mother though thought the gifts frivolous and wasteful, asking, "Why should I care about these things? They are of no use to me . . . I need a hoe. That is what I need. I do not need these things. I think I should take my picture back."[32] The point is that what seems fairly normal as a gift for a child in a developed nation may seem wasteful in the eyes of someone living in extreme poverty and struggling for daily survival. Imagine how you would feel as a mother, unsure of where your child's next meal would come from, and having someone give you a "gift" of colorful stickers and pencils. Would you feel valued and empowered by those who claim to want to help? Would you feel that their actions were thoughtful and had your best interests in mind? Would you not resent never being asked what your needs were?

When we presume to know what people need and do not involve them in the process of developing a compassionate response then we diminish their dignity as those created in God's image. If we are not careful, we can also make people strangers to their own culture. Dr. Chun Wai Chan writes of the orphanage he grew up in:

> It was a very regimented and totally insulated environment . . . We were stigmatized . . . and treated like aliens . . . We had gates right in front of the school, with a sign saying 'ORPHANS

31. Steve Roa, "Community Based Care," 21–22.
32. McDonic, "Witnessing, Work and Worship," 74.

HOME.' There was barbed wire—it was more or less like a cor-
rectional institution . . . Each time I returned home, I felt less
and less like I belonged there . . . Little by little, I noticed how
different I was becoming from the rest of my family.[33]

The central problem in all of these examples is that a solution was
imported into a cultural context very different from that of the donor. By
not properly considering these cultural differences, we create the perception
that in order to become a Christian people need to adopt our values and
way of life. What is needed instead is cooperation in which issues are discussed openly and honestly between the missionary and those they serve. It
is incredibly arrogant to think that we can properly assess, much less solve,
the problems faced by children without input from them, their parents, and
their community. As Louis Gosling explains:

> The least powerful, visible and assertive people (women and
> children, for example), should have as much opportunity to be
> involved as those with more confidence and status. Extra effort
> is needed to enable them to become equal parties in the exercise.
> Moreover, a rights-based approach to development requires the
> active, free and meaningful participation of those affected by the
> work. In the case of children, they are considered as active hold-
> ers of human rights which they can exercise in accordance with
> their maturity and experience. This includes the right to express
> their views on decisions that affect them.[34]

Gosling goes on to explain that the benefits of cooperation are numerous.
They include a broader perspective on the relevant issues as more voices offer greater insight. When people have a say in the things that directly affect
their lives, they are far more likely to take ownership. If the project is to be
sustainable, ownership is simply a necessity. Plus, involving local people in developing appropriate responses builds the capacity of local people and moves
beyond the over-under paradigm that has sometimes characterized compassionate missions. When everyone has an equal voice and an equal say, then
no one is in a position to make the other feel subservient or indebted. This is
always a danger in compassionate missions, that through our efforts we would
contribute to feelings of uselessness or dependency among those we are trying
to help.[35] Only by approaching issues related to children in cooperation with
the children and their communities can we avoid this pitfall.

33. Tise, A Book About Children, 45–46; cited in Watson and Clarke, 68.

34. Gosling, Toolkits, 10.

35. Ibid., 11.

Empowerment

The essence of empowerment is realizing that all people have gifts and are deserving of basic dignity and human rights because they are created in the image of God. The overarching issue with responses to the needs of children that are funded entirely (or even mostly) by outsiders and that are designed and run by outsiders is that they do nothing to empower local people. Compassionate missions exists fundamentally for equipping local believers to willingly and joyfully respond to the needs around them (Acts 11:26–29). We once asked a group of Zambians what things missionaries do that annoy them. One responded, "don't treat us like a project." Whenever we engage in compassionate missions in ways that fail to empower people, we become guilty of treating them as projects and not people. Even the word "empowerment" itself can have a paternalistic ring to it, and we must be careful to embody a biblical understanding of our own reality. This means as Paul says, we should "do nothing from selfishness or empty conceit, but with humility of mind regard one another as more important than yourselves" (Phil 2:3 NASB). We are all broken and needy, but we may have access to resources that others lack. Empowerment simply means that we come together as mutually broken people seeking to help each other.

STREET CHILDREN: A CASE STUDY

Imagine that you are living in city in the majority world, and in that city there are large numbers of children living on the streets and begging. Many of them are addicted to drugs, and they range in age from as young as 6 up to age 18. Every day you see these children. They come to your car window when you stop at traffic lights asking for spare change. They are dressed in rags and their eyes are bloodshot from drug use and lack of sleep. You see these children and you imagine how you would feel if your own son or daughter was in their place, sleeping in drainage ditches and rummaging through trash for food. Your heart breaks for them.

By some estimates there are as many as 100 million children around the world who live on the streets.[36] One way of responding to this would be to personally take the children into one's own home, to rescue them directly and become their primary provider. We knew an American medical doctor in Zambia who had done just that, and had taken nearly 30 children off the streets and into her home.

36. UNICEF, "State of the World's Children: 2006."

For missionaries, this may not be the best approach because it falls short in the three key areas—contextualization, cooperation, and empowerment. First, missionaries should focus primarily on planting and strengthening local churches. This requires that we not be the primary agents of compassionate outreach. Second, our first question as missionaries when it comes to helping street children should not be "what can I do?"—but "what can the churches in this area do?" Third, if we are the sole provider then there is little chance that our efforts will last beyond our time in that country. Visas and work permits get cancelled all the time for missionaries.

The following questions are a basic guide for starting an outreach to street kids. These same questions could also be easily applied to any number of projects designed to help needy children in a missions context.

1. *Who else in this city is involved in similar work?* By knocking on a few doors or making a few phone calls, we can usually find other organizations that are addressing the problem. You are probably not the first person to notice the problem and probably not the first person to want to address it. Talk to these organizations. Find out what they are doing that works and what is not working. Does their approach align with the missional approach we have been describing? If so, you may want to explore ways to partner with these organizations.

2. *What are churches doing?* As a missionary, there are presumably churches or at least other believers in the area where you work. Do these churches see this issue as a problem? Do they see it as something they are capable of addressing? Why or why not? These questions should form the fundamental basis for your approach. Your goal, remember, is not to do this alone but to do it in cooperation with others. The first thing you do then may be to hold a meeting with representatives from several of the churches that are in your network. Begin by briefly sharing your burden for street children. Then sit back and listen. As a missionary you will have to resist controlling and directing the conversation. You may even want to have someone from one of the churches lead the discussion, so that you can move into the background. Try not to provide all the answers, but ask probing and thought-provoking questions. Finally, you will want to work through ways to begin including these children in local congregations. The goal should be to not only get them off the streets, but also to get them into the church.

3. *What would an indigenous response look like?* This may first require doing some basic assets identification exercises with these churches. We tend to think of assets primarily in monetary terms, but assets can

be anything from medical professionals within the church, government officials, land, building space, volunteers, knowledge, and even
something as simple as having a burden for this type of work. Begin to
help these local believers to identify what they can do with their own
resources. They will likely need to start small, but remind them that
doing something is better than doing nothing.

4. *What do the children themselves see as their greatest need?* By involving
children in the process we avoid fostering already existing notions of
inferiority and dependence. Start right from the beginning by doing
things that show you value the input and thoughts of those you wish
to help. They too are created in God's image, and have valuable insights
that outsiders are likely to miss.

5. *Are you willing to let go?* If a project is to be truly indigenous, then at
some point the missionary must let go, step back, and allow the project
to develop the way local believers see fit. This will almost certainly
mean that it will look different than the way the missionary envisioned,
and it may take longer for things to happen.

This is not a comprehensive guide but it should at least help you get started.
We recommend that you also refer back to chapter 5 and consider the essential aspects of development when formulating a response to the needs of
children.

CONCLUSION

Few things move us more than the suffering of children. We must be careful
though that our emotions do not cause us to focus on short-term results at
the expense of long-term effectiveness. We must closely guard our mission
as it concerns the local church. As missionaries we simply do not have the
freedom to engage in all manner of activity simply because there is a need.
We should instead remember that the Great Commission in Matt 28:18–20
was first and foremost a commission to make disciples. This does not mean
that we have to choose between serving the needs of children and making
disciples. We can do both. To accomplish that, our first question as missionaries then should be: how do we make disciples who have a burden for
the needs of children in their community? What tools will local believers
need and how can we develop those tools in a non-controlling manner? By
focusing on the needs of children in this way, we help ensure that compassion becomes a fundamental part of the lives of local believers. In doing so,
we exponentially multiply the benefits to children for generations to come.

11

Health Issues and the Church's Response

Karen Herrera and Paula Ireland

National governments and development organizations have long recognized that religious leaders can play a crucial role in community health and development. They are a trusted source of information that can impact the knowledge and behaviors of people in the community. During West Africa's Ebola crisis, it was recognized that mobilizing and equipping pastors was an essential element in containing the epidemic.[1] The following section discusses global health issues in a general way, and provides some guidelines for how local churches can play a role in improving their community's well-being.

Many factors combine together to affect the health of individuals and communities. Whether people are healthy or not is often determined by their circumstances and environment. Some of these elements include:

- Income and social status-higher income and social status are linked to better health. The greater the gap between the richest and poorest people, the greater the differences in health.

- Education—low education levels are linked with poor health, more stress and lower self-confidence.

1. CAFOD, "The Pivotal Role of Faith Leaders in the Ebola Virus Disease Outbreak in West Africa."

- Physical environment—safe water and clean air, healthy workplaces, safe houses, communities and roads all contribute to good health. Employment and working conditions—people in employment are healthier, particularly those who have more control over their working conditions.

- Social support networks—Strong support from families, friends and communities is linked to better health.

- Culture—customs, traditions, and the spiritual beliefs of the family and community all affect health.

- Genetics—inheritance plays a part in determining lifespan, healthiness and the likelihood of developing certain illnesses.

- Personal behavior and coping skills—balanced eating, keeping active, smoking, drinking, and how we deal with life's stresses and challenges all affect health.

- Health services-access and use of services that prevent and treat disease influences health.

A holistic approach to health includes addressing the total person: body, mind and spirit.

This chapter will discuss some of the major health conditions and disabilities that are impacting people in many areas of the world. As previously discussed in this volume, before the church initiates a compassionate outreach an assessment should be done to determine the greatest needs in the community. People in the church and the targeted community need to be involved in all aspects of the planning process.

HIV/AIDS

In many ways today, HIV/AIDS has the same stigmas as leprosy did in the days of the Bible. Leprosy was considered a death sentence. Victims were considered unclean and shunned by their families and communities. Yet Jesus reached out to them, touched them, loved them, and healed them.[2] This is the perfect representation of how the church should respond to "people living with HIV/AIDS" (PLWA).

---

2. See Matthew 8:3.

Facts about HIV/AIDS

The Human Immunodeficiency Virus (HIV) is a tiny germ that causes the disease called the Acquired Immunodeficiency Syndrome (AIDS). HIV is passed from person-to-person by contact with body fluids (sexual secretions, blood, and breast milk) which contain the virus. There is no risk of contracting HIV through casual contact with people who are HIV positive. HIV lives and multiplies in the body for many years before AIDS develops. During this time, the person will appear to be in good health. However, he or she can still pass HIV to another person. There is still no cure for HIV/AIDS. However, researchers have developed antiretroviral therapy (ART) that can suppress the virus to the point where victims can now add years to their lives. Accessing this treatment is crucial for PLWA, as it will greatly improve their quality of life and decrease the transmission of the virus to others. HIV testing is very important so people can learn their status and seek health care as soon as possible. Unfortunately, millions of people are not faithful to their spouses and put themselves at risk just for a moment of pleasure. Christians are called to live by a higher standard. Like Jesus, we must warn those who are putting themselves at risk and have compassion for those who are infected.

Church Response to People with HIV/AIDS

Persons infected with HIV or who have AIDS are in desperate need of physical and spiritual caregivers who can compassionately assist them to live during the process of dying. The church needs to reach out in God's love to provide what the PLWA needs to live life to the fullest. Spiritual and emotional support is critical in every aspect of a church's response. Caregivers should be sensitive to where the person is today, and help the person understand that in the midst of great uncertainties about the future, some things are certain: God's faithfulness and love, and your own constant support and friendship.

Helping people adhere to their ART is also critical to assure the longest life span possible. There are many practical things that church members can do to support PLWA in this process:

- Make daily phone calls and text messages or other reminders to take medicine
- Provide a welcoming place for observed dosing of medicines
- Make home visits to check on PLWA
- Accompany and provide transport to the clinic visits

- Provide food to assure the PLWA is getting the nutrition needed with ART
- Offer emergency financial assistance in time of a life crisis
- Train community outreach workers to identify people who have missed an appointment or become lost to follow up.
- Arrange for shelter if needed
- Provide child care services to allow people to get needed rest and/or make clinic appointments

An excellent resource for churches wishing to engage in ministry to persons with HIV/AIDS is the HIV/AID Initiative developed by Saddleback Church.[3] Another valuable source for training curricula and resources is the Global AIDS Partnership (GAP).[4] This site has tools specifically developed for holistic ministry in an international context.

TUBERCULOSIS

Since the 1980s, the number of cases of tuberculosis has increased dramatically because of the spread of HIV. The risk of developing tuberculosis (TB) is estimated to be between 26 and 31 times greater in people living with HIV than among those without HIV infection.[5] Infection with HIV suppresses the immune system, making it difficult for the body to control TB bacteria. Therefore, communities which are seeing a rise in TB cases need to engage in a concentrated effort to identify people with HIV/AIDS.

Facts about Tuberculosis

Tuberculosis is caused by bacteria that spread from person to person through microscopic droplets released into the air. This can happen when someone with the untreated, active form of tuberculosis coughs, speaks, sneezes, spits, laughs or sings. Although tuberculosis is contagious, it is not easy to catch. You are much more likely to get tuberculosis from someone you live with or work with than from a stranger. Most people with active TB who have had appropriate drug treatment for at least two weeks are no longer contagious. Tuberculosis remains a major killer because of the increase

3. See www.hivaidsinitiative.com.
4. See www.globalaidspartnership.org.
5. World Health Organization, "HIV and Tuberculosis."

in drug-resistant strains of the bacterium. Drug-resistant strains of tuberculosis emerge when an antibiotic fails to kill all of the bacteria it targets. The surviving bacteria become resistant to that particular drug and frequently other antibiotics as well. Some TB bacteria have developed resistance to the most commonly used treatments, such as isoniazid and rifampin.

A healthy immune system (the body's defense against infectious organisms and other invaders) often successfully fights TB bacteria. However, the body is unable to mount an effective defense if the person's resistance is low. Several factors put people at risk for developing TB:

- lack of medical care
- A weakened immune system due to HIV/AIDS, cancer or diabetes
- substance abuse-IV drug use, tobacco or alcohol
- being exposed to TB at home or at work; for example, health care workers, and people living or working in a residential care facility
- poor nutrition and living conditions

Testing is critical for anyone suspected of being infected with TB and all close contacts. A tuberculin skin test determines if a person has been exposed to TB bacteria by detecting antibodies to TB. However, this test can provide false results, for example among people who have received the BCG vaccine and those who had TB in the past but were since successfully treated. Other methods of testing are blood test, sputum culture and chest x-ray.

Church Response to People with Tuberculosis

Even though TB is often found in people with HIV/AIDS, it is important for people to not make wrong assumptions concerning people diagnosed with TB. The church's response should to be similar to that described for HIV/AIDS. The treatment period for TB is several months and people can be very ill during this time—leading to the need for well-coordinated physical and spiritual support.

MALARIA

After decades of research and large-scale interventions, malaria remains one of the leading causes of death in many parts of the world. Most deaths occur among children living in Africa, where a child dies every minute from malaria.[6]

6. World Health Organization, "Malaria Fact Sheet."

Facts about Malaria

Malaria is caused by *Plasmodium* parasites which are spread to people through the bites of infected *Anopheles* mosquitoes, called "malaria vectors," which bite mainly between dusk and dawn. The intensity of transmission depends on factors related to the parasite, the vector, the human host, and the environment. Human immunity is another important factor, especially among adults in areas of moderate or intense transmission conditions. Partial immunity is developed over years of exposure. Although it is not complete protection, it does reduce the risk that malaria infection will cause severe disease. Therefore, most malaria deaths in Africa occur in young children, whereas in places with less transmission and low immunity, all age groups are at risk.

Malaria is an acute febrile illness. In a non-immune individual, symptoms appear seven days or more (usually 10 to 15 days) after the infective mosquito bite. The first symptoms—fever, headache, chills and vomiting—may be mild and difficult to recognize as malaria. If not treated within 24 hours, *P. falciparum* malaria can progress to severe illness often leading to death. Children with severe malaria frequently develop one or more of the following symptoms: severe anemia, respiratory distress in relation to metabolic acidosis, or cerebral malaria. In adults, multi-organ involvement is also frequent. Early diagnosis and treatment of malaria reduces disease and prevents deaths. It also contributes to reducing malaria transmission. The best available treatment, particularly for *P. falciparum* malaria, is artemisinin-based combination therapy (ACT).

Vector control is the main way to reduce malaria transmission at the community level. It is the only intervention that can reduce malaria transmission from very high levels to close to zero. The main ways to reduce or eradicate malaria in a community include:

- For individuals, personal protection against mosquito bites represents the first line of defense for malaria prevention—the use of window screens, insect repellents (such as DEET) and wearing light-colored clothes, long pants, and long-sleeved shirts.

- Long-lasting insecticidal nets (LLINs) are the preferred individual protection and most cost effective means of protection.[7]

- Indoor residual spraying (IRS) with insecticides is a powerful way to rapidly reduce malaria transmission. Its full potential is realized when at least 80 percent of houses in targeted areas are sprayed.

7. UNICEF, "The Global Malaria Burden."

- Mosquitoes require water to breed. It is also very important to remove or poison the breeding grounds of the mosquitoes. Anywhere water stands such as ditches, tire tracks, old tires, rice fields, or latrines are potential breeding grounds.

Church Response to People with Malaria

There are a number of ways that churches can become involved in controlling malaria:

- Assess the malaria problem in the community.
- Find out what services are already being offered, and what is lacking. Initiate a community clean-up day and focus on eliminating areas of stagnant water.
- Organize and provide educational opportunities for malaria prevention, and early treatment intervention. If needed, network with local clinics to assist with the training.
- Participate in the distribution of long-lasting insecticide bed nets.
- Provide practical support for people struggling with malaria, as well as emotional and spiritual support.

MALNUTRITION

Proper nutrition is powerful: people who are well nourished are more likely to be healthy, productive and able to learn. Good nutrition benefits families, their communities and the world as a whole. However, malnutrition is a serious problem throughout the developing world. It is associated with about half of all child deaths worldwide.[8] Malnutrition can be defined as the insufficient, excessive or imbalanced consumption of nutrients. Globally, as well as in developed, industrialized countries, the following groups of people are at highest risk of malnutrition:

- elderly people, especially those who are hospitalized or in long-term institutional care
- individuals who are socially isolated
- people living on low incomes (poor people)

8. UNICEF, "Unlocking Children's Potential."

- women who are pregnant or breastfeeding
- children under 5, especially around the time of weaning
- people recovering from a serious illness or condition

In some developing countries chronic malnutrition is widespread simply because people do not have enough food to eat. Malnutrition in children often starts from birth. The lack of breastfeeding, especially in the majority world, leads to malnutrition in infants and children. In some parts of the world, women have been led to believe that bottle feeding is better for the child. In other cases, women discontinue breastfeeding due to lack of knowledge and support regarding how to breastfeed. Additionally, some mothers lack adequate nutrition to support the production of breast milk.

Many malnourished children suffer lifelong cognitive and physical defects that significantly reduce their earning potential as adults, invariably leaving them in poverty and reducing their capacity to fully contribute to society. These effects in turn contribute to a cycle in which their poverty leads to their own children and grandchildren being malnourished. Malnourished children have lowered resistance to infection; they are more likely to die from common childhood ailments like diarrheal diseases and respiratory infections; and for those who survive, frequent illness saps their nutritional status, locking them into a vicious cycle of recurring sickness.

Church Response to Malnutrition

Churches are extremely important for promoting the moral importance of the issue of hunger and food security. Reducing malnutrition in a community requires a long-term, comprehensive plan to improve the general health in the community and reduce childhood mortality. The church can provide a starting point to initiate the plan by:

- assessing the current malnutrition problem in the community
- identifying assets in the community that are not being utilized appropriately
- determining what is currently being done by other groups—where are the gaps?
- establishing a working relationship with other groups and determine how the church can be involved

- offering educational programs on topics such as the importance of breast feeding, basic nutritional needs, food preparation and storage, gardening, etc.

- providing information and opportunities to utilize appropriate technology to increase food production in the community (for example, a community vegetable garden)[9]

DIARRHEA

Diarrheal disease is the second leading cause of death in children under five years old, and is responsible for killing around 760,000 children every year.[10] Diarrhea (passage of three or more loose or liquid stools per day) that lasts for several days can leave the body without the water and salts that are necessary for survival. Most people who die from diarrhea actually die from severe dehydration and fluid loss. Children who are malnourished or have impaired immunity as well as people living with HIV are most at risk of life-threatening diarrhea.

Diarrhea is usually a symptom of an infection caused by bacterial, viral or parasitic organisms in the intestinal tract. Infection is spread through contaminated food or drinking-water, or from person-to-person as a result of poor hygiene. Each episode of diarrhea deprives the child of the nutrition necessary for growth. As a result, diarrhea is a major cause of malnutrition, and malnourished children are more likely to experience diarrhea. Dehydration is the most severe threat because during a diarrheal episode water and electrolytes are lost. When the water and electrolytes are not replaced, then death can occur.

Church Response to Diarrheal Disease

Both treatment and prevention are vital responses to diarrheal disease. Churches can take a lead especially if there is a community-wide problem. Educational programs that raise awareness and provide training in treatment and prevention are extremely valuable.

Treatment must focus on rehydration (replacement of water and electrolytes) with oral rehydration solution (ORS). In many countries, ORS can

9. Sustain Hope is a Christian missions organization that promotes tools and training for community development. See their resources on gardening at sustainhope.org/resources/gardening.

10. World Health Organization, "Diarrheal Disease Fact Sheet."

be purchased from local pharmacies. People can also be taught how to make ORS at home using clean water (1 liter or 5 cups), salt (1/2 level teaspoon) and sugar (6 level teaspoon).[11] It costs only a few cents per treatment. ORS is absorbed in the small intestine and replaces the water and electrolytes lost in the feces. Emphasizing the need for nutrient-rich foods is very important to break the vicious circle of malnutrition and diarrhea by continuing to give nutrient-rich foods—including breast milk—during an episode of diarrhea, and afterwards when the person is well. This is especially important for children. When diarrhea is a reoccurring problem in a community, prevention has to be a community-wide project that includes:

- Exploring water sources and determining if the water is safe to drink
- Locating water sources away from livestock or garbage pits
- Improving sanitation in homes and community
- Providing health education on how the infection is spread.

People can take responsibility for their personal and family health through:

- Frequent hand washing with soap
- Exclusive breastfeeding for the first six months of life
- Good personal hygiene
- Safe preparation and storage of food

Community Health Evangelism, as discussed in previous chapters, provides an excellent framework for churches wishing to engage in addressing health issues in their community. The training material include thousands of lesson plans written by qualified personnel in various disciplines, updated regularly and shared within the network of participants.[12]

DISABILITIES

> *"Go out quickly into the streets and alleys of the town and bring in the poor, the crippled, the blind and the lame . . . and compel them to come in, so that my house will be full"*
> *(Luke 14:21,23)*

11. Rehydration Project, "Oral Rehydration Solutions: Made at Home."
12. See the Global CHE Network.

Current research indicates that over a billion people, or approximately 15 percent of the world's population, live with some type of disability.[13] That figure rises sharply when the focus is narrowed to people living in poverty—almost one in five persons. Tragically, there exists a strong and complex link between disability and poverty in that they reinforce and perpetuate each other. People living in poverty are more at risk than others of acquiring a disability, and people with disabilities are among the poorest of the poor. They are, according to disability organization *Joni and Friends*, "the highest proportion of the world's disadvantaged population."[14] Consider the following realities pertaining to children living with disabilities around the world, as documented by UNICEF:

- Out of 100 million children with disabilities under 5 years of age worldwide, 80 percent live in developing countries.

- Only 5 percent of children with disabilities worldwide finish primary school.

- 250,000 to 500,000 children become blind every year from consequences of Vitamin A deficiency, mostly in Africa and South Asia.

- Afghanistan alone has over a million children who have been disabled as a result of years of armed conflict.

- Compared to other children, children with disabilities have a 3 to 4 times greater likelihood of experiencing physical and sexual violence and neglect.

This is just a glimpse into the dark reality that colors the lives of many people living with disabilities around the world. The document summarizes: "Children with disabilities experience discrimination and social exclusion in every aspect of their lives . . . a consequence of the combined impact of rejection of difference, poverty, social isolation, prejudice, ignorance and lack of services and support."[15]

The Social Factor

The term *disability* generally refers to physical, cognitive, developmental or emotional impairments that limit a person's ability to participate in normal, everyday activities. Perhaps even more disabling, however, is the

---

13. World Health Organization, "World Report on Disability," 8.

14. Rene, *BASICS: Fundamentals of Disability Ministry.*

15. UNICEF, "Children and Young People with Disabilities Fact Sheet."

response of communities and society as a whole. Disability activist and educator Michael Oliver argues: "In our view, it is society which disables physically impaired people. Disability is something imposed on top of our impairments by the way we are unnecessarily isolated and excluded from full participation in society."[16] Though their experiences and conditions are diverse and unique, people with disabilities often share in "a profound sense of devaluation and wounding."[17] Jeff and Kathi McNair explore multiple "wounds of disability" in an article published by the Christian Institute on Disability. Beyond the actual physical or mental impairment and resulting limitations, deep, invisible wounds can exist:

- being relegated by society into a low social status
- experiencing rejection in almost every social context
- considered and treated as "less than fully human"
- being blamed for their own or other's hardships
- an absence of natural, authentic relationships
- a loss of personal autonomy
- "having one's life wasted"—that is, being deprived of the opportunity to discover one's potential and purpose in life[18]

These wounds can result in deep insecurity, behavioral issues, and desperation. How can we, as "ministers of reconciliation," be oblivious to such woundedness? [19]

Much of the suffering experienced by persons living with disabilities flows from social stigmas, religious beliefs, and cultural traditions that link disability to punishment for wrong-doing, evil spirits or other spiritual causes. This is especially true of mental disabilities, which are often a source of great shame for the family. Consequently, people with special needs are often hidden, prisoners in their own homes, further compounding the challenges faced by them and their caregivers. Ignorance about physical and mental impairments further compound the dilemmas faced by people with disabilities. For example, in some contexts it is believed that persons with learning or cognitive disabilities are "contagious," thus increasing their isolation. Hissa Al-Thani, former UN Special Rapporteur on Disability, describes another example of culturally-based stigma. She notes that women

---

16. McNair, "Disability and Human Supports."

17. Tada and Bundy, *Beyond Suffering Study Guide*, 30.

18. McNair and McNair, "Wolfenberger's 18 Wounds of Disability," Module 1.

19. 2 Cor 5:18–21.

with disabilities suffer double discrimination owing to their gender as well as their disability. Women with disabilities in Arab regions, she observes, suffer triple discrimination. Considered unmarriageable, these women are cut off not only from men but also from other women, in a culture where marriage and motherhood are paramount.[20] Generally speaking, in much of the majority world, people with disabilities are hidden in homes or visible mostly on street corners, are treated as objects of "charity" and tossed a few loose coins.

Overcoming Barriers

Many churches fail to engage in disability ministry because they have not recognized the genuine need. Others have seen the need, but believe this type of ministry is too complex, and is somehow beyond their capacity. Fear is at the root of many barriers. What should we say . . . or not say? What if we do the wrong thing? We feel awkward and uncomfortable, and are afraid of being confronted with challenges that we are not prepared to handle. Addressing these barriers may not be easy, but the starting point is simple—building relationships, and beginning to identify with men, women, and children who have disabilities. Kim Kargbo directs Women of Hope International, serving women with disabilities in West Africa. Visitors who want to assist with this ministry must first spend an entire day in the home of a disabled woman, witnessing firsthand the challenges she faces, and becoming acquainted with her as an individual with unique gifts and abilities.[21] Without a foundation of personal relationship, "ministry" will never be genuine or fruitful.

Another barrier is the often unconscious perception that people with disabilities are not acceptable as they are. Somehow, it is thought, this person needs to be fixed, in order to find a place of acceptance in our community. Steve Bundy, who serves as the Vice President of Joni and Friends, shares a deeply personal experience concerning his son, born with serious physical and cognitive disabilities.[22] One night as he cried out to God for his son's healing, the Lord gently spoke to him, "Son, aren't you glad that I didn't require you to be fixed before I accepted you?" That evening, says Steve, he came to realize his own brokenness, and recognized that *he* was the one in need of healing. Likewise, the Holy Spirit must enable us to see beyond physical or mental brokenness, and see a person made in the image of God,

20. Al-Thani. "Disability in the Arab Region: Current Situation and Prospects."
21. Kim Kargbo, email message to author, April 16, 2016.
22. Bundy, "Does My Child Need to be Healed?" Module 2.

treasured by God, and worthy of unconditional love and acceptance, *just as they are.*

Not only must people with disabilities be seen as whole persons, capable of having a personal relationship with Christ, but also as essential co-laborers in mission. A friend told me about a recent conversation with a pastor in India. The pastor had never considered that disabled people should become disciples who make disciples and was both intrigued and confounded by the idea. Missionaries and Christian workers often have this same blind spot: we are eager to lead disabled people to Christ, but slow to equip and integrate them into a place of service in the body of Christ. We fail to see their full potential, to recognize their spiritual gifts, and to empower them to engage in and not merely receive ministry.

Again, we realize that the bigger issue is not the physical or mental impairments, but the *restrictions* which hold people back from what they desire to do and be. This is an essential change in focus. Our aim is no longer "fixing" people, but rather helping them overcome these restrictions. While physical barriers such as narrow doorways and stairs and lack of adaptive equipment may be realities that need to be addressed, the more restrictive barriers are the invisible ones. When and if misperceptions, attitudes and cultural biases are addressed, people with disabilities can experience unprecedented opportunities and freedom. What better context for this to take place than the church?

Disabled People and the Gospel

Studies show that disabled persons are much less likely to attend religious services due to both physical and social barriers. According to a special paper presented to Lausanne Committee for World Evangelization, the global community of people with disabilities comprise one of the largest under-reached, and hidden, people groups on the planet. The article estimates that only 5 to 10 percent of this global community has been reached with the gospel.[23] Door International, an organization that ministers to the deaf community, estimates that less than 2 percent of the world's 70 million deaf people are believers.[24] While statistics are often unreliable and never disclose the full picture, one thing is certain—millions of people living with disabilities have never heard the gospel, and are far less likely to be reached by traditional approaches. The barriers are too high and too deep, and must

23. Tada and Oppenhuizen, "Hidden and Forgotten People: Ministry Among People with Disabilities."

24. Door International.

be intentionally bridged. In a familiar story in Mark 2, a handful of men went to significant effort to bring their paralyzed friend to Jesus, overcoming no small challenges and barriers. Jesus was deeply touched by their faith, and healed the paralyzed man's body and soul. This story most assuredly impacts and influences the Church. Followers of Jesus should still be committed to overcoming barriers and bringing people to Jesus, the sole source of abundant life.

PRINCIPLES FOR EFFECTIVE MINISTRY TO PEOPLE WITH DISABILITY

Ownership and Participation by the Church

In the world of community development, there exist diverse players and modes of engagement: non-government organizations, faith-based organizations, para-church organizations, community-based organizations and associations, etc. Each have their advantages and disadvantages and different roles to play. While many of the principles may apply in other contexts, our discussion will focus on ministries that flow out of a local church or body of believers. In her book *From the Roots Up,* JoAnn Butrin makes a strong case for why the church should be the source and center for all compassionate outreach. In short, *the church is present*—it is permanent, physical, tangible, and often connected to a larger network of churches in urban and rural areas. *The church understands the context,* much more deeply than outsiders possibly can. Cultural issues are *their* reality. Further, *the church has influence.* The church is an insider, having a degree of authority and respect within the community that is vital to creating an atmosphere for change. Most of all, the church is God's chosen means of bringing His life-transforming power to bear on a lost world.[25]

Throughout this volume we have strongly emphasized the essential nature of community participation and ownership for any effective development initiative. For disability ministry, the "community" that must own the process is twofold—the church, as well as the ones affected by disability. The local church, first of all, must grow into a vision and capacity for ministry that is inclusive and that values the vulnerable. They must come to recognize that opening their doors and hearts to people with special needs is not some exceptional ministry, but rather something that should be normative, and characteristic of God's people. Growing in this area of ministry will

---

25. Butrin. *From the Roots Up,* 50–52.

require exploring and sharing God's heart for this vulnerable population through preaching, teaching, and relationship-building.

Several passage from the Bible are especially relevant to this topic:

- Gen 1:26: Everyone, including those with disabilities, are created in the image of God

- Ps 139:13, Exod 4:11: People with disabilities are created by God and have purpose

- John 9:1–5: Disabilities are not the result of personal sin

- 1 Cor 12:22–23: Those that "seem to be weaker are *indispensable*" and worthy of "special honor"

- 2 Cor 12:7–9: God's strength is perfected in human weakness

In fact, a careful study of the Old and New Testaments will reveal that God has much to say about disability.[26] Through a process of awareness-raising, training and modeling, church leaders and members must take the lead role in planning, carrying out, and evaluating their ministry efforts. The process will require prayerfulness and patience.

Ownership and Participation by People with Disabilities

A second level of ownership also applies: the very population that we desire to serve. People with disabilities must themselves play a key role in the development of any ministry that relates to them. Ministry should not be done *for* disabled persons, but *with* and *alongside* them. Whether or not individuals choose to be directly involved, their voices should be heard and valued. The most effective disability ministries will be led by people coming from within this community.

Genuinely Holistic Ministry

Holistic ministry has been emphasized throughout this book, but is worth revisiting in this context. Genuine holistic ministry goes far beyond just making sure there is a spiritual component, and a social component, and a physical component. It involves realizing the complexities that exist within and between people and God and society; it involves opening the door for the Holy Spirit to touch people in every part of their being. This is the basis of *shalom*—the wholeness that results from living in harmony with oneself,

---

26. For a good overview of this topic see Deuel, "Disability and the Kingdom of God."

with others, with God and with our environment. In *Walking with the Poor*, Bryant Myers discusses "poverty of being," noting that "a lifetime of exclusion, deception and exclusion is internalized by the poor" and results in them "believing that they are and will always be without value and without gifts."[27] Shattered relationships exist on every level, compounding the burden. This is the context for the holistic ministry that is so vitally necessary for transformed lives.

Reflecting on her own ministry experience, Kim Kargbo observes that "when people have been told their whole lives that they are worthless and half-human and cursed, no measure of economic aid, even from a sustainable perspective, is going to work for them, as they do not believe they have the capacity to succeed."[28] They may benefit from the provision of a wheelchair and vocational skills training, but they need to be touched at a much deeper level. They need to become disciples of Jesus, and specifically, be helped to see their profound value to God as persons made in the very image of God. Their whole identity needs to be transformed from the perception of being *no one*, having *nothing*, to treasured children of God, invested with gifts to share. The shift could not be more radical. Genuinely holistic ministry requires that we begin with, and continue to be, gospel-centered and not needs-driven. Massive and overwhelming needs exist on every side, far more than we are even aware. We are called, however, to make disciples, not just to meet needs. Staying true to this focus will require prayerfulness and wisdom, and will result in greater outcomes than one can imagine.

Earning Trust through Partnership and Perseverance

Those that have worked successfully in cross-cultural disability ministries insist that effectiveness requires great perseverance and a commitment to long-term engagement. Issues are complex, and are not going to change overnight. Working in Togo, we have repeatedly heard this sad testimony from village pastors: outside organizations come and go, often leaving behind broken promises and unfinished projects. That is why church-based initiatives are so vital. Trust is not easily won among those who have been repeatedly abused and disappointed. Trust is precious, and costly. It is only built over time, as genuine concern and reliability are demonstrated and proven. This kind of trust is best cultivated in the process of engaging in ministry together. That is, it flourishes in the context of true partnership, as we work *with*, and not *for*, people with disabilities.

27. Myers, *Walking with the Poor*, 76.

28. Kim Kargbo, email message to author, April 16, 2016.

Assessment

Assessment of needs and assets has been discussed in chapter 5. It bears re-
peating that this is an essential step for disability ministry as well. It should
start from the inside, within the local church. What barriers exist (visible
and invisible)? Who are the people with disabilities who attend, or who used
to attend, or who live in the neighborhood, or who are related to church
members? What are their ideas for reaching out to people with disabilities?
Concerning assets, are there people who already have an interest or burden
for this community? Who do we know that has professional skills or first-
hand experience working in this domain? Looking beyond the church, what
organizations or associations exist in the immediate or larger community
for people with disabilities? What support services are available pertaining
to health, education, vocational training, etc.? While one may not work directly with these organizations/services, it is important to be aware of them
for possible networking and referral.

Training

Any ministry involved in transformational development must have a strong
training component. Training must be uniquely focused for every level of
engagement, including pastors and church leaders, the hands-on volunteers,
and the members of the group needing aid. Training must be practical,
action-oriented, and transferrable so that it can multiply to other churches
and communities. An important starting point for disability ministry is an
awareness seminar to elicit the support and input of leaders such as pastors,
church leaders, and missionaries. After that, a more general training for the
entire congregation should be offered, to help them feel more prepared and
comfortable with entering into this new area of ministry. More extensive
training will be needed by the volunteers who will be actively engaged, with
the content obviously determined by the nature of the outreach.

Starting Small

As with any development ministry, disability ministry should start small.
For example, before planning a community outreach, a church should begin
by addressing needs within their own congregation. With time, the work
can grow into something larger and more encompassing. An excellent starting point is a uniquely designed "seed project." A seed project is a small
scale project that can be done within a few days and uses local resources.

It provides the church with the opportunity to meet a practical need and demonstrate Christ's compassion in the community. In this case, it would most likely focus on needs related to disability. Some examples include:

- hosting a sports/recreation day for youth or children with disabilities
- a VBS for children with disabilities
- a mother's day out for mothers of children with special needs
- a Luke 14 banquet—a special meal and program designed especially for people with disabilities
- constructing a wheelchair ramp in a public place in need of greater accessibility
- a training seminar on an issue pertinent to people with disabilities

All of these ideas and more are described in greater detail in the document created by the Lausanne Issue Group on Disability Ministry.[29] Seed Projects gain visibility, demonstrate compassion, and help build bridges with the community. They also help churches gain experience and confidence in new areas of ministry, and serve as a good entry-point for further ministry.

What Every Church Can Do

Empowering local churches for valuing and integrating persons with disabilities into their fellowships is the essential first step in any transformational ministry to persons with disabilities. At whatever level one chooses to engage, and whatever special population one chooses to serve, churches must be prepared to receive persons with disabilities into a place of fellowship, discipleship, and ministry. Attitudes and cultural biases will have to be addressed, especially concerning persons with cognitive disabilities.

Many excellent resources exist for discipling both children and adults with intellectual disabilities. In the words of one special educator who works with Joni and Friends, "Since spiritual truths are spiritually—not intellectually—discerned, these students have the same potential for spiritual growth as other church members. Spiritual maturity may look different . . . but it is just as real."[30] Should people with special needs be separated into a special classroom or included with everyone else? Cultural issues and context will color the way churches choose to respond. Whatever the starting point, the

---

29. Tada and Oppenhuizen, "Hidden and Forgotten People."
30. Tada and Bundy, *Beyond Suffering*, 191.

goal must be clear—not mere *presence*, but full *integration* into the life of the church. As people with disabilities begin to find their place in the church, their very presence sends a loud message to the larger community: that they are both *valued* and *valuable*. It is only when they are *present* in the church that relationships with them can begin to grow and barriers can begin to crumble. Until the church recognizes people with disabilities as being *gifts* to the Body, and not burdens, or objects of ministry, the ministry is not yet mature. We are called to live and experience genuine relationships and community. Churches are strengthened and enriched as they experience God's grace flowing through a Body composed of diverse and special parts, each using their gifts to serve one another.

More Specialized Ministries

The possibilities for church-based disability ministry are as limitless as the churches they represent. These ministries do not necessarily require a lot of special training or finance. They do require patience, commitment, and love. A friend of mine hosts a support group for mothers of children with disabilities. The group meets one Saturday morning a month. There are no special facilities or equipment, just a spacious room with some simple children's toys. Moms sit on the floor, relieved to be surrounded by other moms that understand them, in a context where their children are no longer "different." For some parents, it has provided their first occasion to learn how to play with their children, and to just enjoy being with them. After a time of fellowship and play, there is worship, prayer, and teaching from the Bible. Sometimes a short teaching on a health topic is offered, if requested by the moms. Sometimes special guests visit the group and offer specialized training, like how to make adaptive equipment, or how to do appropriate exercises and activities that could help prepare some children for walking. But most often, it is a just a time and place of encouragement, acceptance and love. My friend has seen lives and families changed by Jesus' love working through this special group.

Community Health Evangelism (CHE) has developed training materials that focus specially on issues pertinent to persons with disability. Some CHE programs have chosen to reach out specifically to persons with disabilities, and have witnessed firsthand how Christ-centered compassion and development training can transform lives. Women of Hope International has used and adapted CHE materials and strategies for working with disabled women in Sierra Leone. Disabled women are not merely the focus of ministry, but are themselves the core of this ministry, serving as the trainers, the managers, and the community health evangelists—now empowered, now reaching out to others.

The story of Pastor Georgian Ugah is an example of how disability ministry can expand to a national church level. Both Georgian and her husband are ordained ministers with the Assemblies of God of Nigeria, central Africa. Nigeria is Africa's most populated nation and home to an estimated one million deaf people. During her studies at Bible school, Georgian felt God calling her to minister to the deaf. She learned sign language and began working as an educator and deaf advocate in a high school for the deaf. As her heart and capacity for this ministry became evident, the general superintendent of the Assemblies of God asked her to lead the national church's initiative in compassionate ministry. Over the past fifteen years, the fruit of this ministry has grown to include the planting of twenty-five Deaf Culture Fellowships, a Bible School for the deaf, a special needs school which includes vocational training and rehabilitative services, as well as specialized ministries for other vulnerable populations. Tens of thousands of lives have been deeply touched by the mercy of Jesus.

Reaching out to persons affected by disability may not be as complicated as one may think. Ministries of compassion have a way of evolving as we respond to opportunities the Lord sets before us. Rather than trying to devise complex projects and programs, we begin by investing in relationships with people who are so often overlooked, wounded, and alone. We trust God to demonstrate His mercy and transforming power to us, in us, through us. As a result, no one, most of all ourselves, will be the same.

12

Natural Disasters and the Church's Response

JEFFREY HARTENSVELD

WE LIVE IN AN increasingly unpredictable world. According to a study published in *The New England Journal of Medicine* on the impact of natural disasters and armed conflict on human health, the scale and scope of natural disasters have increased markedly since the 1990s.[1] This increase, coupled with a rising global population, means greater numbers of people are being affected by natural disasters, as illustrated in the following graph:[2]

---

1. Leaning and Guha-Sapir, "Natural Disasters, Armed Conflict, and Public Health."
2. *EM-DAT: The National Disaster Database.*

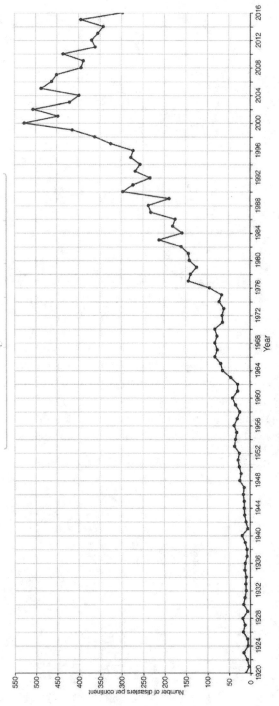

EM-DAT: The OFDA/CRED International Disaster Database - www.emdat.be - Université Catholique de Louvain, Brussels - Belgium

If volunteers plan to be a global Christian worker for any length of time, chances are they will live through some type of disaster. Obviously, the longer the tenure in country, the greater the chance of experiencing a disaster in the host country. Volunteers also have a greater chance of being in the right place at the right time in order to demonstrate the love of God to those who suffer.

December 26, 2004 changed our lives and ministry forever. On that fateful day the nation where we were living, Indonesia, experienced its worst natural disaster to date. An oceanic earthquake off the northwest coast of the island of Sumatra, registering at least 9.1 on the Richter scale, created a devastatingly large tsunami, killing an estimated 170,000 people in Indonesia alone. This all took place in a few hours. As I watched events unfold on television, I began to realize that possibly the worst natural disaster in human history was happening right before my eyes and that God had strategically placed us there "for such a time as this."

Prior to this particular disaster, we had done relief work and community development following the social and religious unrest and economic fallout of the Asian monetary crisis in the late nineties. Yet nothing prepared us for the scale of natural disaster the nation now faced. Our initial reaction was a desire to contribute to relief efforts, so within a week we were on the ground in Banda Aceh, the capital of Aceh province in Indonesia, ready to give away a twenty-foot container of food, and assess further needs. Aceh province had been closed to all foreigners, and no outside humanitarian organization, religious or nonreligious, had any work stationed there. Therefore, we had an opportunity not only to help, but also to share our faith through compassionate acts and personal prayer for people who had experienced tragedy and devastation beyond imagination.

Because of my fluency in the Bahasa Indonesia language, the U.S. Navy aircraft carrier, USS Abraham Lincoln, which was operating off the shores of West Sumatra, asked me to be a translator for their helicopter missions that were delivering food and bringing back severely injured people to the capital. Imagine, every time I went to a town or village and stepped off that helicopter, I was quite possibly the first Christian ever to set foot in those places. For Christians working in some of the most difficult places around the world, disasters will present unprecedented opportunities to share your faith with people who have never heard the good news of Christ. Many people were not only wanting, but begging for prayer and any help we could offer. We certainly do not hope for natural disasters to strike, but we know we live in a world where human tragedy and its effects surround us, and we need to be salt and light at all times.

After our initial food distribution and translation assistance, we realized we would be helping with disaster relief for the long haul. We settled on working in a town outside the capital, away from the majority of relief agencies. Aid agencies from around the world descended on Aceh province. Even in our small setting, over four hundred relief agencies initially registered with the local government to do some form of relief. By September 2005, because of the town's unique and difficult situation, we remained one of over forty agencies still operating in that part of the province. Some agencies finished what they came to do and left, others departed after finding conditions too difficult. Others like us stayed, focusing on long-term relief goals that can take years to achieve after a major disaster. We appreciated those who came short-term, but we were serving our home country and were committed to staying.

No one is as valuable in disaster recovery as someone who speaks the local language, has local or provincial contacts, understands the cultural and religious landscape, and most importantly, is considered trustworthy. Unfortunately, scores of local opportunists show up after a disaster, trying to take advantage of unknowing foreign relief agencies. Sometimes people's naiveté surprised me; I could tell too many stories about well-meaning agencies that showed up with nothing more than a stack of $100 bills and left with nothing to show for it.

This section will discuss some key elements of disaster relief that will help a global worker. If the disaster is large-scale and internationally known, you will probably interact with major aid agencies that may want to partner with and resource you. However, even after a smaller-scale disaster, you can still find ways to participate in relief work and contribute to the recovery effort.

BEING PREPARED

The worst time to plan for a disaster is in the midst of it. Depending on location, preparedness will look different. One need not prepare for a flood in the Sahara or a volcanic eruption in the United States Midwest.

Preparation begins with getting other interested helpers together and talking about "what-ifs." The group should discuss what disasters could potentially happen in the area. List them, and then focus on the most-probable three for this part of the world. Next, discuss the relationship assets in the community and how those could be leveraged for help in relief efforts. For example, several in our group had strong ties to the government plus access to and knowledge of transportation. Some knew how to purchase large amounts of essentials rapidly and at low cost. These people were on call so at a moment's notice they could mobilize, because, when it comes to disaster relief, time is of the essence.

Search and Rescue

Search and rescue is a specialized skill that should be left to professionals during disaster relief. However, a global worker could still be in a situation where one is the only person available to rescue people, so prepare ahead of time for the unlikely event that this involves a search-and-rescue effort. First, keep basic tools on hand such as pry bars, sledgehammers, shovels, wheelbarrows, or other tools that could help remove rubble to reach someone who is stuck. Second, become certified in basic first aid, which can help rescued people plus team members who need simple, immediate care, such as for a cut or wound; people needing serious medical attention will, of course, require professional medical help.

Food and Water

Disasters often leave people without the means to provide food and water for themselves and their families. The West has a well-developed economic system plus aid agencies that can get food distributed quickly, but people in the developing world already live day-to-day. A natural disaster that wipes out crops, livestock, and the means to buy food can immediately devastate an already at-risk population. Therefore, consider these points about food and water.

First, when a local church is present, that should be the primary distribution point. Second, the type of food distributed should be simple to prepare and eat. Try not to hand out foods that requires cooking, because the disaster may have wiped out the community's means of doing so. Third, make sure the food is not religiously or palatably offensive to the people of that culture. For example, after the tsunami an aid agency sent a container of canned pork meat to a nation with an almost purely Muslim population. That effort was not well-received. Finally, pay attention to water. Wells and water supplies can become more tainted than they were pre-disaster, not to mention that people may have lost the means to boil water. Setting up water filtration or providing families with a pan and small Sterno stove may save lives, especially the most vulnerable, namely the children and the elderly.

The importance of using the local church as a starting point for relief work is illustrated by a story about the 2009 Padang earthquake. In September

2009 the city of Padang, Indonesia, was rocked with an earthquake that dev-astated much of the city, knocking down buildings and houses and killing hundreds of people. We arrived about three days after the earthquake and went immediately to the one local church we were associated with in the city. Roughly a third of the church building was destroyed or falling over. While we came with about $10,000 in cash, we were also armed with linguistic knowledge and cultural understanding, plus we had brought a local Chinese businessman who commanded the marketplace wherever he went.

A quick meeting was set up with the pastor and church leadership, and we established two important facts: (1) The congregation's members were well and their homes intact, but many of their neighbors' homes were devas-tated, and (2) this was a heavily persecuted church. I had noticed some front windows were destroyed and boarded up; the pastor explained they were broken by large rocks thrown at them during Sunday worship, not from the earthquake. Not only that, but the church's ten cell groups, or house churches, were persecuted so intensely that, while they were permitted to meet, they were not allowed to sing or pray out loud in their homes.

The relief plan here was easy to see. We would assemble two thou-sand relief packets valued at $5 each and use the ten cell groups as distri-bution points to the two hundred destroyed homes in the area. The team also promised to help remove a destroyed wall and rebuild, doubling the church's seating capacity to accommodate all the new people who would be coming. As a result of these relief efforts, the church doubled in attendance and received enormous favor in the community. The church also became a tremendous resource during later relief efforts, when other disasters hap-pened in that area.

Shelter and Comfort

Along with basic food and water, getting people out of the elements is criti-cal. Situations can vary greatly, however. Many will not leave their property because they are afraid of losing their few valuables buried in the rubble, or they fear losing their stake to their small piece of property to a squatter. Others leave out of fear—as was the case with the tsunami, people were afraid to be within a kilometer of the ocean.

When whole communities are devastated, refugee camps often form as people gravitate to temporary shelters that have been set up. Creating these camps is usually the responsibility of the local government or military, and it is best to steer clear of forming them. Instead, focus on the needs of those living in them.

For those who are trying to stay close to their devastated homes rather than join a refugee camp, help can come in the form of distributing tents or tarps and poles from local materials (which can at times be salvaged from the wreckage of previously existing structures), plus rope so people can tie up their tarps. Comforts such as blankets, flashlights, plastic dishes, bug repellent, and other items people request can make a huge difference for someone living outside and exposed to the elements.

Rubble and Debris Removal

Disasters generally leave one big mess in their wake. Buildings have either completely or partially collapsed, and before people can rebuild, they need to clean things up. This is where longer-term disaster relief really takes place.

Imagine taking a few days to help someone take care of clearing away debris so they can rebuild. The impact on those people's lives is many times more significant than the short-term relief of one meal. Helping clear rubble offers the opportunity to spend a few days with a specific family or families, and serious conversations can start happening. Also, it is not terribly specialized work; no construction skills are needed to haul away rubble, so this type of relief is open to unskilled helping hands. A word of caution is in order though: partially broken-down structures can be unstable, so be careful. If a building has been flattened, it is probably okay to move pieces of it.

Two other practical ways to provide aid include the gifting of tool kits and the recycling of building materials. Following the 2004 tsunami, Aceh province initially banned rebuilding within half a kilometer of the beach. However, the local government was unable to enforce this with people who had lost their family and literally all their material possessions in these locations.

One afternoon after a long day of visiting refugee camps, I was in the deserted beach area trying to catch a moment of peace, and I saw a man foraging through the rubble and occasionally sitting by himself. I approached him and saw he had obviously been working on what remained of a dwelling, using a rock to try and dislodge nails from the boards. He was also holding and petting a cat. He told me his name was Biduan[3] and that cat was all that remained of his family. I reminded him that the government said he could not build there, and without looking up, he said, "My wife and daughter died here. I'm never leaving here, no matter what."

That night I went to the hardware store and bought him a whole set of carpenter's tools. Eventually the government lifted the ban, and Biduan was

---

3. Not his real name.

the first to rebuild in that area. We supplied him with more tools and materials. This was only one of many heartbreaking stories from this disaster, but this encounter prompted me to keep carpentry and masonry tool kits in our pickup so we could give them out whenever we saw someone in need.

Sometimes it is necessary to recycle destroyed homes and reuse the materials. In the 2010 tsunami that destroyed much of the Mentawai Islands, the islands were so remote and logistically hard to reach that our team spent a week in the jungle specifically looking for wood planks, roofing, doors, windows, and door frames—remnants of the village that had been swept away. This was cleanup and rebuilding at its most extreme.

Health

Depending on the situation, health care can play a key role in the disaster relief process. Something amazing happens when someone who is injured receives care. People are so grateful. Medical professionals who bind up broken bodies can seem like angels to those hurting people.

Before employing health care in disaster relief, consider two possible approaches: (1) hosting a foreign team, or (2) contacting and utilizing a local team. There are distinct advantages and disadvantages to each. A local team can usually get to a disaster area more quickly and may be familiar with what medicines are available. On the other hand, a foreign team may offer more advanced medical practice, be able to diagnose and handle extreme medical emergencies, and exhibit a dedication to their craft and a passion to work in a disaster situation that are unmatched. The disadvantages are that foreign medical teams are challenging to figure out legally, may need translators, and may be unused to working in less-developed and unsterile locations.

CONCLUSION

As a Christian worker, no matter where you live, you will probably experience disaster on some level and at some time. You cannot singlehandedly help everyone affected by the disaster, but figure out where your gifts and talents might work best and fill that niche. After the Indonesian tsunami I learned that I could not compete with USAID when it came to food distribution to refugee centers, but I could utilize my own skills to help people during the crisis. Do not let your relief efforts be driven by others who do not consider your skill set or the needs of the people, even if they have a great idea and money to fund it.

Most importantly, ask communities what they need. Amazingly, many agencies do not. If you are going to give out food, first ask what the people eat. If you are going to give out shoes, find out what sizes people wear—or if they wear shoes at all. By simply asking, you show compassion for them as people, which is a type of personalized caring many lack after enduring devastating losses from a disaster.

If a disaster occurs while you are serving somewhere around the globe, remember that the Lord has placed you there "for such a time as this." Disasters present an opportunity to show the love of Christ in both practical and spiritual ways as we help people and bear witness to the love of Christ.

13

The Local Church and Faith-Based Organizations

Jason Paltzer

THE LOCAL CHURCH AND its members in resource-limited countries may interact with faith-based as well as secular non-profit, non-governmental organizations. This chapter will focus specifically on faith-based, non-profit organizations and assume there is alignment and understanding about the motivation and theological understanding of compassion described in chapters 1 and 2. Christian faith-based organizations (FBOs) are an important part of facilitating external resources and skills in partnership with a local church. The challenge that many FBOs face is that the local church may have a different understanding of compassion and look to the FBO staff for exclusive assistance to the members based on religious affiliation and denomination. In return, the FBO may succumb to these requests driven by efficiency and return-on-investment to maintain the financial engine of the organization rather than taking the time to develop a contextualized relationship and mutually beneficial partnership with a local church.

As a local church, the following questions might come up when discussing the needs and potential areas of compassion in the community in partnership with a Christian FBO:

1. What if the community's needs do not match the local church's capacity?

2. What happens when the local church's goals are not aligned with the FBO's goals?

3. What happens when the FBO's push for efficiency and return-on-invest are in conflict with the local church (resources, time, and outcomes)?

In this chapter, we will look at how an effective partnership can be built between a local church and an international FBO. Going into a partnership with awareness, clear expectations and guidelines can help both groups enjoy a collaborative ministry of compassion and grow together as the one body of Christ.

Christian FBOs play a unique role as supporters and facilitators of a delicate relationship between a local church and the community. In many communities, the local church is a focal point of faith and identity as a member of that particular congregation or denomination. FBOs must recognize this and work to enhance or strengthen the role of the local church in the community and not the FBOs own identity. This can cause a point of tension because the FBO also wants to show impact and tell a moving story of improving and transforming lives physically and spiritually.

The impact of FBOs has been receiving greater global recognition because of the connection and opportunity to work in remote communities through the local churches.[1] In 2002, USAID established the Center for Faith-Based and Community Organizations stating, "Working closely with faith-based and community stakeholders is critical to the success of USAID's mission."[2] These additional external partnerships can add another layer of complexity and influence to an already sensitive relationship between the FBO and local church. Another value such external partners recognize in collaborating with FBOs is that the relationship with the local church provided greater community involvement due to the Christian moral motivation for acts of compassion in God's kingdom as described in the other chapters. [3] Government and secular donors are collaborating with FBOs to increase the effectiveness of their development funding. Because of this, it is imperative for the FBO to have its policies and strategies in place in advance so they are able to effectively honor their partnership with the local church and also leverage the financial resources and training from governmental and secular partners.

---

1. Lipsky, "Evaluating the Strength of Faith," 25–36; Schmid, et al., "The contribution of religious entities to health in sub-Saharan Africa."

2. USAID, "Center for Faith-Based and Community Initiatives.".

3. Ferris, "Faith-based and secular humanitarian organizations," 311–325; Lipsky, "Evaluating the Strength of Faith," 25–36.

THE FORM OF A PARTNERSHIP

Christian community development requires an honest dialogue between people. Without trust, an open and honest discussion cannot take place and the FBO will assert its assumptions as the community's reality, which may not be correct. This circle of trust should start with the local church leaders, pastors, and members and allow them to slowly expand their circle of trust to others in the community. Christian FBOs and local church leaders can take specific actions to help this process along and facilitate healthy church-community relationships.

The local church plays an important role in the community by providing a place for the integration of the sacred and the secular, the spiritual and the physical. The local church is a centerpiece in the community and often recognized as a safe and trusted entity. It has the opportunity and responsibility to connect Christ's love with the hurts and struggles of people in this physical world. This physical, social, mental, and spiritual brokenness often found in communities throughout the world is exacerbated in impoverished countries, and the local church quickly becomes a central entity in navigating this physical and social conflict and struggle. The local church is a place where reconciliation can take place and forgiveness received as a foundation for future development.

It is in this context where a local church partners with an FBO to work together on a holistic and integrated strategy for serving people with compassion and love. Figure 1 shows the general relationship between the FBO and the local church in relationship with the national church body and other public service providers and donors.

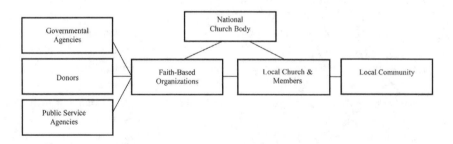

Figure 5: Relationship between the faith-based organization and the local church (Source: author)

The FBO is often but not always a primary link between government and other public service agencies as well as compassion ministry donors to the local church. In many relationships, there will also be a relationship with national church leaders in that specific country of focus. The national church or secretariat can be a valuable connection when the time comes to replicate and scale up service to other local churches in the country. Ultimately, the local church and its members form the primary relationship with the community members. The link between the FBO and the local church and the link between the local church and the community are significant relationship points. The FBO and local church need to be in agreement as to what the relationship will look like between the local church and the community and what role the FBO will play in assisting the local church in this relationship.

An important aspect of this relationship between the local church and a FBO is that the local community does not necessarily associate the acts of compassion with the FBO but with their friends and family that are part of the local church. This indirect association with the activities is one of the most challenging aspects of a FBO working alongside a local church. Impact and outcomes should be important to the local church as well as the FBO and connected to the values established in the partnership rather than a short-term output of a specific activity. At the end of the chapter, a utilization-focused evaluation approach is suggested that also includes the local church in the evaluation of a project.

FBOs generally provide three different types of local church support. Each of these can be appropriate depending on the current environment, structure, or need in the community and the status of the local church in the community.

1. Financial—in this relationship the FBO provides a one-way financial transaction, grant, or gift to the local church to provide some type of assistance or relief either within the church and/or the community.

2. Knowledge—in this relationship the FBO provides a one-way transaction of knowledge (i.e. health education) to members of the local church, which they can then use to serve their families, other church members, and other individuals in the community based on their personal interests and desires.

3. Mutual Growth & Discipleship—in this relationship the FBO and local church agree to enter a long-term relationship with a desire to grow together in Christ while helping each other serve the needs of the community around them. The FBO understands they may not have all of the resources required to meet the needs of the community but is committed to leveraging other external resources. The local church

members commit to leveraging internal assets and understand their call to be good stewards of their skills, gifts, and talents.

Within these categories, there are variations of FBOs based on size, geographical focus, service delivery capacities, and level of commitment to a particular denomination and evangelism efforts.[4] Similarly, local churches can also vary depending on size, traditions, and rituals, worship and fellowship practices, and member skills and talents. McGinnis distinguishes a local congregation as an entity that is focused on "doctrines, rituals, and other matters directly related to the shared experience of worship."[5] FBOs compliment a local church by focusing on some sort of community service delivery such as health care, education, sanitation, disability services, or relief. As mentioned earlier, FBOs also provide a bridge between the local church and other governmental or public service agencies and resources. This link is especially important in low-resource settings where individuals may not have access to such agencies or officials to advocate for their physical, social, or mental health needs.

THE FUNCTION OF A PARTNERSHIP

Christian FBOs have a responsibility to recognize and develop the God-given potential in people. An aspect of a Christian's view of compassion is the recognition that every individual is a unique child known by God (Psalm 139). The reality is that God has called his people to live in fellowship and provide opportunities for others to live in a right relationship with him, others, themselves, and creation through Jesus. All Christians living in low-or high-resource settings experience challenges in living this out. This is an important realization in building a local church-FBO partnership. FBOs are an important mechanism through which Christians throughout the world can connect and share resources, ideas, and time in helping one another live out this fellowship and Christian community.

Resources and networks are available to both local churches and FBOs looking to build Christ-centered church-community relationships. The Community Health Evangelism (CHE) model led by the Global CHE Network and Tearfund's *Umoja* model and training manuals are both widely used as approaches and processes to leverage resources for the local

---

4. Olarinmoye, "Faith-Based Organizations and Development," 1–14.

5. McGinnis, "Religion Policy and Faith-Based Organizations: Charting the Shifting Boundaries between Church and State."

church to show compassion in the community around them.[6] Both models are based on participatory models of engagement, asset-based community development, and Christian servant leadership, which are important components of sustainable and impactful compassionate ministry.

The relationship between the FBO and the national church body can be utilized to scale a program horizontally. Horizontal scaling is the process of replicating effective programs in more communities thereby providing the service to more people. Vertical scaling is building on an existing program and integrating additional services so the community is receiving a greater number of services. FBOs that are generalists in nature tend to scale vertically by focusing on process and community engagement bringing together other technical providers as needed and appropriate. FBOs with a specific focus service area, tend to scale horizontally and look to replicate their service to more people. Both types are important but realizing what to expect from each is important for the local church to not get frustrated or confused with what the FBO may or may not be providing. It is unlikely that one FBO will be able to deliver everything a local church is looking for to help them be a more compassionate body of Christ in the community.

A FOCUS ON PEOPLE, NOT PROJECTS

The need that many local churches face is the fact that their communities lack the basic services and infrastructure required for improved health and wellbeing. The local church is an existing group embedded in the community and experiencing the same challenges of that community. This adds to the challenge but also offers a unique opportunity to show selfless sacrifice and compassion. The FBO is in a position to leverage external resources with internal assets through equipping leaders in the local church based on a mutual understanding of compassion. The collaborative benefits between an FBO and a local church can be extremely significant if both enter the partnership with open eyes and a willingness to communicate openly.

FBOs do well to remember that all people are uniquely equipped to serve God in His kingdom. 1 Peter 4:10 states, "Each of you should use whatever gift you have received to serve others, as faithful stewards of God's grace in its various forms."[7] All of God's people have been given unique mission fields and should receive support, training, and equipping through

6. See The Global CHE Network, www.chenetwork.org; F. Njoroge, et al., *Umoja: Transforming Communities: Coordinator's Guide.*

7. All Scripture references in this chapter are from the NIV Bible (2011) unless otherwise noted.

their spiritual leaders to use their personality and vocation as instruments in God's kingdom. Peter goes on to describe the over-arching responsibility all Christians have as the royal priesthood in declaring the praises of God in this world. "But you are a chosen people, a royal priesthood, a holy nation, God's special possession, that you may declare the praises of him who called you out of darkness into his wonderful light" (1 Pet 2:9). FBOs play an important role, especially for Christians in resource-limited areas where basic needs are often competing for people's time and talents. The early church realized their limitations in being able to address the physical needs of its members and identified seven leaders to oversee this specific area of ministry. Acts provides a description of how the early church responded to issues of need and equity among its early members. "So the Twelve gathered all the disciples together and said, 'It would not be right for us to neglect the ministry of the word of God in order to wait on tables. Brothers and sisters, choose seven men from among you who are known to be full of the Spirit and wisdom.'" (Acts 6:2–3). The individuals chosen needed to be "full the Spirit and wisdom" given the importance and implications of their task. Compassion is a heart-felt behavior motivated by a genuine love for your neighbor as well as a service with significant implications for physical and spiritual well-being. Many FBOs have gone out with good intentions to carryout "works of service" without seriously considering the implications of their actions and the people involved. Compassion is not just an activity or a project but a process and a journey between people. Compassion motivated by Christ affirms and recognizes the royal priesthood of all believers and trust in a loving God who equips his people with unique gifts and skills for the benefit of his kingdom on earth.

CULTURAL ADAPTATION

In order to be a sensitive partner, FBOs need to invest the time in adapting any training or program to the unique context of the local church. Many international organizations fail to adequately contextualize health programs, instruments or tools to the cultures within which they are being implemented.[8] Forward and backward language translations are one part of the overall adaptation process but not a complete process. Adaptation should include a critical participatory review of the available evidence-based models and tools that have been developed. Each item within that model or tool should be reviewed for acceptability, interpretability, and understandability. If they fail in any of these areas, they should be removed or changed appropriately.

8. Paltzer, et al., "Measuring the Health-Related Quality of Life," 1177–1187.

The reality is that this process might reduce the overall comparability of the program when it comes to validating it with other similar programs but it will make it a better model or tool for use in the target community. It will also strengthen the ownership of the local church in the development and execution of the program.

This process takes time and is often frustrating for everyone involved. The staff and local leaders will receive pushback for the delay in implementation but the process is well worth it in terms of understanding the various components, activities, inputs, outputs, and expected outcomes of the program or activity. It will also strengthen the overall relationship by forcing both partners to invest time an energy up front to ensuring a high-quality, culturally adapted program is going to be conducted. This approach also leads into the concept of reverse innovation.

VALUES

All communities struggle with some level of internal conflict and distrust. FBOs can unintentionally add to the conflict by providing resources to certain individuals or families without understanding the larger community dynamics. FBOs need to be aware of power differentials in economics and resource allocation, knowledge, political influence, and decision-making.

FBOs need to be clear and transparent about their values to help navigate these internal conflicts. Local congregations also need to be accountable and transparent in clarifying what values they are looking for in a partner for their ministry of compassion. Some values to consider as part of a FBO and local church partnership include:

- Accountability for the resources the organization and local church have been given to provide long-term impact regardless of the service being delivered/offered
- Respect for the local knowledge and truth in learning with the local church and community
- Humility in recognizing mistakes and the learning required to work with a cross-cultural partner
- Servant leadership based on a daily reflection of Scripture and application of the biblical truths of grace and forgiveness
- Authenticity in communicating with partners focused on building trust and loving relationships

It can be easy for a FBO to fall into a paternalistic role as donor influence or organizational metrics and outcomes supersede the relationship with the local church members. In many cases, this shift will happen over time and neither partner will formally recognize it because neither wants to cause offense. The local church will be reluctant to confront the shift out of respect for the relationship. This shift limits the effectiveness of the ministry and potential for learning in the community of the local church as well as in the other countries where the FBO is working. If the values listed above are held to, there is greater likelihood of learning and evidence-based practices to develop flowing to and from the local church.

EVALUATION & ACCOUNTABILITY

Evaluation is another area of support often neglected by FBO-local church partnerships either because of limited bandwidth to carryout it out, lack of knowledge in how to conduct an evaluation, or low priority among the organizational leaders to commit to evaluation. Evaluation is a critical element of accountability to ensure both the local church partner and the FBO's stakeholders that the organization's values and services are aligned with its outcomes. Evaluation takes time and resources to carryout but yields valuable lessons for the long-term relationship. The reality that many FBO-local church relationships are based on relief or some other short-term humanitarian services leads to the thinking that evaluation is not an appropriate use of resources. If the opportunity cost of $1,000 for evaluation activities results in $1,000 less for direct services, the popular choice is to use those funds for direct services assuming they are achieving the expected impact.

In many situations, we realize only well after the fact that such services led to greater long-term harm than the initial realized benefit.[9] Evaluation can be integrated into an organization's processes but requires the value of accountability integrated into the culture of the organization and partnership. Without this, evaluation is not likely to happen consistently or be utilized by the field staff or local church leaders to inform and improve the services on the ground and ultimately strengthen the relationship with the local church. The basic components to evaluate partnership activates are:[10]

---

9. Moyo, *Dead Aid*; Corbett and Fikkert, *When Helping Hurts*.
10. Innovation Network, "Evaluation Plan Workbook."

INPUTS → OUTPUTS → OUTCOMES

Clarifying the inputs, outputs, and outcomes for each activity will create a firm foundation for subsequent implementation, process and outcome evaluations to take place through the life of the partnership. Given the technology today, electronic baseline and follow-up surveys can be collected offline via mobile tablets, encrypted, and synced with a server to be accessed by a team anywhere in the world.

Such partnerships can offer a lot in moving toward global health and compassionate ministry evidence-based practices. There is a need to be comfortable with some level of ambiguity when it comes to the adaption, application, and execution of such practices on the local level. All the pieces will not be figured out prior to execution, which requires trust between the FBO staff the local church lead team. This involves appreciating and respecting truth in the bi-directional learning process.

ELEMENTS TO A HEALTHY FBO-LOCAL CHURCH PARTNERSHIP

A healthy FBO-local church partnership is important in moving forward with effective ministries of compassion that recognize and strengthen the faith of the members and provide impactful service opportunities in the community. This is a list of common elements and actions that should be carried prior to moving ahead with a partnership:

1. Focus on partner strengths but recognize weaknesses. Carrying out a basic SWOT (strengths, opportunities, threats, and weaknesses) analysis or another participatory learning tool such as Dr. Ravi Jayakaran's Holistic Worldview Analysis and Ten Seed Technique can identify unrealized opportunities.[11] Following a SWOT analysis, the team can then categorize the various opportunities through an opportunity matrix or Eisenhower's Decision Matrix (popularized by Covey in 7 *Habits of Highly Effective People*) to identify and agree on those opportunities that will lead to the greatest good for the greatest number in the community given the assets and resources available.[12]

11. Jayakaran, "Wholistic Worldview Analysis: Understanding Community Realities," 41–48; i Jayakaran, *The Ten Seed Technique*.

12. Rosenberg, et al., *Real Collaboration*; Covey, *The 7 Habits of Highly Effective People*.

2. Write and sign a formal partnership agreement. The agreement does not have to be complex or long but listing a few expectations in writing can assist both parties in having ownership in the partnership. A partnership agreement will not avoid all misunderstandings but it is useful when leaders change or projects change. The agreement allows for greater accountability and can also set a time horizon on how long the partnership will last. A partnership agreement is not meant to be a hindrance or limiting step but rather a step that creates flexibility and improves the communication process and accountability. The tendency is for Christian partnerships is to rely on Christian "niceness" but often this results in conflict and misunderstanding. Cross-cultural communication barriers and different expectations can get in the way of a healthy, God-pleasing relationship. A basic agreement can have the following parts:

   A. Primary contacts—use titles in addition to names in case of changes in leadership

   B. Key objectives of the partnership and expectations of each partner

   C. The overall governance of the partnership and affiliated activities including the process for major decision-making

   D. The time horizon of the agreement. This can be a single year agreement with the option to renew or a multi-year agreement with the understanding that a new agreement can be written if both parties agree

   E. Termination process—this allows for either party to terminate the agreement within a given communication process and timeframe.

   F. Signatures of both entities

3. Clarify financial accountability and funding expectations. The partnership will require money and funds. Estimate what the expected costs will be and how the funds will be raised before any work is started. Grant opportunities or fundraising campaigns should be identified in advance even if the specifics of who will write the grant or funding appeal is not yet clarified. This discussion should result in a financial action plan that will cover the length of the partnership agreement. If funding is already procured, discuss how the funds will be distributed and accounted for on the ground by the individuals making the purchases. Clarify how receipts will be managed and communicated.

4. Identify specific leadership roles. Leadership within the partnership can cause friction and frustration if roles are not clarified. Individuals

from the local church and the FBO should be in specific leadership roles such as the visionary, the strategist, team builder, and convener.[13] Each role does not have to be filled but clarifying these roles up front can improve communication and strengthen the partnership along the way. These leaders can also learn from each other as it says in Prov 27:17, "As iron sharpens iron, so one person sharpens another."

5. Communicate. When in doubt, ask, then clarify whether you are asking the right question and ask again and then clarify the answer. Cross-cultural communication is one of the biggest challenges in healthy FBO-local church relationships. Even when the same language is used, a dysfunctional partnership can be the result. Respect face-to-face communication, use electronic communication when it is appropriate but do not rely on it as the primary means for relaying important information.

Figure 6 shows a step-by-step process that can be carried when moving forward with specific program planning and execution once the basic partnership and governance aspects have been discussed and agreement reached. The goal is for the FBO to support the local church members in their service of compassion working alongside others in their communities. The Local Lead Team (LLT) consists of members from the local church who desire to express their faith through compassion in people's lives. They desire to have a partner to help recognize, plan, equip, and develop a local, contextualized program of compassion. The FBO consists of staff able to facilitate the process to achieve impact resulting in high-quality initiatives implemented and sustained by the LLT.

Step one is assessing and defining the purpose of the opportunities within the local church and community. The LLT commits to gathering information and developing a vision based on their shared knowledge, interest, and competencies. Step two involves analyzing and prioritizing the information gathered by the church members from the community as well as the FBO staff from the existing literature and experience. The analysis and prioritization will be done through participation learning processes. Step three moves the team into the program planning and development stage. This step should conclude with a logic model and specific program strategy. Step four involves two parts; part one is to organize any training or workshop to better equip the team to implement the plan and part two is to recruit other key members to fill specific roles and functions. Step five is all about engaging members in the service opportunity thereby strengthening

13. Rosenberg, *Real Collaboration*, 128.

internal fellowship as well ensuring the service is carried out with collective compassion. Step six creates space for the LLT to engage other community groups or individuals to help with the service and program. It also involves marketing the program to others in the community to create awareness and a broader level of support. Step seven is to evaluate the service either during the implementation, the process or after it is completed to learn any lessons for future services.

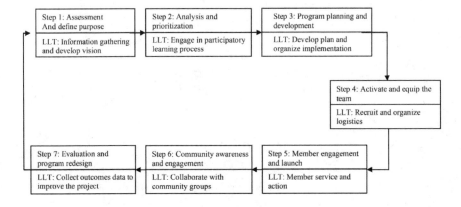

Figure 6: Step-by-step program development and implementation tasks by FBO staff and local lead teams

QUESTIONS FOR FORGING A HEALTHY PARTNERSHIP

As a FBO, answer:

1. What is our capacity to provide what is expected of us in this relationship?

2. How long are we planning to be a partner and will our involvement be helpful in the long-term for this local church and the local community?

3. What do we expect to learn in this partnership?

4. Who on our team is the best equipped to add value to this partnership and why?

5. What tools or resources do we currently have that will help us be a good partner? Which ones are we able to procure if needed?

6. How will we grow in our relationship with Jesus through this partnership?

As a local church lead team, answer:

1. What is our capacity to provide what is expected of us in this partnership?

2. How long are we expecting the FBO to work with us and will it be helpful for our local community in the long-term?

3. How will this partnership equip us to be better examples and ambassadors of Christ in our community?

4. What do we expect to learn from the FBO in this partnership?

5. Who in our local church is the best person to be our primary liaison in this partnership and why?

6. How will we communicate our concerns to the FBO if things are not going well?

Key Points:

1. The local church and partnering FBO needs to be clear on what they each can offer and realize that other partnerships may be required for the church members to carry out their ministry of compassion.

2. An FBO and a local church need to have a process for engagement that honors each other's position and their ability/responsibility to act as the body of Christ in the community.

3. Together, the FBO and local church leaders can leverage bi-directional learning for the adaptation and implementation of evidence-based models and programs around ministries of compassion.

14

Conclusion
For the Love of God

Jerry M. Ireland

Joseph T. Gibson once wrote that "a cold compassionless man is essentially un-Christian, and a compassionless church cannot be a Christian church."[1] If modern missions movements are to succeed in the area of compassionate missions, we would do well to keep this in mind. While it may be easier and more expeditious to take the lead role in compassionate outreach, we must remember that doing so wreaks havoc on the growth and maturity of local congregations.

Jesus said "a city on a hill cannot be hidden" (Matt 5:14). He was talking about good works performed by His followers as they expressed love for God and neighbor. "Let your light shine before men in such a way that they may see your good works, and glorify your Father who is in heaven" (Matt 5:16). His words anticipated the character and nature of the church He was calling into existence (Matt 16:18). His point was that the gathered people of God should be a visible expression of the kingdom of God on earth. Compassionate service is done fundamentally for the love of God. In this, the word "for" means both "because" and "by." God's love provides both the motivation and means for our own loving action (1 John 4:7, 10–11).

Twice in Matthew 5:13–16 Jesus warns against doing anything to hinder the outward movement of the church into the world as it engages in

1. Joseph Thompson Gibson, *Jesus Christ: The Unique Revealer of God*, 205.

244

"good works." He warns against salt becoming tasteless and he warns against hiding the light that should radiate from those who are his disciples. His point is that the mission of his followers requires their movement into the world. This is evident in the phrases "salt of the earth" and "light of the world." Christ followers are sent into the world, but are to be radically different from it. Far too often though, compassionate efforts in missions hinders this essential movement of the church into the world. We do this by not working in ways that equip local churches to be the primary agents of compassionate outreach to their communities. In short, we sometimes cause salt to become tasteless and we hide the light of the church under a basket.

Jesus says that "if salt becomes tasteless" it becomes useless (Matt 5:13; Luke 14:34). The Greek word used for tasteless is *moraino*, which can also mean "foolish." From this we get the modern word, *moron*. Whether the double meaning is intended is uncertain. Either way, we should be careful not to miss the severity of Jesus' warning. Plus, it would not be an exegetical stretch to say that hindering the work of the church is simply foolish, given the centrality of the church in God's redemptive plan.

Sometimes the good works of local churches become obscured by missionaries seeking the spotlight for themselves. This often results from simply wanting to make a difference in the world. Though a noble desire, we must remember that there are short-term differences and long-term differences and we should strive for the latter. If we take Jesus' warning seriously, we must avoid hiding the light of the church under a basket of individualism or self-importance. Jesus said "a city set on a hill cannot be hidden" (Matt 5:14). We should remind ourselves that a "city" can never be one person. A city by definition consists of many people. Our goal is the glory of God and Him alone. If the church is to shine like a city on a hill, then the collective nature of the church must take center stage. The brightness of the city depends on many lights shining all at once.

There are other ways too in which we hide the good works of the church. Sometimes this happens when good intentions create systems that overshadow the church. Several years ago a national church in Kenya entered into a partnership with an NGO to respond to various humanitarian needs. Since that partnership was first begun though, this national church had grown to become one of the strongest national churches on the continent. Yet, whenever a humanitarian need arose, the national church continued to call upon the NGO for a response, even though it was well within the capacity of that national church to respond out of their own resources. The problem was that the national church had relegated a fundamental part of its identity to another organization, and was quite happy to continue that relationship as long as funding and resources were available. The missionaries working with this church realized that the partnership had a long-term negative effect on the maturity of that church and now were faced with trying to figure out how to undue decades of bad practice.

It is important that we reflect carefully and consider what structures we have erected that cast a shadow over the local church. What towers of Babel have we built in order to make a name for ourselves? Whether the shadow cast is from an NGO or from our own missionary presence, if it causes the church to be less than it should be, then we are clearly guilty of ignoring Jesus' warning. It further means that correction is essential.

The above chapters are not meant to solve every challenge in the arena of compassionate missions. To even attempt such a thing would be quixotic to say the least. Rather, this volume is meant as a *guide*, as a starting point, to help missionaries—rookies and veterans alike—to begin rethinking how we can do compassion in ways that strengthen local churches. It is further intended as a means for pastors, missions committees, and NGOs to reconsider their engagement with a hurting world in ways that guard, rather than hinder, the forward momentum of missions as fundamentally a church-planting and disciple-making movement.

No one likes to be told that they have been doing things wrong. We recognize that some of what is said in this text may strike some readers as just that. In previous eras, many missionaries went to the field of their calling and were told simply, "do whatever your hands find to do." Many did just that and accomplished great things for the Lord. We must also admit, nevertheless, that a number of compassionate efforts by missionaries around the world have not always worked in ways that strengthened the capacity of local believers. In many cases this was simply because there were few guidelines and helps available. People had to figure it out as they went. It is no surprise that mistakes were made. Yet, in recent times, compassionate missions has far too often been guilty not only of mistakes but gross shortsightedness. This is evident in the tendency toward donor driven projects that do little or nothing to strengthen local churches. They are often "feel-good" efforts that lack sound ecclesiology and missiology. This has been true not only of missionaries but equally of the churches that send and support them. It is high time for a paradigm shift.

Whatever successes we may have found in modern missions we owe to those who have gone before us. As Isaac Newton famously said, "if I see further, it is by standing on the shoulders of giants." So too with this text. This contribution to a better way for compassionate missions comes only because we stand on the shoulders of giants in the fields of theology, missiology, international development, and Christian ethics. We have attempted to marshal their collective insight. In doing so, we have found remarkable agreement on the centrality of the local church to God's redemptive plan, and on the need for capacity building in compassionate outreach. If we see clearly in these matters, it is only because generations of missionary practitioners and scholars before us have labored and loved, and some have given their lives, for the cause of Christ around the world. We have benefited and learned from their successes and from their mistakes. We can best honor their efforts and sacrifices by likewise laying a solid foundation for future generations who answer the call of God in compassionate missions.

Bibliography

Allen, Roland. *The Spontaneous Expansion of the Church-and the Causes Which Hinder It.* Cambridge: Lutterworth, 1927.

Al-Thani, Hissa. "Disability in the Arab Region: Current Situation and Prospects." *DVV International,* 2007. https://www.dvv-international.de/adult-education-and-development/editions/aed-682007/adult-education-for-persons-with-disabilities/disability-in-the-arab-region-current-situation-and-prospects/.

Allison, Greg R. *Sojourners and Strangers.* Wheaton: Crossway, 2012.

Asset-Based Community Development Institute, 2009. http://www.abcdinstitute.org.

Baggett, David, and Jerry L. Walls. *Good God: The Theistic Foundations of Morality.* Oxford: Oxford University Press, 2011. Kindle.

Baker, Quinten, et. al. "An Evaluation Framework for Community Health Programs," *The Center for the Advancement for Community-Based Public Health,* June 2000. http://prevention.sph.sc.edu/Documents/CENTERED%20Eval_Framework.pdf.

Banks, Robert. *Paul's Idea of Community: The Early House Churches in Their Cultural Setting.* Revised edition. Peabody, MA: Hendrickson, 1994.

Barber, Owen. "What Is Development?" *Center for Global Development,* August 16, 2012. http://www.cgdev.org/blog/what-development.

Barna. "Research Shows That Spiritual Maturity Process Should Start at a Young Age." November 2003. https://www.barna.org/component/content/article/5-barna-update/45-barna-update-sp-657/130-research-shows-that-spiritual-maturity-process-should-start-at-a-young-age#.VowmymO2_Kw.

Bebbington, David. *Evangelicals in Modern Britain.* London: Routledge, 1993.

Bessenecker, Scott. *Overturning Tables: Freeing Missions from the Christian-Industrial Complex.* Downers Grove, IL: InterVarsity, 2014.

Blomberg, Craig L. *Neither Poverty nor Riches: A Biblical Theology of Possessions.* Downers Grove, IL: InterVarsity, 1999.

Blomberg, Craig L., and Mariam J. Kamell. *James.* Exegetical Commentary on the New Testament. Grand Rapids: Zondervan, 2008.

Bosch, David J. *Transforming Mission: Paradigm Shifts in Theology of Mission.* American Society of Missiology Series, vol. 16. Maryknoll, NY: Orbis Books, 1991.

Brown, David L. "People-Centered Development and Participatory Research." *Harvard Educational Review* 55 no. 1 (1985) 69–75.

Bundy, Steve. "Does My Child Need to be Healed? A Father's Reflections." *Beyond Suffering Course Reader*, Module 2. Agoura Hills, CA: Christian Institute on Disability, 2011.

Burnside, Jonathan. *God, Justice, and Society: Aspects of Law and Legality in the Bible.* Oxford: Oxford University Press, 2011.

Bush, Luis. "The 10/40 Window, Getting to the Core of the Core." Paper presented to Lausanne II, Manila, July 1989.

"Business as Mission." www.businessasmission.com.

Butrin, JoAnn. *From the Roots Up: A Closer Look at Compassion and Justice in Mission.* Springfield, MO: Roots Up Publishers, 2010.

———, ed. "Taking a Stand against Human Trafficking." http://www.nuturehope.net/assets/nhn-tool-kit-hr-rev-6.pdf.

Cable News Network. "US Missionaries Charged with Kidnapping in Haiti." http://edition.cnn.com/2010/CRIME/02/04/haiti.arrests/.

CAFOD. "The Pivotal Role of Faith Leaders in the Ebola Virus Disease Outbreak in West Africa." http://cafod.org.uk/content/download/21487/149541/ file/CAFOD %20Ebola%20Faith%20leaders%20policy%20paper%20111114%20(2).pdf.

Cambridge Dictionaries Online. S.v. "Best Practice." http://dictionary.cambridge.org/us/dictionary/british/best-practice.

Carpenter, Jeffrey. "Moral Hazard, Peer Monitoring, and Microcredit: Field Experimental Evidence from Paraguay." Working Paper at the Federal Reserve Bank of Boston, no. 10–6, June 28, 2010.

Carr, Alan. "When and How Often Should You Brush Your Teeth." *Mayo Clinic; Healthy Lifestyles*, May 14, 2013. http://www.mayoclinic.org/healthy-lifestyle/adult-health/expert-answers/brushing-your-teeth/faq-20058193.

Centers for Disease Control. *Writing SMART Objectives.* http://www.cdc.gov/healthyyouth/evaluation/pdf/brief3b.pdf.

Chitando, Ezra. "HIV and AIDS and Theological Education: Mainstreaming HIV and AIDS in Theological Education." In Dietrich Werner, et. al. eds, *The Handbook of Theological Education in World Christianity*, 242–250. Oxford, UK: Regnum Books International, 2010.

The Chalmers Center. www.chalmers.org.

Charities Aid Foundation. "World Giving Index 2014 Report," November 1, 2014. https://www.cafonline.org/publications/2014-publications/world-giving-index-2014/infographic.aspx.

Cohen, Monique. *The Impact of Microfinance.* CGAP Donor Brief. Washington, D.C.: CGAP, July 2003.

Collins, Daryl, Jonathan Morduch, Stuart Rutherford, and Orlanda Ruthven. *Portfolios of the Poor: How the World's Poor Live on $2 a Day.* Princeton, NJ: Princeton University Press, 2009.

Collins, Kenneth J. *Power, Politics, and the Fragmentation of Evangelicalism.* Downers Grove: IVP Academic, 2012.

Community Tool Box. http://ctb.ku.edu/en/table-of-contents/structure/strategic-planning/vmosa/main.

Copleston, Frederick. *The History of Philosophy.* Volume 4, *Modern Philosophy: Descartes to Leibniz.* New York: Doubleday, 1963, 208. Cited in John Douglas Morrison, *Has God Said,* 40. Eugene, OR: Pickwick, 2006.

Corbett, Steve, and Brian Fikkert. *When Helping Hurts*. Chicago, IL: Moody, 2009.

Coulter, Paddy. "Pretty as a Picture." *New Internationalist*. Issue 194, April 1989. https://newint.org/features/1989/04/05/pretty/.

Covey, Steven. *The 7 Habits of Highly Effective People: Powerful Lessons in Personal Change*. New York: Simon & Schuster, 2013.

Crawley, Winston. *Global Mission: A Story to Tell*. Nashville, TN: Broadman, 1985.

Cray, Graham. "A Theology of the Kingdom." In Vinay Samuel and Chris Sugden, editors. *Mission as Transformation*, 26–44. Oxford: Regnum, 1999.

Davids, P. H. "Rich and Poor." In *Dictionary of Jesus and the Gospels*. Edited by Joel B. Green, Scot McKnight, and I. Howard Marshall. Downers Grove: InterVarsity, 1992.

Davis, Billie. "I Was a Hobo Kid," *Saturday Evening Post*, 225, no. 24 (1952) 25.

Disasters Emergency Committee. "Haiti Earthquake Facts and Figures: Haiti before the Earthquake," 2015. http://www.dec.org.uk/articles/haiti-earthquake-facts-and-figures.

Donahue, John R. "The Lure of Wealth: Does Mark Have a Social Gospel?" In *Unity and Diversity in the Gospels and Paul: Essays in Honor of Frank J. Matera*. Edited by Christopher W. Skinner and Kelly R. Iverson, 71–94. Leiden: Brill, 2012.

Door International. https://www.doorinternational.com/mission-and-vision.

Dorfman, Diane. "Mapping Community Assets Workbook." *ABCD Toolkit*. http://www.abcdinstitute.org/docs/Diane%20Dorfman-Mapping-Community-Assets-WorkBook(1)-1.pdf.

Deuel, David. "Disability and the Kingdom of God." May 9, 2016. http://www.joniandfriends.org/media/uploads/PDFs/jcid_gods_story_of_disability-the_unfolding_plan_from_genesis_to_revelation[5].pdf.

Eagleton, Terry. "Was Jesus Christ a Revolutionary?" *New Internationalist* 411 (May 2008) 22–24.

Easterly, William R. *The Elusive Quest for Growth: Economists' Adventures and Misadventures in the Tropics*. Cambridge, MA: MIT Press, 2002.

Elmer, Duane. *Cross-Cultural Servanthood: Serving the World in Christlike Humility*. Downers Grove, IL: IVP Books, 2006.

EM-DAT: The National Disaster Database. http://www.emdat.be/natural-disasters-trends.

Epstein, Paul, et. al. *Results That Matter: Improving Communities by Engaging Citizens, Measuring Performance, and Getting Things Done*. San Francisco: Jossey-Bass, 2006.

Erickson, Millard J. *Christian Theology*. 2nd edition. Reprint, Grand Rapids: Baker Academic, 1983.

Fanning, Don. "Short Term Missions: A Trend That Is Growing Exponentially." *Trends and Issues in Missions*, Paper 4 (2009). http://digitalcommons.liberty.edu/cgm_missions/4.

Federal Bureau of Investigation. "Human Sex Trafficking." https://leb.fbi.gov/2011/march/human-sex-trafficking.

Fee, Gordon. "The Kingdom of God and the Church's Global Mission." In Murray W Dempster and Bryon D. Klaus, editors. *Called and Empowered: Global Mission in Pentecostal Perspective*, 7–21. Reprint, Grand Rapids: Baker, 2015.

Ferris, Elizabeth. "Faith-Based and Secular Humanitarian Organizations." *International Review of the Red Cross* 87, no. 858 (2005) 311–325.

Fielding, Charles. *Preach and Heal: A Biblical Model for Missions*. Richmond, VA: International Mission Board of the Southern Baptist Convention, 2008.

Fikkert, Brian, and Russell Mask. *From Dependence to Dignity: How to Alleviate Poverty through Christ-Centered Microfinance*. Grand Rapids: Zondervan, 2015.

Fikkert, Brian. "How Do We Flourish? The Image of God and Homo Economicus." In *Made in the Image of God: The Importance of the Imago Dei for Issues in International Development*. Edited by Hannah J. Swithinbank, 46–58. London, UK: Tearfund, 2016.

Finger, Reta Halteman. "Widows." In *Dictionary of Scripture and Ethics*. Edited by Joel B. Green. Grand Rapids: Baker Academic, 2011.

Five Talents International. www.fivetalents.org.

Fox, Frampton F. "'Eating the Flesh of Our Sons and Daughters': Mission to Children-at-Risk through Parents at Risk." *Missiology: An International Review* 37, no. 4 (2009) 499–510.

France, R. T. *The Gospel of Matthew*. New International Commentary on the New Testament. Grand Rapids: Eerdmans, 2007. Accordance electronic edition.

Frost, Michael, and Alan Hirsch. *ReJesus*. Peabody, MA: Hendrickson, 2009.

Gallup. "Most Americans Practice Charitable Giving, Volunteerism," December 13, 2013. http://www.gallup.com/poll/166250/americans-practice-charitable-giving-volunteerism.aspx.

Garrison, David. *Church Planting Movements: How God Is Redeeming a Lost World*. WIGTake Resources, 2004.

Gbowee, Leymah. *Mighty Be Our Powers: How Sisterhood, Prayer, and Sex Changed a Nation at War*, 171–172. New York: Beast Books, 2011. Cited in Ron Sider, *Nonviolent Action*, 114. Grand Rapids: Brazos, 2014.

Gener, T. D. "Contextualization." In *Global Dictionary of Theology*. Edited by William A. Dyrness and Veli-Matti Kärkkäinen. Downers Grove, IL: InterVarsity, 2008. Kindle.

Gibson, Joseph Thompson. *Jesus Christ: The Unique Revealer of God*. New York: Fleming H. Revel, 1915.

Global AIDS Partnership. www.globalaidspartnership.org.

Global CHE Network. www.chenetwork.org.

Gonzalez, Justo L. *Faith and Wealth: A History of Early Christian Ideas in the Origin, Significance, and Use of Money*. Eugene, OR: Wipf & Stock, 1990.

Gonzalez, Justo L. *A History of Christian Thought*. Volume 3. Reprint, Nashville: Abingdon, 1987.

Gosling, Louisa. *Toolkits: A Practical Guide to Planning, Monitoring, Evaluation and Impact Assessment*. London: Save the Children, 1996.

Grameen Bank. "Grameen Bank Monthly Update." Statement No: 1, Issue No. 436. May 8, 2016. http://www.grameen.com/data-and-report/2016-04-issue-436-usd/.

Grant, Beth. *Courageous Compassion: Confronting Social Injustice God's Way*. Springfield, MO: My Healthy Church, 2014. Kindle.

Green, Joel B. *The Gospel of Luke*. New International Commentary on the New Testament. Accordance electronic ed. Grand Rapids: Eerdmans, 1997.

Green, Michael. *Evangelism in the Early Church*. Reprint, Grand Rapids: Eerdmans, 2003.

Harris, Murray J. *The Second Epistle to the Corinthians: A Commentary on the Greek Text*. New International Greek Testament Commentary. Grand Rapids, MI: Eerdmans, 2005.

Hebblethwaite, Peter. "In Rwanda, 'Blood Is Thicker Than Water,'" *National Catholic Reporter*, June 3, 1994. Cited in Emmanuel Katongole and Jonathan Wilson-Hartgrove. *Mirror to the Church*, under chapter one, section "Facing the Contradictions." Grand Rapids, MI: Zondervan. 2009. Kindle.

Henry, Carl F. H. *Christian Countermoves in a Decadent Culture*. Portland, OR: Multnomah, 1986.

———. *A Plea for Evangelical Demonstration*. Grand Rapids: Baker Book House, 1971.

———. *The Uneasy Conscience of Modern Fundamentalism*. Grand Rapids, MI: Eerdmans, 1947.

———. *The Uneasy Conscience of Modern Fundamentalism*. Grand Rapids, MI: Eerdmans, 2003.

Hermes, Niels, and Robert Lensink. "The Empirics of Microfinance: What Do We Know?" *Economic Journal*, 117 (February 2007) 1–10.

Hilberg, R. "Opening Remarks: 'The Discovery of the Holocaust." In P. Hayers, ed. *Lessons and Legacies: The Meaning of the Holocaust in a Changing World*. Evanston, IL: Northwestern University. Press, 1991, 11. Cited in Eve Garrand and Geoffrey Scarre, eds., *Moral Philosophy and the Holocaust*, 75. Burlington, VT: Ashgate, 2003.

Hirsch, Alan. *The Forgotten Ways*. Grand Rapids, MI: Brazos, 2006.

Hodgman, Denise. "The Flaw of the Excluded Middle: Among the Cree People of Canada." Abridged Version. MA thesis, Providence Theological Seminary, 2004.

HOPE International, *HOPE International Annual Report* 2015. Lancaster, PA: HOPE International, 2015. www.hopeinternational.org/images/uploads/financials/2015-HOPE-annual-report.pdf.

Innovation Network. "Evaluation Plan Workbook." http://www.innonet.org/resources/files/evaluation_plan_workbook.pdf.

International Labour Organization of the United Nations. "21 Million People Are Now Victims of Forced Labour, ILO Says." Press release, last modified June 1, 2012. http://www.ilo.org/global/about-the-ilo/newsroom/news/WCMS_181961/lang—en/index.htm.

———. "Forced Labour, Human Trafficking and Slavery (Forced Labour, Human Trafficking and Slavery)." http://www.ilo.org/global/topics/forced-labour/lang—en/index.htm.

Ireland, Jerry M. *Evangelism and Social Concern in the Theology of Carl F. H. Henry*. Eugene, OR: Pickwick, 2015.

———. "UPG's and Compassion: Guidelines for Loving the Poor as We Reach the Lost." Unpublished paper, Springfield, MO, October, 2015.

Jayakaran, Ravi. *The Ten Seed Technique*. World Vision China, 2002.

———. "Wholistic Worldview Analysis: Understanding Community Realities." *Participatory Learning and Action* 56 (2007) 41–48.

Jenkins, Philip. *The Next Christendom: The Coming of Global Christianity*. Oxford: Oxford University Press, 2002.

Johnson, Alan. "Analyzing the Frontier Missions Movement and Unreached People Group Thinking, Parts I–V." *International Journal of Frontier Missions* 18, no. 1–3 (2001).

Johnson, Jean. *We Are Not the Hero*. Sisters, OR: Deep River Books, 2012.

Johnson, Paul. *A History of Christianity*. New York: Simon and Schuster, 1976.

Joshua Project. "What is the 10/40 Window?" http://joshuaproject .net/resources/ articles/10_40_window.

Kaiser, Walter C., Jr. "Poverty and the Poor in the Old Testament." In *For the Least of These: A Biblical Answer to Poverty*. Edited by Anne Bradley and Art Lindsley, 39–56. Grand Rapids: Zondervan, 2014.

Kaiser, Walter C., Jr. *Toward Old Testament Ethics*. Grand Rapids: Zondervan, 1983.

Karlan, Dean, and Jacob Appel. *More Than Good Intentions: Improving the ways the World's Poor Borrow, Save, Farm, Learn, and Stay Healthy*. New York: Penguin, 2011.

Katongole, Emmanuel, and Jonathan Wilson-Hartgrove. *Mirror to the Church*. Grand Rapids, MI: Zondervan. 2009. Kindle.

Keller, Tim. *Ministries of Mercy*. 2nd edition. Phillipsburg, NJ: P&R Publishing, 1997.

Kennedy, John W. "The 4/14 Window." *Christianity Today*, July 2004, 53.

Kirk, J. Andrew. *The Good News of the Kingdom Coming: The Marriage of Evangelism and Social Responsibility*. Downers Grove: InterVarsity, 1983.

Kline, Frank J. "Family." In *Baker's Dictionary of Christian Ethics*. Edited by Carl F. H. Henry. Grand Rapids: Baker Books, 1973.

Kotter, David. "Remember the Poor: A New Testament Perspective on the Problems of Poverty, Riches, and Redistribution." In *For the Least of These: A Biblical Answer to Poverty*. Edited by Anne Bradley and Art Lindsley, 60–91. Grand Rapids: Zondervan, 2014.

Kreider, Alan. *The Change of Conversion and the Origin of Christendom*. Eugene, OR: Wipf & Stock, 1999.

Krishna, Anirudh. *One Illness Away: Why People Become Poor and How They Escape Poverty*. New York: Oxford University Press, 2010.

Kunhiyop, Samuel Waje. *African Christian Ethics*. Nairobi: Hippo Books, 2008.

Ladd, George Eldon. *The Gospel of the Kingdom*. Grand Rapids: Eerdmans, 1959.

———. *Theology of the New Testament*. Grand Rapids: Eerdmans, 1993.

Larson, David. "A Leap of Faith for Church-Centered Microfinance." Working paper #204, Chalmers Center for Economic Development at Covenant College.

Lausanne Covenant. Article 5, "Christian Social Responsibility." http://www.lausanne. org/ content/covenant/lausanne-covenant.

Lausanne Movement. https://www.lausanne.org/content/statement/transformation-the-church-in-response-to-human-need.

———. *The Capetown Commitment: A Confession of Faith and Call to Action*, 2011, Part 1, Section 10.B. https://www.lausanne.org/content/ctc/ctcommitment.

Leaning, Jennifer, and Debarati Guha-Sapir. "Natural Disasters, Armed Conflict, and Public Health." *The New England Journal of Medicine*. Vol. 369, no. 19 (November 7, 2013). http://www.nejm.org/doi/full/10.1056/NEJMra1109877.

Lipsky, Alyson B. "Evaluating the Strength of Faith: Potential Comparative Advantages of Faith-based Organizations Providing Health Services in Sub-Saharan Africa." *Public Administration and Development* 31 (2011) 25–36.

Livingston, James C. *Modern Christian Thought*. Minneapolis: Fortress, 2006.

Loewen, Joy. *Woman to Woman: Sharing Jesus with a Muslim Friend*. Grand Rapids, MI: Chosen, 2010.

Lopez, Christine. "Analyzing Root Causes of Problems: The 'But Why' Technique." *Community Tool Box*, Chapter 17, Section 4. http://ctb.ku.edu/en/table-of-contents/ analyze/analyze-community-problems-and-solutions/root-causes/main.

Lupton, Robert. *Compassion, Justice and the Christian Life: Rethinking Ministry to the Poor*. Ventura, CA: Regal, 2007.

———. *Toxic Charity: How Churches and Charities Hurt Those They Help*. New York: HarperOne, 2011.

Marsden, George. *Fundamentalism and American Culture*. New York: Oxford University Press, 1980.

Marshall, I. Howard. *The Gospel of Luke: A Commentary on the Greek Text*. New International Greek Testament Commentary. Grand Rapids: Eerdmans, 1978.

Martin, Jonathan. *Giving Wisely?: Killing with Kindness or Empowering Lasting Transformation*. Sisters, OR: Last Chapter Publishing, 2008.

McDonic, S. M. "Witnessing, Work and Worship: World Vision and the Negotiation of Faith, Development and Culture," 92. Ph.D. diss., Graduate School of Duke University, 2004. Cited in Brad Watson, et al., "Issues in Historical Child Sponsorship." In *Child Sponsorship: Exploring Pathways to a Brighter Future*. Edited by Brad Watson and Matthew Clarke, 74. New York: Palgrave Macmillan, 2014. Kindle.

McGinnis, Michael D. "Religion Policy and Faith-Based Organizations: Charting the Shifting Boundaries between Church and State." Paper presented at the 2011 Annual Meeting of the Association for the Study of Religion, Economics & Culture, April 7–10, 2011, Indiana University, Bloomington, Indiana.

McGrath, Allister E. "Enlightenment." In Allister E. McGrath, *The Blackwell Encyclopedia of Modern Christian Thought*. Oxford, UK: Blackwell, 1993.

McKnight, Scot. *Kingdom Conspiracy: Returning to the Radical Mission of the Local Church*. Grand Rapids: Brazos, 2014. Kindle.

McManus, Erwin Raphael. *An Unstoppable Force: Daring to Become the Church God Had in Mind*. Orange, CA: Yates & Yates, 2001.

McNair, Jeff. "Disability and Human Supports." *Christian Journal for Global Health* [Online] 2, no. 2 (November 2015). http://journal.cjgh.org/index.php/cjgh/article/ view/86/274#ref3.

McNair, Jeff, and Kathi McNair. "Wolfenberger's 18 Wounds of Disability." *Beyond Suffering Course Reader*. Agoura Hills, CA: Christian Institute on Disability, 2011.

Medical Ambassadors International, "Community Health Evangelism Expanded," 2012. http://www.medicalambassadors.org/CHE.html.

Middleton, J. Richard. A New Heaven and a New Earth: Reclaiming Biblical Eschatology. Grand Rapids: Baker Academic, 2014.

Miles, Rebekah. "Children," "Family." In *Dictionary of Scripture and Ethics*. Edited by Joel B. Green. Grand Rapids: Baker Academic, 2011.

Mohamed, Faiza Jama. "Putting an End to Female Genital Mutilation: The Africa Protocol on the Rights of Women." In *African Voices on Development and Social Justice*. Edited by Firoze Manji and Patrick Burnett, 114–116. Dar Es Salaam, TZ: Mkuki Na Nyota Publishers, 2005.

Moo, Douglas J. *The Epistle to the Romans*. New International Commentary on the New Testament. Accordance electronic ed. Grand Rapids: Eerdmans, 1996.

Moore, Art. "The Myth of the Needy Child." *Christianity Today*, May 18, 1998, 17.

Moore, Russell D. *The Kingdom of Christ: The New Evangelical Consensus*. Wheaton, IL: Crossway, 2004.

Moreau, Scott A., et al. *Introducing World Missions: A Biblical, Historical, and Practical Survey*. Monrovia, CA: MARC, 2004.

Morris, Leon. *The Gospel According to Matthew*. Pillar New Testament Commentary. Grand Rapids: Eerdmans, 1992. Accordance electronic edition.

Moser, Paul K. "Faith." In Michael W. Austin and R. Doug Geivett, editors. *Being Good: Christian Virtues for Everyday*, 13–29. Grand Rapids: Eerdmans, 2012.

Mott, Stephen Charles. *Biblical Ethics and Social Change*. Oxford: Oxford University Press, 1982.

Moyo, Dambisa. *Dead Aid: Why Aid is Not Working and How There is Another Way for Africa*. London: Penguin Group, 2009.

Müller, Roland. *Honor and Shame: Unlocking the Door*. Philadelphia, PA: Xlibris, 2000.

Myers, Bryant. *The New Context of World Missions*. Monrovia, CA: MARC Publications, 1996.

———. "State of the World's Children: Critical Challenge to Christian Mission." *International Bulletin of Missionary Research*. Vol. 18, no. 3 (1994) 98–102.

———. *Walking with the Poor; Principles and Practices of Transformational Development*. Maryknoll, NY: Orbis, 1999.

Narayan, Deepa. "Designing Community-Based Development." The World Bank, Social Development Papers, 1. http://siteresources.worldbank.org/INTRANET SOCIALDEVELOPMENT/ 214578–1111660828964/20486383/sdp07.pdf.

Neill, Stephen. *Creative Tension*. London: Edinburgh House, 1959.

Newberry, Warren B. "Contextualizing Indigenous Church Principles: An African Model," *Asian Journal of Pentecostal Studies* 8, no. 1 (2005): 99–102.

The Network: A Called Community of Women. "From Migrant to Doctor: A Life of Learning: An Interview with Billie Davis." http://ag.org/wim/resources/interviews/intrv_0409_davis.cfm.

Njoroge, F., et al. *Umoja: Transforming Communities: Coordinator's Guide*. Teddington, UK: Tearfund, 2009.

Nouwen, Henry J., Donald P. McNeill, and Douglas A. Morrison. *Compassion*. New York: Doubleday, 1982.

Nurture Hope Network of the Assemblies of God World Missions. "Taking a Stand Against Human Trafficking: A Guide for the Local Church and Concerned Christians." *Tool Kit*. Springfield, MO, n.d.

Olarinmoye, Omobolaji Ololade. "Faith-Based Organizations and Development: Prospects and Constraints." *Transformation: An International Journal of Holistic Mission Studie*s 29, no. 1 (2012) 1–14.

Olson, Kerry, Zanele Sibanda, and Geoff Foster. "Raising Community Awareness and Inspiring Action." In *From Faith to Action: Strengthening Family and Community Care for Orphans and Vulnerable Children in Sub-Saharan Africa*. Edited by Laura Sutherland. 2nd edition, 6–8. Santa Cruz, CA: Firelight Foundation, N.d.

Olson, Roger. *The Journey of Modern Theology*. Downers Grove: IVP Academic, 2013.

Organization of the High Commissioner for Human Rights (OCHR). "Protocol to Prevent, Suppress and Punish Trafficking in Persons, Especially Women and Children, Supplementing the United Nations Convention Against Transitional Organized Crime," November 15, 2000. http://www.ohchr.org/english/law/protocoltraffic.htm.

Ott, Craig, and Stephen J. Strauss. *Encountering Theology of Missions*. Grand Rapids: Baker Academic, 2010.

Padilla, C. René. "Integral Mission and its Historical Development." In Tim Chester, editor. *Justice, Mercy, and Humility*, 42–58. Waynesboro, GA: Paternoster, 2002.

Paltzer, Jason, et al. "Measuring the Health-Related Quality of Life (HRQoL) of Young Children in Resource-Limited Settings: A Review of Existing Measures." *Quality of Life Research* 22, no. 6 (2013) 1177–1187.

Parks, Stan. "Changing The Percentages," *Mission Frontiers* (May–June 2013).

Platt, David. *Radical: Taking Back Your Faith from the American Dream*. Colorado Springs, CO: Multnomah, 2010.

Prostitution: Money and Power (Women's Support Project and Zero Tolerance, 2010). http://www.womenssupportproject.co.uk/content/prostitution/205,172/.

Ravallion, Martin, Shaohua Chen, and Prem Sangraula. *New Evidence on the Urbanization of Global Poverty*. Policy Research Working Paper 4199. Washington, D.C.: World Bank, 2007.

Reed, Larry. *Mapping Pathways out of Poverty: The State of the Microcredit Summit Campaign Report, 2015*. Washington, DC: Microcredit Summit Campaign, 2015.

Rehydration Project. "Oral Rehydration Solutions: Made at Home." http://rehydrate. org/solutions/homemade.htm.

Rene, James. *BASICS: Fundamentals of Disability Ministry Training*. Agoura Hills, CA: Joni and Friends International Disability Center, 2009. http://www.joniandfriends. org/media/uploads/PDFs/basics_teacher.pdf.

Rhee, Helen. *Loving the Poor, Saving the Rich*. Grand Rapids: Baker Academic, 2012.

Richter, Linda M., and Amy Norman. "AIDS Orphan Tourism: A Threat to Young Children in Residential Care." *Vulnerable Children and Youth Studies* 5, no. 3 (2010) 217–229.

Rist, Erika A. "When Humans Become Commodities: Minimizing Costs, Maximizing Profit, and the Exploitation Inherent to the Sex Industry." October 2012. http:// media.virbcdn.com/files/15/FileItem-276204-Rist_HumanCommodity2012.pdf.

Ritzer, George. *The McDonaldization of Society*. Los Angeles, CA: Pine Forge, 2009.

Roa, Steve. "Community-Based Care: Africa Models a New Approach to its Orphan Crisis." *Mission Frontiers*, November–December 2011, 21–22.

Rosenberg, Mark L., et al. *Real Collaboration: What it Take for Global Health to Succeed*. Berkeley, CA: University of California Press, 2010.

Rosner, Brian S. "Biblical Theology." In *New Dictionary of Biblical Theology*. Edited by T. Desmond Alexander and Brian S. Rosner, 4–11. Downers Grove: InterVarsity, 2000. Accordance electronic edition.

Ross, Cathy. "Introduction: Taonga." In *Mission in the 21st Century: Exploring the Five Marks of Mission*. Edited by Andrew F. Walls and Cathy Ross, xiii–xvi. Maryknoll, NY: Orbis, 2008.

Rucker, Philip. "Rick Perry, Hungry for Redemption, Says He's a Fundamentally Different Candidate." *The Washington Post*, December 9, 2014, http://www. washingtonpost.com/politics/rick-perry-hungry-for-redemption-says-hes-a-substantially-different-candidate/2014/12/09/3c9c605a-7f20-11e4-81fd-8c4814dfa9d7_story.html.

Ruiz, Heather. "Voluntourism: More Harm than Good." *The Walla Walla University Collegian*, 2014. http://aswwu.com/collegian/voluntourism-more-harm-than-good/.

Rundle, Steve, and Tom Steffen. *Great Commission Companies*. Downers Grove, IL: Intervarsity, 2003.

Rutherford, Stuart. *The Poor and Their Money*. New York: Oxford University Press, 2000.

Saddleback Church HIV-AIDS Initiative. www.hivaidsinitiative.com.

Saddleback Church PEACE Plan. www.saddleback.com.

Sahih al-Bukhari. http://www.sahih-bukhari.com/Pages/Bukhari_1_06.php.

Samuel, Vinay. "God's Intention for the World: Tensions Between Escatology and History." In *The Church's Response to Human Need*. Edited by Vinay Samuel and Chris Sugden, 128–160. Eugene, OR: Wipf and Stock, 2003.

Say Hello. "About." http://sayhelloinfo.com/about/.

Schmid, B., et al. "The Contribution of Religious Entities to Health in Sub-Saharan Africa." Study commissioned by B & M Gates Foundation. Unpublished report, ARHAP, 2008.

Schmidt, A. J. *How Christianity Changed the World*. Grand Rapids, MI: Zondervan, 2009.

Schrag, Brain. "Ethnoartistic Cocreation in the Kingdom of God." In *Worship and Mission for the Global Church: An Ethnodoxology Handbook*. Edited by James Krabill, 49–56. Pasadena, CA: William Carey Library, 2013.

Schwartz, Glenn. *When Charity Destroys Dignity: Overcoming Unhealthy Dependency in the Christian Movement*. Lancaster, PA: World Mission Associates, 2007.

Sells, Heather. "In the Midst of Hardships, Cubans Catch Missions Fever." Christian Broadcasting Network, 1 January 2016. http://www1.cbn.com/cbnnews/world/2015/September/In-Midst-of-Hardships-Cubans-Catch-Mission-Fever.

Shediac-Rizkallah, Mona, and Lee Bone. "Planning for Sustainability of Community-based Health Programs: Conceptual Frameworks and Future Directions for Research, Practice and Policy." *Health Education Research*, 13, no. 1 (1998) 87–108.

Shenk, Wilbert R. "The Origins and Evolution of the Three-Selfs in Relation to China." *International Bulletin of Missionary Research* 14, no. 1 (1990) 28–35.

———. "Rufus Anderson and Henry Venn: A Special Relationship?" *International Bulletin of Missionary Research* 5, no. 4 (1981) 168–172.

———. "The Whole Is Greater Than the Sum of the Parts: Moving Beyond Word and Deed." *Missiology: An International Review* XX, no. 1 (1993) 65–75.

Sider, Ron. *Good News and Good Works*. Reprint, Grand Rapids: Baker, 2011. Kindle.

Slimbach, Richard. "First Do No Harm." *EMQ* (October 2000). www.emqonline.com. Paraphrasing David Bosch, *Transforming Mission*. Maryknoll, NY: Orbis, 1993. http://members.optusnet.com.au/newportcrisps/mistcd/files/First_do_no_harm.pdf.

Smith, Steve. "CPMS: The Counter-Intuitive Ways of Growing God's Kingdom." *Mission Frontiers* (May–June 2013) 28–31.

Smither, Ed. "Foreword." In Jerry M. Ireland, *Evangelism and Social Concern in Theology of Carl F. H. Henry*. Eugene, OR: Pickwick, 2015.

Smithers, Nicola. "The Importance of Stakeholder Ownership for Capacity Development Results." *World Bank Group*, May 1, 2011. https://wbi.worldbank.org.

Soul Destruction. "Voices of Prostitution Survivors." http://soul-destruction.com/voices-of-prostitution-survivors/.

Spadaro, S. J., Antonio. "Francis: A Big Heart Open to God." *America*, September 30, 2013. http://americamagazine.org/pope-interview. Cited in William T.

Cavanaugh. *Field Hospital: The Church's Engagement with a Wounded World*, 1. Grand Rapids: Eerdmans, 2016.

Synder, Howard. *The Community of the King*. Downers Grove: InterVarsity, 1977. Kindle.

Stark, Rodney. For the glory of God: How Monotheism Led to Reformations, Science, Witch-hunts, and the End of Slavery. Princeton, NJ: Princeton University Press, 2003.

Stassen, Glen H., and David P. Gushee. *Kingdom Ethics: Following Jesus in Contemporary Contexts*. Downers Grove, IL: IVP Academic, 2003.

Stott, John, ed. *Making Christ Known: Historic Mission Documents from the Lausanne Movement* 1974–1989. Grand Rapids: Eerdmans, 1996.

Stowasser, Barbara Freyer. *Women in the Qur'an, Traditions, and Interpretation*. New York: Oxford University Press, 1996.

Sugden, Chris. "What is Good about Good News to the Poor?" In *Mission as Transformation: A Theology of the Whole Gospel*. Regnum Studies in Mission. Edited by Vinay Samuel and Chris Sugden, 236–260. Irvine, CA: Regnum, 1999.

Sugden, Chris. "Mission as Transformation–Its Journey Among Evangelicals Since Lausanne I." In Brian Woolnough and Wonsuk Ma, editors. *Holistic Mission*, 31–35. Oxford: Regnum, 2010.

Sundquist, Scott W. *Understanding Christian Mission: Participation in Suffering and Glory*. Grand Rapids: Baker Academic, 2013. Kindle.

Sustain Hope International Community Development. "Gardening." http://sustainhope.org/gardening.html.

Swanson, Allen. "The Money Problem." *World Encounter* 6, no. 5 (July 1969) 28.

Swartley, Willard M. "Peace." In *Dictionary of Scripture and Ethics*, 583–586. Edited by Joel B. Green. Grand Rapids: Baker Academic, 2011.

Tada, Joni Eareckson, and Steve Bundy. *Beyond Suffering Study Guide*. Augora Hills, CA, Joni and Friends, 2011.

Tada, Joni Eareckson, and Jack Oppenhuizen. "Hidden and Forgotten People: Ministry Among People with Disabilities." Lausanne Occasional Paper No 35B, (2004). https://www.lausanne.org/wp-content/uploads/2007/06/LOP35B_IG6B.pdf.

Tearfund. www.tearfund.org.

Tennent, Timothy C. *Invitation to World Missions: A Trinitarian Missiology for the 21st Century*. Grand Rapids: Kregel, 2010.

Teterud, Wesley M. *Caring for Widows: You and Your Church Can Make a Difference*. Grand Rapids: Baker, 1994.

Thornhill, A. Chadwick. "Poverty." In *The Lexham Bible Dictionary*. Edited by John D. Barry, et al. Bellingham, WA: Lexham, 2015.

Tise, L. E. *A Book about Children: The world of Christian Children's Fund* 1938–1991, 45–46. Falls Church, VA: Hartland Publishing, 1993. Cited in Brad Watson, et al., "Issues in Historical Child Sponsorship." In *Child Sponsorship: Exploring Pathways to a Brighter Future*. Edited by Brad Watson and Matthew Clarke, 68. New York: Palgrave Macmillan, 2014. Kindle.

Tizon, Al. *Transformation After Lausanne*. Eugene, OR: Wipf & Stock, 2008.

Tolbert, Mary Ann. "How the Gospel of Mark Builds Character." *Interpretation*, 47 (1993) 347–357.

Trousdale, Jerry. *Miraculous Movements*. Nashville: Thomas Nelson, 2012.

UNICEF. "Children and Young People with Disabilities Fact Sheet." May 2013. http://www.unicef.org/disabilities/files/Factsheet_A5__Web_NEW.pdf.

———. "Child Protection: Current Status + Progress." http://data.unicef.org/child-protection/child-labour.html.

———. "The Global Malaria Burden." http://www.unicef.org/prescriber/eng_p18.pdf.

———. "Orphans." http://www.unicef.org/media/media_45279.html.

———. "Unlocking Children's Potential." http://www.unicef.org/nutrition/.

———. "State of the World's Children: 2006." http://www.unicef.org/sowc06/profiles/street.php.

United Nations. *The Millenium Development Goals Report* 2015. New York, NY: United Nations, 2015.

United Nations. "Sustainable Development Goals." http://www.un.org/sustainabledevelopment/poverty/.

———. "Widowhood: Invisible women, secluded or excluded." *Women* 2000. December 2001. http://www.un.org/womenwatch/daw/public/wom_Dec%2001%20single%20pg.pdf, 2.

United Nations Office on Drugs and Crime. "Global Report on Trafficking in Persons 2014," 10 (2014). https://www.unodc.org/documents/data-and-analysis/glotip/GLOTIP_2014_full_report.pdf.

United to End Genocide. "Syria Backgrounder." http://endgenocide.org/conflict-areas/syria-backgrounder.

USAID. "Center for Faith-Based and Community Initiatives" (2014). https://www.usaid.gov/faith-based-and-community-initiatives.

Van Engen, Charles. *God's Missionary People: Rethinking the Purpose of the Local Church*. Grand Rapids: Baker Academic, 1991. Kindle.

Verhey, Alan. *The Great Reversal: Ethics and the New Testament*. Grand Rapids: Eerdmans, 1984.

Verkuyl, Johannes. "The Kingdom of God as the Goal of Missio Dei." *International Review of Mission* 68 no. 270 (1979): 168–175.

Walls, Andrew. "Demographics, Power, and the Gospel in the 21st Century." Paper presented, SIL International Conference and WBTI Convention, June 6, 2002.

Walsh, Janet. "Women's Property Rights Violations and HIV/AIDS in Africa." *Peace Review: A Journal of Social Justice* 17, no. 2/3 (2005): 189–195.

Wan, Enoch. *Diaspora Missiology: Theory, Methodology, and Practice*. Portland, OR: Institute of Diaspora Studies—U.S. Western Seminary, 2011.

Watson, Brad, et. al. "Issues in Historic Child Sponsorship." In *Child Sponsorship: Exploring Pathways to a Brighter Future*. Edited by Brad Watson and Matthew Clarke, 66–95. New York: Palgrave Macmillan, 2014. Kindle.

Watson, Brad, and Matthew Clarke. "Introduction to Key Issues in Child Sponsorship." In *Child Sponsorship: Exploring Pathways to a Brighter Future*. Edited by Brad Watson and Matthew Clarke, 1–18. New York: Palgrave Macmillan, 2014. Kindle.

Watson, David. "Church Planting Essentials—Exploring Contextualization and Deculturalization." http://www.davidlwatson.org/2010/02/12/church-planting-essentials-%E2%80%93-exploring-contextualization-and-deculturalization/.

"WB-IMF Report Gauges Progress on Development Goals," last modified October 18, 2014. http://www.worldbank.org/en/news/press-release/2014/10/08/wb-imf-report-progress-development-goals-promoting-shared-prosperity.

Webb, William J. *Slaves, Women and Homosexuals: Exploring the Hermeneutics of Cultural Analysis*. Downers Grove: InterVarsity, 2001. Kindle.

Weber, Linda J. *Missions Handbook*. 21st Century edition. Wheaton: EMIS, 2010.

"What is T4T?" http://t4tonline.org/about/what-is-t4t/.

Winter, Ralph D. "The Future of Evangelicals in Mission: Will We Regain the Vision of Our Forefathers in the Faith?" *Mission Frontiers* (September–October 2007) 15.

———. "Six Spheres of Mission Overseas." *Mission Frontiers Bulletin* (1998) 16–45.

———. "The Two Structures of God's Redemptive Mission." In *Perspectives on the World Christian Movement: A Reader*. Edited by Ralph D. Winter and Steven C. Hawthorne, 220–230. Pasadena, CA: William Carey Library, 1999.

Witherington, Ben, III. *The Acts of the Apostles: A Socio-Rhetorical Commentary*. Grand Rapids, MI: Eerdmans, 1998.

Witherington, Ben, III. *The Indelible Image: The Theological and Ethical Thought World of the New Testament. Volume 1*. Downers Grove: InterVarsity, 2009.

Woodberry, Robert. "The Missionary Roots of Liberal Democracy." *American Political Science Review*, 106 no. 2 (2003) 244–274

———. "Reclaiming the M-Word: The Legacy of Missions in Non-Western Society," *International Journal of Frontier Missions* 25, no. 1 (2008) 17–23.

"World Development Report, Chapter 2." http://siteresources. worldbank.org/ INTPOVERTY/Resources/335642-1124115102975/1555199-1124115187705/ ch2.pdf.

"World Bank Group: Poverty Overview," last modified April 6, 2015. http://www. worldbank.org/en/topic/poverty/overview.

World Food Programme. "Hunger Statistics." https://www.wfp.org/hunger/stats.

World Health Organization. "Democratic Republic of Congo," 2012. http://www.who. int/maternal_child_adolescent/epidemiology/profiles/neonatal_child/cod.pdf.

———. "Diarrheal Disease Fact Sheet." http://www.who.int/mediacentre/factsheets/ fs330/en/.

———. "Female Genital Mutilation." http://www.who.int/mediacentre/factsheets/ fs241/en/.

———. "Global Health Observatory Data: Child Health." http://www.who.int/gho/ child_health/en/.

———. "Health Promotion and Community Participation," 2012. http://www.who.int/ water_sanitation_health/hygiene/emergencies/em2002chap15.pdf.

———. "HIV and Tuberculosis." http://www.who.int/hiv/topics/tb/about_tb/en/.

———. "Malaria Fact Sheet." http://www.who.int/mediacentre/factsheets/fs094/en/.

———. "World Report on Disability." 2011. http://www.who.int/disabilities/world_ report/2011/report.pdf (2011).

World Missions Associates. http://wmausa.org/resources/article/.

World Relief. www.worldrelief.org.

Wright, Christopher J. *The Mission of God's People: Unlocking the Bible's Grand Narrative*. Grand Rapids: Zondervan, 2010.

———. *Old Testament Ethics for the People of God*. Downers Grove, IL: InterVarsity, 2011.

Wydick, Bruce "Want to Change the World: Sponsor a Child." *Christianity Today*, June 2013, 20–25.

Wydick, Bruce, et al. "Does International Child Sponsorship Work? A Six-Country Study of Impacts on Adult Life Outcomes." *Journal of Political Economy* 121, no. 2 (2013) 393–436.

Yamamori, Tetsuanao, and Kenneth A. Eldred, eds. *On Kingdom Business: Transforming Missions through Entrepreneurial Strategies.* Wheaton, IL: Crossway Books, 2003.

Yaylor, John V. "What Is Man?" *The Ways of the People: A Reader in Missionary Anthropology.* Edited by Alan Tippet and Doug Priest, chapter 6. Pasadena, CA: William Carey Library, 2013.

Yunus, Muhammad. *Banker to the Poor: Micro-Lending and the Battle against World Poverty.* New York: Public Affairs, 1999.